A HOLE
IN THE WIND

A HOLE
IN THE WIND

A Climate Scientist's Bicycle
Journey Across the United States

DAVID GOODRICH

PEGASUS BOOKS
NEW YORK LONDON

A HOLE IN THE WIND

Pegasus Books Ltd.
148 W. 37th Street, 13th Floor
New York, NY 10018

First Pegasus Books paperback edition August 2018
First Pegasus Books hardcover edition June 2017

Interior design by Maria Fernandez

Interior maps by Lara Andrea Taber

Library of Congress Cataloging-in-Publication Data is available.

ISBN: 978-1-68177-788-7

10 9 8 7 6 5 4 3 2 1

Printed in the United States of America
Distributed by W. W. Norton & Company

For Concetta

Though I sometimes wander off to far reaches of the solar system,
you are the sun that pulls me back.

CONTENTS

MAPS

Prologue

One day in May, a few weeks after I retired, I turned left out of our Maryland driveway and rode my bicycle to Oregon. Three months would pass before I'd see home again. The hardest part of the ride was, surprisingly, Kansas. I had assumed that riding across the great ocean of the Plains would be where the miles would rack up, where eighty- or hundred-mile days would be the rule. I hadn't counted on the big winds. For a cyclist, they are almost identical to hills but less predictable, and, unlike a hill, you cannot see the top. To further drive home my underestimation of the prairie, temperatures on the ride across Kansas hit 105°F that June, enough for dehydration to be a real concern. My legs began to feel hollowed out. It was a struggle to stay upright. I broke the ride into three-mile stretches those days, and after each I would stop and pour water down my throat. I longed for a break in the blast-furnace conditions—a hole in the wind.

What I also found on my way across the country, along with heat and wind and mountains and snow, were stories. Land stories, to be more precise. I spent four years at sea during my career, and on board ship there is a fine tradition of the sea story. It is said that the difference between a fairy tale and a sea story is that one begins "Once upon a time . . ." and the other "This is no shit . . ." In this sense I accumulated more than a few land stories, and you may choose your own preamble.

For me, though, there was more to the ride than the collection of stories. As a climate scientist, I can see a hard time coming, for our country and our world, as climate change continues to unfold. For some things the effects are quite clear and predictable, as in the case of temperature change. While there will be interludes, the warming trend is both relentless and easy to see from the long-term records. Sometimes things are less predictable, like insect outbreaks and frequency of storms. What I seek to do in these pages, along with telling land stories, is connect the predictions of the science community with the people and places I've seen from the seat of my bicycle. I'd like to consider what the future might look like, and what we might do about it. To look for where there might be a hole in the wind.

After my time on research ships, I worked in climate science for over twenty-five years at the National Oceanic and Atmospheric Administration (NOAA). Three of those years were in Geneva, Switzerland, as director of the UN Global Climate Observing System office at the World Meteorological Organization (WMO). After driving ships, this was my best job. WMO is headquartered in a beautiful glass building looking out over Lake Geneva and the French Alps. My task was coordinating the global network of land, atmosphere, ocean, and space instruments that we use to track climate change. Though WMO can be slow moving and bureaucratic, there's something genuinely inspiring about people coming from around the world to work together. Soon after I arrived, I had a meeting upstairs with one of the vice presidents, who was also the head of the Iran Meteorological Organization. Going up the stairwell, I was both nervous and excited. I remember thinking, *The Great Satan meets the Axis of Evil. How cool is this?* Of course, they were gracious and professional, good folks, concerned about the same things I was. Climate doesn't know anything about national boundaries.

Along the way, I also ran the U.S. Global Change Research Program office in Washington, D.C., the coordinating body between the various federal agencies involved with climate change research. In the early part of my career, climate change was pretty esoteric science, though one with many universities and government agencies fully engaged. With time, climate became a full-fledged political issue, replete with spin and distortion. But fundamentally, the questions about climate haven't changed. They're still about the science, about what quantifiable observations tell us about how the Earth is changing and what our best understanding can tell us about what changes lay in store. As the years went on, I grew frustrated with the dismissal of climate change or any possibility that humans could have a role in it. This notion has come to be known as climate denial, and it's prominent in the popular and political discussion.

Climate's not really that complicated, and I thought that I could explain it if given the chance. As I approached retirement, the idea came that maybe I could just ride my bike across the country and talk with people. My inspiration came from the movie *Animal House*: "This situation requires a really futile and stupid gesture on somebody's part, and we're just the guys to do it."

So on the ride across, I gave seventeen presentations in eight states about the science of climate change, mostly to school groups, typically high school or college students. The short version of the talk: it's for real. More on that later. Showcasing the cross-country bike rig in the process, well, the medium was a bit of the message. Or maybe it was dislike of airline food taken to the extreme.

But the journey really started a decade before. I had been commuting to work by bike for some time. I gradually came to be aware of this thing called bicycle touring, the idea that there were people who cycled across states, countries, or even continents. At about the same time, I became fascinated with the tragic story of the 1877 Nez Perce War, when the US Army pursued a Native American band for 1,170 miles across the Northwest, with the Nez Perce caught just forty miles from refuge in Canada. The two ideas connected, and it occurred to me that the route of the Nez Perce was probably paved and rideable today. So for my first tour, in 2000, I attempted the Nez Perce trail. What I didn't realize was that I would be riding into one of the great fire seasons in the West, seasons that have grown increasingly severe as the climate has warmed. That story is told in chapter 16.

Other bicycle journeys followed. After a while, the kids would begin to ask where Dad's next adventure would be. Following the ride across to Oregon, I went from riding the Iroquois Warriors Path down the Appalachians to an Underground Railroad route, to a search for the site of the Lakota Ghost Dance. All of these form part of the story to come, and are shown on the map on first page of the image insert. The main route, and the thread of this book, leads across the country, east to west, Delaware to Oregon. But as in life, there are a few detours along the way.

The main cross-country ride was almost ruler straight across the middle of the United States until Colorado, when I jogged north into Montana to avoid the deserts, as shown on the map on page 1 of the image insert. For the numbers, my 2011 cross-country ride was 4,208 miles, averaging fifty-six miles and two thousand feet of climbing per day (though averaging climbs between Kansas and Colorado seems a little odd). It took three months. I carried about fifty pounds in four panniers (bicycle packs) and split my evenings between campgrounds and motels. Usually in the campgrounds, I stayed in the "Primitive Area" (no RVs). One might expect that this would be Where the Wild Things Are, but in fact tent camping was fairly sedate.

I also rode solo most of the time, less from some grand philosophical decision than from the difficulty of recruiting someone else with the time and inclination to do such a quirky thing. My mother wouldn't have approved of solo riding, but it was a lot less dangerous than one might think. It was a bit of an internal journey as well. Thoreau wrote, "Be a Columbus to whole new continents and worlds within you. Explore the private sea, the Atlantic and Pacific of one's being alone." And I certainly had plenty of time to think.

Despite years of planning and romantic notions from winter readings in coffee shops, a fair part of the journey involved not simply getting outside but living wet. Lewis and Clark, the explorers whose 1803–06 path I would follow for much of the cross-country route, provided some inspiration. They traveled this way two hundred years ago without benefit of Gore-Tex and survived. So between rain and sweat, I spent most of May soaked. Coming up on Cincinnati on a wet Sunday morning, I drew some looks walking into the Dunkin' Donuts, where I proceeded to monopolize the bathroom by hugging the World Dryer. My motto was modified from Viking Cruises: "Exploring the World in Discomfort."

Yet there is a certain magic in having to spend a moment upon waking figuring out just where you are and realizing, despite the best planning, that there will be something remarkable and unexpected coming at you before the sun sets: a person, a town, a thunderhead, a red-winged blackbird. After the passage of several years, I find that even now, I can remember where I was that summer, almost hour by hour.

A HOLE
IN THE WIND

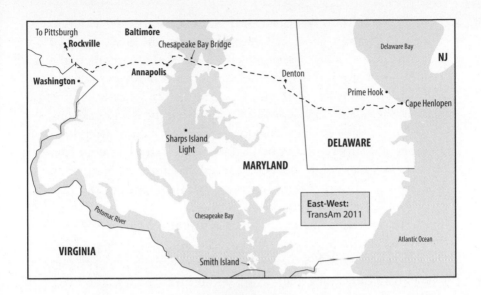

DELAWARE:
THE SEA APPROACHES

The Doppler radar showed a perfect pinwheel of storm clouds off Cape Hatteras, drawing energy from the warm waters of the Gulf Stream. A nor'easter was spinning up, a classic East Coast winter storm named for its ferocious winds from the northeast. Down on an asphalt shoulder on Maryland's Eastern Shore, I could feel the storm growing. I wondered if perhaps March was a little early to start.

My bicycle was fully loaded for the cross-country ride, with four bright yellow bags, a tent, and a headlight that I reflexively switched on. The ride across to Oregon was westbound, the direction of the pioneers. But for a true coast-to-coast journey, I needed to ride east three days from my home in Maryland to symbolically dip my tire in the Atlantic. I stopped in Annapolis at the Naval Academy Museum, simply to warm up. On the wall was a quote from John Paul Jones, father of the American navy: "I wish to have no connection with any ship that does not sail fast; for I intend to go in harm's way." Except that my bike was slow and I rode timidly, J.P.J. and I were pretty much on the same page.

By the next day alongside the highway's rumble strip, the east wind was dead into my face, light rain starting to sting. Low, gray, scudding clouds streamed over the horizon. I was warm enough with legs spun up into a steady riding rhythm, but if I pulled over, I would get very cold, very fast. Stopping wasn't an option. This wouldn't be a fun night to camp out, and the first of many recalculations had me headed to a motel in Denton. The wind was picking up. Ten miles from the motel, I was making 10 MPH. Six miles out, I was at 6 MPH. No matter how hard I worked, I was an hour away. This was getting irritating.

On Maryland's Eastern Shore that day, the only choice was to slug it out. As the rain began to sweep across the road, I balled up, got low on the bike, and powered through. This was only the short eastbound prologue, with another four thousand miles west yet to go. I began my road tradition of a designated Song of the Day. With rain dripping off my nose, the song was "Surfin' Safari." I forced myself to be hyperconscious of traffic, knowing that my rig was a yellow dot on someone's streaky windshield. Cold gray miles inched past. Then, paradise in red plastic:

PIZZA HUT

BEST WESTERN

The Denton exit came into view. I got under the motel's white aluminum awning and shook the water off like a spaniel. The lady at the front desk peered over her glasses and watched as I dripped puddles on the check-in counter. Later, in the room, I left a sopping pile of clothes on the bathroom floor and let the shower dump steaming water over my skin. I decided to lie down on the bed for a moment. Three hours later, dinnertime was almost past. It was with some pleading that a last-call pizza appeared.

After a pure black night's sleep, I awoke feeling battered, aching, stiff. Heading down the corridor for breakfast, the odor was hard to place at first, but there it was: hair spray. Clouds of it. And giggles and screeches coming from the theater-sized meeting room up ahead. Little girls in sparkly dresses and shiny shoes were scooting by, with jittery moms in tow, cans of hair spray poised, ready to fire. I was walking through a toddlers' beauty pageant. *They sure do dress funny*, thought the old guy in spandex.

Outside, the morning was brisk and clear, the sky washed clean after the storm. I flew across the flat fields of Delaware, driven by a tailwind toward the ocean. Concetta had come to meet me for the weekend at a bed-and-breakfast in the coastal town of Lewes. In the coming season, my bride of thirty-four years would be alone for a Mother's Day, a Memorial Day, and a Fourth of July. She'd learn to use a chain saw for the tree branches down in the back yard after a storm. With our son Andrew, Concetta would meet me in Yellowstone National Park and, on a later ride, trail me in a car over the Going-to-the-Sun Road in Glacier National Park. And she'd be on the other end of a phone line each night before bed.

The B&B was sweet and cozy, with our room done up in bright Key West colors with a blue four-poster bed. Big soft quilts and a bottle of wine were just what I needed. The next day we rode together through the salt marshes and scrub forests of the state park at Cape Henlopen. Over the last dune, Concetta and I pedaled into a bright, cloudless vista at the shore. Off that same coast some years before, storm waves had almost capsized a ship I was on. This day it was quiet, shimmering. On a chilly early spring day, no one else was in sight. Only horseshoe crabs crowded the beach, some flipped on their back in the surf. In the distance stood Cape Henlopen

Lighthouse. Outbound tankers crawled along the horizon. The Atlantic. I walked into the wet sand carrying the bicycle and dipped the front tire in the water. It was westbound from here.

I thought of John Steinbeck's *Travels with Charley*. He left on his cross-country journey at the same age as me—fifty-eight. Our sentiments were similar: "I had conveniently forgotten how incredibly huge America is." The Alleghenies and Rockies and Cascades awaited, not single mountains but dozens of them. Concetta picked up a shell and put it in my handlebar bag. She told me to drop it in the Pacific.

We took a side trip not far up the Delaware coast to a place where climate and the rising sea are on display, a pretty little beach community called Prime Hook. There isn't much there—a small store, an ice cream stand, a park, and some beach houses, from bungalows to multifamily rentals, strung along the shore. It's the kind of place where you'd imagine spending a barefoot summer. But it has a problem. Prime Hook is a barrier island, a long, sandy strip of land fronting the sea, typical of oceanfront land on the East and Gulf Coasts. And it's a little lower than most. The high-tide line comes just below the dunes. The access road to the island is just inches above the level of the surrounding water on both sides.

We stopped behind the island at Prime Hook National Wildlife Refuge. It's a sunny, quiet salt marsh, a major stopover for migratory birds on the Atlantic Flyway. But like many places along the coast, things are changing. In 2008, a storm cut several inlets through Fowler Beach, an uninhabited barrier island north of Prime Hook Beach. I was looking for someone at the refuge to speak with about how things had changed since that breach.

"That would be Annie," the man at the desk said. "You need to talk to Annie."

Annabella Larsen, the staff biologist, wore sunglasses and a parka, with white hair tucked under a Fish and Wildlife Service baseball cap. She's blunt, sometimes crusty, eminently knowledgeable, with the impatience that comes from watching the sea chew away at her refuge for twenty years. Before the breaches, the refuge was fresher and shallower, attracting what Annie called dabbling ducks, like pintails and mallards.

"We're just going through huge change here. Colossal. It used to be we were the pintail capital of the East Coast in the winter," said Annie. "We would have thirty thousand to forty-five thousand pintails in a season. Now those numbers are way down. Sea level rise is happening faster than the flow of new sediment. Now what's happening is mainly benefiting wading birds. Last August we had five thousand to ten thousand of them in here. I don't think we'll ever see the numbers of ducks that we used to have."

Nearby, there was a lady in a blue sweatshirt with a knitting bag who was a volunteer at the refuge office. I asked if she lived on the island. She did.

"Must be a beautiful place to live. What's it like during a storm?"

"It can get pretty nasty, but we're not here year round, so we usually miss the bad weather. But sometimes we watch the weather on TV and have to hold our breath. Then we take a ride back out and clean up afterward. It's a lot of work, but we don't mind it."

"Are you seeing sea level rise?"

"I don't know about that, but the bay has certainly moved in. What's killing us is the flood insurance. They keep jacking up the premiums, year in and year out. Getting harder and harder to stay."

I'd heard this before. A friend in Florida with oceanside property complains often about flood insurance costs. In Florida, Delaware, and along the coast, people get coverage from the National Flood Insurance Program, underwritten by the federal government. A 2012 law, passed after Hurricane Katrina had bankrupted the program, provided that insurance premiums would be recalculated to accurately reflect risk. In reaction to complaints from homeowners and builders after the premium increases, Congress passed a 2014 law rolling back many of those increases and reinstating discounted rates. Private insurance companies, who make it their business to assess risk, won't touch flood insurance by the sea. Do they know something we don't?

Prime Hook Beach's predicament came into better focus with a visit to the uninhabited Fowler Beach. Fowler once had beach houses, but they're long washed away. It's now part of the refuge. The access road led to a small parking lot, with shards of asphalt strewn about. A section of guardrail from the road hung out into space over the beach. On either side of the crumbling lot were breaches in the island, new inlets formed by the 2008 storm. Clearly there used to be much more land here. The bay behind Fowler was freshwater a few years ago, but now salt water moves in with the tides through the many inlets. Much of the marsh has been replaced by four thousand acres of open water—salt water—and an entirely different ecosystem.

The barrier island problems aren't limited to Delaware, or the Atlantic coast, or North America. Dealing with sea level rise is common, from Miami Beach to Bangkok. London has built the Thames Barrier to protect it, while in Egypt, the Nile Delta is eroding rapidly. It is all very much tied to the warming climate. Global sea level is rising steadily virtually everywhere. Warmer temperatures are melting glaciers, and satellites record the melting of the great ice sheets of Greenland and Antarctica. Their meltwaters account for better than half of global sea level rise. Satellites can actually measure the weight coming off the land as the ice melts. In addition to this ice melt, as the ocean warms, it expands, which also adds to the sea level rise. Again, satellites have shown the distinct increase over the last twenty years. Since 1992, the rate of global sea level rise has been roughly twice the rate observed over the last century.[1] The rate of increase is increasing. In other words, sea level rise is accelerating.

It wasn't an easy subject for the Prime Hook homeowner to discuss with me, but people with beach houses aren't the only ones to avoid the topic. In Virginia in 2012, a study on the response to sea level rise only passed the General Assembly because its title was changed to "recurrent flooding."[2] In the same year, North Carolina passed a law banning the state from basing policies based on the latest predictions of how much sea level will rise.[3] And in

Florida, the state most threatened by sea level rise, Department of Environmental Protection officials were instructed to replace the phrase *sea level rise* with the term *nuisance flooding*.[4] As with other aspects of climate change, many people just don't want to talk about it.

During my time at sea, I developed an appreciation for the ocean's power in this part of the world. Back when I was still working aboard research vessels, my ship once rode out a November storm off Delaware's Atlantic coast. We were waiting for the waves to die down enough for us to pick up some scientific instruments. For three days, the ship would head straight into the twenty-foot seas, sometimes burying her nose, then surging up from underwater. Everyone was nauseous and exhausted. Simply standing on the rolling deck required constant balancing, shifting from side to side. To return to the same position, after eight hours the ship would need to turn around and go back the other way. The maneuver, known as *coming about*, put the ship broadside to the waves during the turn.

I was a 25-year-old junior officer, driving the ship that morning as we readied to come about. There is a descriptive nautical phrase for the conditions we were facing: *confused seas*, meaning the waves were coming at us from all directions. I was pacing the bridge deck, anxiously looking for some calm space in the confusion. The captain watched from behind, hands gripping the armrests. By tradition the skipper is the only one on the bridge allowed to be seated. Seeing what looked like an opening, I threw in all the engines and all the rudder we had. Halfway through the turn, a massive wave rose up to our right. I had a flashback to a dry chalkboard lesson on nautical architecture, about how far over a vessel can roll before the point of no return. Capsizing is how ships disappear without a trace. If you turn turtle, no distress call goes out, and chances for survivors are slim.

I caught a glimpse of the clinometer, a bubble level that measures the ship's angle of roll. We were at 40 degrees. In the moment we were heeled over, the ship had a sickening hang. Then, agonizingly slowly, we began to right. The skipper, gray-haired and stoic, had no shortage of years at sea. He was a pretty unflappable guy.

"Let's not do that again, Dave," he said as he straightened himself in his chair.

Speaking unscientifically, the ocean is a relentless and indifferent thing. Boxcar-sized waves from the Atlantic turned seaside New Jersey mansions into matchsticks during 2012's Hurricane Sandy. Those monsters were built on a sea level that was rising and continues to rise. The ocean doesn't care whether it's called "sea level rise" or "nuisance flooding." By any name or no name at all, the waves will come.

The future doesn't look good for Prime Hook, or for other low-lying barrier islands of the East and Gulf Coasts. Although Sandy only gave Delaware a glancing blow, it was brutal for Prime Hook, severing the access road and flooding dozens of houses, as well as creating new inlets in Fowler Beach.

Annie Larsen, the Prime Hook Refuge biologist, had seen it before. "On the refuge our biggest climate-related habitat changes came way before Sandy. Our major storms have always been nor'easters. We used to get a big one every five years or so. Around the mid-nineties, we started to get them every year instead of every five. They tore apart the base of the dunes. Sandy was just the last blow. People with beach houses do not want to hear about climate change and rising seas. Probably the refuge will be underwater by the end of the 21st century."

There's been an attempt to help the Delaware shore community. In the wake of Sandy, Congress approved a $39.8 million federal project to fill the island breaches, build a new elevated road to the beach, and rebuild the marsh. Annie says, "What we're trying to do is buy some time—fifteen to thirty years max—and get the salt marsh to recolonize, to act as a shock absorber for the next storms that will be coming along. We were excited to get the money after Sandy. You don't get money like this for marsh restoration. But after thirty years, all bets are off as to where the water will be."

I love the beach. Who doesn't? If I had a house on the beach, I would do everything I could to protect it, including camping out in my senator's office. Alas, it will take one more big storm to wash over any of our remaining low barrier islands, leaving new channels for the ocean. Those storms are coming. From climate model projections, it is not clear that a warming climate will necessarily generate more storms. But our best estimate is that the storms that are generated will be more severe, fed by the warming ocean waters. Observations bear this out. The intensity, frequency, and duration of nor'easters and North Atlantic hurricanes have all increased since the early 1980s.[5] And it jibes with what Annie sees firsthand at the refuge.

But what to do about it? There are many good reasons to stop our loading of the atmosphere with carbon dioxide, and not the least is to begin to put the brakes on sea level rise. The link between carbon dioxide, global warming, and sea level rise is quite firm. Carbon dioxide, the principal greenhouse gas, warms the atmosphere, which melts the glaciers and expands the water. This rise, superimposed on stronger storms, means that events like Hurricanes Katrina and Sandy are bound to become more familiar and more destructive. People will tire of rebuilding structures only to have them washed away again, and eventually these communities may be abandoned.

There are hundreds of Prime Hooks and dozens of Miamis and Bangkoks, vulnerable seaside locales around the world. For some densely populated places and high-value real estate, coastal protection involving sea walls and pumps is possible. The Netherlands has been doing this for some time.

But protection on the scale of the entire Atlantic or Gulf Coast isn't feasible. Ultimately there will be some kind of withdrawal from large stretches of low coast. In some places, a planned retreat is already happening. At Cape Cod National Seashore in Massachusetts and Assateague Island National Seashore in Virginia, popular beaches are being relocated to higher ground. Of course, it's easier when private property isn't involved. But the ocean doesn't care who owns the property. Michael Oppenheimer, a Princeton professor who studies the intersection of climate change and policy, put it this way:

> The concept of retreat, which is sort of un-American, has to be normalized. It has to become part of the culture. Because there are some places where we're really going to have to retreat.[6]

Consider Sharps Island in the Chesapeake Bay, mapped by John Smith in the 1600s and home to a grand hotel with six gables in the early 20th century. Now the hotel is gone and the island itself long washed away. A leaning rusted steel lighthouse is all that remains, presiding over a three-foot shoal. Regardless of our best efforts, this is the fate of our low barrier islands. Ultimately, we must face that there are places like Sharps, like Fowler Beach, that we have abandoned, and others will follow. The manner of retreat, whether catastrophic or planned, is a choice for us to make.

Leaving the Delaware beaches behind, Concetta and I loaded the bikes in the car and headed back to Maryland. March had been a little raw for my taste. But I'd shaken down the equipment and tested my legs. The main event, the journey west, waited in May.

MARYLAND:
THE WAY TO GET TO OREGON

April was a month of preparations for the journey that would start on the first day of May. The first decision I had to make was which way to go: starting from Maryland or from the West Coast. Westbound wasn't necessarily the best direction. If I rode west, the prevailing westerlies meant I would be fighting the winds more often than riding with them. The ride would get exciting in

Kansas, where the full force of the howling Great Plains winds would come to bear. But my reasons for a westbound route were both romantic and practical. It was the direction of the pioneers and of European settlement. I would follow much of Lewis and Clark's Corps of Discovery route from 1804–06, and the notion of retracing some of their path to the Northwest was appealing. Heading west meant that the morning sun would not be in my eyes or those of drivers passing me. From the other direction, starting east in early May from the Oregon Coast would put me on the high passes of the Cascades and Rockies in late May to early June, when snow could still close the roads. If I cleared the passes, the heat of the East in July would be waiting. Embarking from Oregon would be the worst of both worlds. So I prepared for a few thousand miles of headwinds.

In addition to the physical challenge of the ride, one of the goals for the ride across the country was to talk with people about climate. Before leaving, I took the month of April to try out my presentation to groups near our home. By far the most fun was the talk at Bradley Hills Elementary School, where Concetta was the media specialist and librarian. Her class group would be following me on Skype during the first part of the ride west, and we would have a memorable encounter in Kansas. The climate change parts of the discussion were easy for the kids, unburdened by politics, to understand: climate change is for real; things people do are largely responsible for the global warming trend; and there are solutions.

But their real interest was focused more on the bike parked at the front of the room. Typical of any group of third-graders, the question session tended toward expositions on their bike, their trip, or their dog. But a few of their questions were on point.

"I love to bike ride, too. Where do you change clothes?"

"Where do you sleep?"

"I think that what's most important is that you eat a good breakfast."

The prizes were in the kids' thank-you notes. Alison said, "I would love to ride across the conty to but I don't think I wuld ever make it." Sam had drawn a detailed outline of the United States with a thick black line across it. The legend: Black—Follow. White— Don't Follow. It was titled "Map to Help You Get You to Oragan."

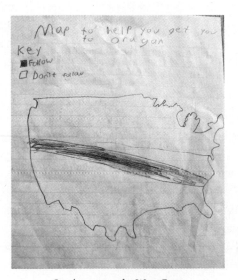

Sam's route to the West Coast

Upper-level school presentations were tested out well before the ride, too. I spoke at the State University of New York at Cortland and George Mason University in Virginia, and at several Washington, D.C.–area high schools. In each case someone I knew worked inside the school. Setting up high school presentations during the ride itself was more difficult, and I came to realize that in many places climate is a controversial topic. Usually the "cold" email to a science teacher along the route was ignored.

One exception was at Gateway High School in Monroeville, Pennsylvania, south of Pittsburgh. Marc Gigliotti is an energetic science teacher who'd been to American Meteorological Society meetings and on the Greenland ice sheet helping with research projects. He arranged a presentation in the school auditorium. The stage was set up for that night's production of "Horton Hears a

Who." Horton the Elephant was peeking out behind the podium. The students had a wide range of questions, from climate change in Pennsylvania to life on the road.

As I was leaving, Marc mentioned that he was showing a film entitled *The Great Global Warming Swindle* to his classes the next day. I assumed that he wanted to avoid appearing to be on any one side of a political issue in case of flak from parents. It's not surprising. The default way of presenting climate change, including in the media, is to depict it as a debate, "fair and balanced." Except that on one side are the National Academy of Sciences, the international science community, and 97 percent of climate scientists.[1] On the opposite side are the other 3 percent of climate scientists and a lot of loud, well-financed pundits. For a student seeing such a "debate," a reasonable conclusion is that all is uncertain. The fog machine works. As I came to realize, high school science classes looked less like the science community and more like the country at large: polarized.

The first place I'd taught and done research was in my home state of Maryland. Coming back from dipping the tire in the Atlantic, we had driven across the Chesapeake Bay Bridge. Concetta doesn't let me drive across that bridge, as I have a bad habit of looking out across the water. At the beginning of my career, I spent two years on a National Oceanic and Atmospheric Administration (NOAA) ship on the bay and wrote my dissertation on currents and wind there. The Chesapeake, one of the largest estuaries and richest in the world, splits Maryland down the middle. H. L. Mencken called it "the great protein factory," and few around the bay have missed out on its crabs and oysters. It's part of the state's identity. But it has a long-standing problem, one with its origins outside of climate change but which stands to be strongly influenced by it in the future.

Our job on the NOAA ship in the early 1980s was to measure the currents, maintaining the instruments in the water. From time to time I was on a dive team assigned to replace these current meters with recharged ones. On a flat, calm, hot summer day, we took a small open boat out and tied off to a buoy, in sight of that same Bay Bridge. Below us was the string of instruments suspended up from the anchor by a subsurface sphere, basically a big steel balloon. Our task was to unbolt the old meters and replace them with new ones.

This would be an easy dive. It was like jumping into bathwater, but we couldn't go in with only bathing suits. We wore coveralls to keep stinging jellyfish off our skin. As we descended, we saw that the wire of the mooring was covered with algae and sea grass, grown over the months the instruments had been in place. Fish darted in and out. Pulses of our air bubbles drifted up toward a bright, rippled surface.

At about fifteen feet down, there was a striking change. The growth and the fish disappeared. By the time we reached the bottom at eighty feet, the anchor, which had been covered with rust when it went in the water, was shiny clean. We had entered the dead zone.

For divers, there was no risk, since we carried air tanks. But nothing moved or grew. Life in a coastal estuary is usually a busy, jumbled, murky thing, with the water full of plankton and fish. The dead zone is remarkable for what's not there. It's strikingly clear. At the bottom of the Chesapeake in summer, the deep water of the bay is stripped of its dissolved oxygen. This happens because excess nutrients run off the land in rivers and into the bay, leading to a spring bloom of algae. As the algae fall to the bottom, bacteria consume them, using up the oxygen. At that point in the summer, nothing that uses oxygen can survive. Even the rust on the anchors is chemically broken down.

Climate change didn't cause this dead zone, but humans are still responsible. These dead zones happen because of excess nutrients from sewage treatment plants and agricultural fertilizers. A significant part comes from chicken manure from the Eastern Shore's poultry industry. Development of this dead zone has become more frequent and severe since the 1960s, as warming temperatures act to reduce the amount of oxygen that can be dissolved in the water. Think about how quickly a soda loses its fizz on a hot summer day. Warmth also increases the rate of respiration, using up the oxygen faster. In addition, the higher future river flow into the bay projected by most climate models will mean that the lighter, fresher, and more oxygenated surface water will be less able to mix with the heavier, saltier bottom water.[2]

Blue crabs, the bay's most famous bounty, and the watermen who catch them know all about the dead zone. They avoid it. In the summer, at the peak of the oxygen loss, buoys marking crab pots would be in the shallows, where oxygenated water could still be found. When the fall storms would break up the dead zone, the crab pots would move, with the crabs, into the deep water.

I saw the crabs during the winter in a very different setting. During January in Norfolk, my dive buddy and I waited for two weeks for that one day calm enough for a dive on the instruments from a small open boat. It became a ritual that winter. Each morning we opened the hatch and stepped out on deck. Some kind of weather would be going on.

"Looks nasty," he'd say.

"Yep," I'd say. "Have to scrub the dive." And we'd go back into the nice warm galley.

Then came the day we dreaded: calm, cold, perfect. Our sixteen-foot boat roared out through Hampton Roads, past the aircraft carriers at the navy base, past where the *Monitor* and *Merrimac* had fought, out to the edge of the ocean, the mouth of the Chesapeake Bay. Frigid spray coming off the bow would cut like a knife. We tied off to the buoy with the current running strong, air and water temperature in the low forties. My buddy and I were in dry suits, designed to keep the cold water out, but they always leaked. A leak in the winter was exactly like getting a glass of ice water poured down your back. Only neoprene gloves covered our hands, so we filled them with water as hot as we could stand. In the bay in January, we had about fifteen minutes of usable hands; after that, the cold would render them numb and stiff.

We held our face masks on and rolled backward off the boat and into the water. Hitting the cold left me breathless, but there was no time to be shocked. The current was immediately sweeping us from the boat out to the open sea. We swam hard, got to the array wire, and got into the deep as fast as we could, out of the strong surface current. We were close to the ship channel, and in my chest I could feel the lum-lum-lum of the house-sized container ship propellers. At the bottom, we followed a well-practiced choreography: grab wrenches, unbolt instruments, slap in new ones, tighten them down. I dropped a bolt from my thick gloves, but no matter; spares were stuck in the sleeves, as numbing hands got increasingly clumsy. Then all done, with plenty of air left and not yet in the cold's grip. Time to be a tourist.

Tiny starfish littered the sea floor, and I stuffed a couple in my pocket for my son. Down in the mud, two eyes on stalks were gazing at me. I reached to dig them up. The eyes belonged to a female crab, buried for the winter. She made a sleepy attempt to pinch me, but the cold had slowed her down, too. I laid her back down and she slowly dug herself back into the mud. I followed my bubbles to the tiny boat far over my head, up to the place of air and life and a thermos of coffee.

Climate is slowly changing the ground rules everywhere, from the high Arctic to the bottom of the bay. As the bay warms, we can expect that the crabs will no longer dig into the mud for the winter. In warmer bays and estuaries farther south, this isn't part of the crabs' winter behavior, so they likely would adapt in the Chesapeake as well. Another effect of climate change is that increased carbon dioxide in the atmosphere is making the oceans more acidic. That sharp taste of soda water on your tongue is carbonic acid, from the dissolved carbon dioxide. The ocean's acidity has increased at a rate faster than any known change in ocean chemistry for at least eight hundred thousand years.[3] As the ocean grows more acidic, there is less carbonate ion available in seawater. Thus the ecosystem will tend to shift away from species that build calcium carbonate shells, like diatoms, coral, and crabs. We'll see the effects of ocean acidification more clearly when we reach the Pacific coast. For Chesapeake Bay crabs, it's difficult to isolate one threat—acidification—from others like ocean warming, overfishing, or habitat loss. But threats there are.

I have waded through eelgrass in the bay and watched crabs skittering away past my feet. I've seen the way they dance around pilings under the cone of a dock light at night, and realized how they got their Latin name, *Callinectes sapidus*: beautiful swimmer. I've dived through more than one bushel basket of red spiced steamed crabs. The blue crab is as iconic to the Chesapeake Bay as the salmon is to the Columbia River. Its decline would be a truly sad thing.

For the Chesapeake watershed, the bordering states and the EPA have made a multidecade effort to reduce the nutrient pollution coming into the bay, with some success. It would seem that the summer dead zone that I dove into should have gotten smaller as a result. It hasn't.[4] But the statement implies that the bay has at least stayed the same over those decades. It hasn't either. Warmer temperatures, altered wind patterns, and rising sea level have all changed the bay. Like the rest of the planet, it's in a different world.

Crabs need oxygen and people need land. For low-lying coast, the battle against the sea isn't limited to barrier islands. It goes on in earnest in Chesapeake Bay. Out in the bay is a waterman's isle, a low place of salt marshes and crab shanties called Smith Island. Residents still speak a dialect of Cornish, tracing back to the English colonists of the 17th century. It's a slow, timeless place, cut off from the world. But the island is low and rapidly eroding from sea level rise. Many residents have relocated to the mainland, with population down from a peak of 700 in 1960 to 176 today. One elementary school closed in 1996; the remaining school has eleven students. Marshes are all that remain of flooded, abandoned nearby islands with names like Holland, Bloodsworth, and South Marsh. The lighthouse, the leaning tower of Sharps Island Bar, sits not too far up the bay.

Smith Island, like Prime Hook Beach in Delaware, faces the fate of these lost islands. It was recently granted something of a reprieve. With post–Hurricane Sandy funds, a new $9 million jetty is being built along the Martin National Wildlife Refuge on Smith Island, with another $2.4 million coming from Somerset County to build a second jetty near the town of Rhodes Point. These jetties will slow some of the dramatic, rapid, wave-driven erosion of the island. But they will do nothing about sea level rise. There are soaked, spongy back yards on the island, with salt water near the surface. Land is in the process of turning into salt marsh.

Down the bay, problems involve far more people and infrastructure. Along with sea level rise, land in the Chesapeake region is also subsiding, making the situation more difficult. Projections from the Virginia Institute of Marine Science are that the sea in Norfolk will rise by three to five and a half feet by the end of the century, with "recent trends suggesting we are on the 'high' curve.'"[5] This was the same study that the Virginia General Assembly insisted be on "recurrent flooding" rather than "sea level rise."

Norfolk is home to the largest naval base in the United States. I often used to drive my ship past the fleet back when I worked on the bay. The base has begun raising its piers. But by 2040, Hampton Boulevard, the main road into the base, will be impassable every high tide, two to three hours a day, according to Larry Atkinson, an oceanographer at Norfolk's Old Dominion University. There are a few other problems. At five feet of sea level rise, the National Mall, all the way in Washington, D.C., 120 miles from the ocean, will be flooded.[6] Of course, the story has multiple endings. Sea level at the end of the century depends very much on the level of greenhouse gases that we put into the atmosphere today.

Though it had been poignant to reflect on the changing Chesapeake, a ride to Oregon was in front of me now. April brought the training days. It's possible to start a long ride in poor condition and ride into shape, but it involves a week or more of pure misery on the road, something I wanted to avoid. So I went to my friend Jan's house south of Syracuse, New York, in search of hills. Except for rain, snow, sleet, wind, frost heaves, and roadside sand, training conditions were ideal.

The rides around my Maryland home were less dramatic. There is a nearby neighborhood awash in speed bumps, all with 15 MPH warning signs. Part of my riding routine was to pour it on and hit every bump at over 15 MPH, just to be on the wild side. Stopping for lunch on the cold days was usually counterproductive. Sweat on the inside of the clothes would cool me down so fast I'd be shivering by the time I got back on the bike. In the middle of my ride I would break out of the trees into a flat, windswept stretch of farmers' fields. In my mind, that stretch had a name reminding me of what was to come: Little Kansas.

Along with the Lewis and Clark route, much of the cross-country ride would be on cycling's TransAmerica Trail—the TransAm—a route pioneered in 1976 as part of a celebration called Bikecentennial. Old photos from those rides of guys in too-short shorts and girls in perms adorn the website of Adventure Cycling, the Montana organization that grew out of Bikecentennial. Adventure Cycling's exquisite maps would guide me across.

On my route, the truly nasty mountains for a cyclist rise up early in the ride. The Rockies can involve two-day climbs on a bike, but generally the roads don't have an extreme grade thanks to extensive switchbacks. But the Appalachians, particularly the Alleghenies of Pennsylvania, pose a more formidable challenge. The climbs are not high but very steep, and they come one after another in quick succession. A single day can bring as many as four thousand-foot ridge ascents.

I sought out advice on the internet from people who had made the crossing before. Rich Vertigan, a lean engineer, had ridden across solo the prior year. His detailed, well-thought-out packing list is in the appendix. It features a perfect tool kit with spares for breakdowns in the middle of nowhere, balancing the substantial weight of metal tools with the indispensable items for getting back on the road. Rich even figured out how to keep camping gear on one side of the bike, to avoid unpacking completely on motel nights. He also contributed a last bit of advice for a long bike trip: "Keep the rubber side down."

The days before starting west began to drop away. The contents of the bike bags were strewn across the bedroom floor, my personal Everest Base Camp. Much of the weight on the bike would be tools.

The guiding principle of packing was the Crowheart test. I wanted to be able to fix the majority of problems on the most remote roadside: Crowheart, Wyoming. There is a 125-mile stretch of central Wyoming with no motel, so I needed camping equipment on the bike: tent, sleeping bag, pad, stove, cook kit, and a stash of food. More weight came from water. I had racks for three bottles for the West's open spaces, though with refills some days I would go through five.

Another substantial part of the equipment was electronics. I brought a camera and laptop for blog posts, and a smartphone for navigation and calls home. Though alone, I would almost never be out of touch, and, thanks to GPS, I would almost always know my location. It was a little sad, as getting lost has its own pleasures. I'd never know the sense of Jim Bridger, the mountain man of the 1800s who said, "I was never lost. I just didn't know where I was for a couple of months."

Good foul-weather gear was a critical part of outfitting. To get across the country in a reasonable amount of time, there could be very little weather that would keep me off the road. As the ride unfolded, a few exceptions emerged: gale-force winds. Big electric storms. Tornadoes.

It was almost inconceivable that I could load up all this gear and roll down the road. I tried to think of every detail, down to sealing the seams on the tent. I fiddled with packing, adding things and dropping things at the last minute. After reading one too many stories of dog encounters on the road, I bought a can of pepper spray, which would wait until Missouri for its star turn. I changed every battery, filled every prescription, and oiled the chain one last time. I was anxious. The bike sat in front of me, a collection of skinny little spokes and cables and wheels. It seemed implausible that such a thing could get me across a continent. I could feel a bad case of cold feet coming on. But that week a fortune cookie came with a Chinese dinner: "You are going to take a trip to the seaside." I was ready.

We had a big party in our back yard the night before departure, full of teenagers. One of my avocations is coaching a high school quiz bowl team. This was the annual end-of-year cookout. Some diving saves kept the volleyball out of the potato salad, and happily there were no injuries. Leaning up against the back fence was the loaded bike, panniers stuffed tight with too much gear. One of the kids munched on a hamburger and checked out the bike.

"Dr. G, you sure you can stay upright with all that?"

"I sure hope so."

Late that night I finished Joshua Slocum's book *Sailing Alone Around the World*. In 1899, he was an aging sea captain, awash in debts and legal problems, who laid the keel for the *Spray*, "a private ark, designed to float free of the irksome land." He set sail from Fairhaven, Massachusetts, and returned three years later. His closing advice:

> To young men contemplating a voyage, I would say go. The tales of rough usage are for the most part exaggerations, as also are the stories of sea danger. Dangers there are, to be sure, on the sea as well as on the land, but the intelligence and skill God gives to man reduce these to a minimum.

Similarly, contemplating a coast-to-coast ride was a little daunting. I had ridden multiday tours of a few hundred miles, but the TransAm was about ten times as long as my longest. These tours had always been within a day's drive for Concetta to come pick me up if something bad happened. This time, well, Plan B wasn't all that robust. Like Slocum, I'd be on my own. So I resolved to think only about getting the first sixty miles down the road the next day, when April rolled into May, and see what the next day brought, and the day after that. All spring the kids on the team had threatened me with a going-away present: a Life Alert bracelet ("Help! I've fallen and I can't get up!"). Maybe I wanted one after all.

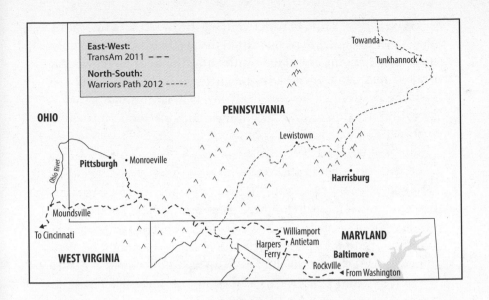

East-West:
TransAm 2011 – – –

North-South:
Warriors Path 2012 - - - - -

OHIO

PENNSYLVANIA

Towanda

Tunkhannock

Lewistown

Pittsburgh • Monroeville

Harrisburg

Moundsville

To Cincinnati

WEST VIRGINIA

Williamport
Harpers Antietam
Ferry

MARYLAND

Baltimore •

Rockville

◄ From Washington

THE PENNSYLVANIA GOLD RUSH

May Day dawned gray and chilly as we turned left out of our driveway. Concetta rode with me the first ten miles, past all the neighborhood schools and parks and strip malls, now oddly unfamiliar, as though I were already a thousand miles away. The road smelled of dirt on damp pavement as we dodged through traffic. Panniers on the front of the bike frame made for sluggish steering. It would be four days in Maryland before I crossed into Pennsylvania.

I'd had worse starts to bike trips. On the first day of one of my first long rides, in eastern Washington State, I hit a patch of gravel after the pavement had suddenly and unexpectedly disappeared. I skidded and went down, skinning my leg and forearms. *Road rash* is the cycling term. I was picking little pebbles out of my flesh and painfully cleaning up with alcohol wipes, dusting off and aching everywhere. I had a certain epiphany. Then, as now, I felt old. But I didn't feel weak.

Gears, wheels, and patience are magical things. Now here I was heading out on the road again. As the sky brightened on an overcast day, Concetta and I were rolling down toward the Potomac River, heading toward a place on the Chesapeake & Ohio Canal where I would return in my mind many times in the coming months. Pennyfield Lock is buried in the forest, an old lockkeeper's building the only structure in sight. The C&O Canal is a national park built around George Washington's dream of a water route from the Chesapeake across the Appalachians to the Ohio Valley. Today it's a packed-dirt footpath along the Potomac that runs for 184 miles, straight and with virtually no incline, ideal for cycling. It was one of our favorite places, and where we would part. She wore a bright yellow jacket that stood out against the gray of the day. We held each other on the towpath. The rain began to fall as we parted and I turned west.

I rode three days along the river across Maryland to Cumberland, the western terminus of the canal. Not far off the first day's route, I stopped by the St. Paul Community Church, the spiritual heart of the community of Sugarland Forest. Sugarland was founded in 1871 by freed slaves and purchased from a former slave owner for $25. The village is long gone now. Some say that it was named for the sugar maple trees that grew there, and others because its founders believed that "the women here were as sweet as sugar." But I wondered if it might not be the name for a place where people first came to live in freedom. If you breathe deeply, you can catch a faint whiff of old joy.

By that first day's end, I'd put in a respectable seventy miles through the rain and mud of the C&O, roughly following Robert E.

Lee's 1862 route in his first invasion of the North during the Civil War. In the now-driving rain, a warm dry bed rather than a sleeping bag sounded ever more inviting, so I climbed away from the canal and the river toward the town of Sharpsburg. Out of the mist in gathering darkness, black shapes: cannons. I was passing through the Antietam battlefield, site of the bloodiest day in American history. One of the Confederates described that day as "a converging storm of iron." All was perfectly quiet, dark, and wet that night in Sharpsburg, with everything closed but the tavern. Bar food on a linoleum table would be a princely meal, but first I needed a place to stay. I pulled up under an awning in a downpour, streetlights reflecting in puddles, trying to get in touch with a B&B owner while keeping my phone dry. It was a late call because of the rain. On the third try she picked up.

"I had called earlier. Will I be able to stay at your place tonight?" I asked.

"Sure, but we won't be there. The key's under the mat, and there's breakfast stuff in the fridge."

"Any Wi-Fi?"

"Sometimes off the firehouse across the street if the conditions are right."

"Uh, okay. How do I pay you?"

"Would you mind just leaving cash on the table when you leave?"

Of course not. Doesn't everyone? In a day's ride, I had made the transition from the Washington, D.C., suburbs to small-town America, where I would live for the next three months.

I rode out of town the next morning with wet clothes pinned to my bags to dry. The day had dawned sparkling clear, and I asked the convenience store clerk what happened to the dismal forecast.

"It's Monday. It's always sunny on Monday," he muttered. I'd have to pass that on to my friends at the National Weather Service.

Back on the canal, I was still creaking after a long, wet first day. After twenty miles on that tunnel through the forest, clothes and bike had pretty well dried out. A few hours on the trail led to a search for lunch. Just up from the river in Williamsport, a cluster of flower pots fronted the Desert Rose Café. Something special was going on. It was opening day for the café, and Rose Harris and her mom, the co-owners, were adding the finishing touches. They were readying for friends and well-wishers but took time out to talk. Rose had a bright smile under wavy dark hair and shared the reason for the name of the café.

"My parents were hippies," she said. "I was born in Tennessee in a camouflage school bus, and we moved to the desert when I was thirteen days old. They had to name me before they took me out of Tennessee." Rose paused, then laughed, "So they named me Desert Rose."

That day, Rose's mom, Beverly Kipe, wore a cowboy hat. Her hair was coming back in after chemo. Concetta and I stopped in to the café five years later. Rose said her mom had no sign of the cancer's return. And the Desert Rose is bustling right along, the beating heart of Williamsport. It seemed that all three of us were starting in on dreams that day.

Two more days on the C&O Canal brought me to Cumberland, and by the fourth day the weather was once again closing in. Raindrops began to bead up on my jacket as I took on the climb out of town. Leaving the C&O was an uphill grade to the Mason-Dixon Line and the Pennsylvania border. I had turned onto a converted railroad bed, a rail trail called the Great Allegheny Passage. The Allegheny ridges came one after another: Haystack Mountain, Dans Mountain, Meadow Mountain, Big Savage Mountain. These were the first real hills of the transcontinental ride, and my legs felt the weight of every pound in the four bags I was carrying. I took shelter in the half-mile-long Big Savage Tunnel for lunch and quickly started shivering as rain and sweat cooled on my skin.

The Alleghenies are a great arch of ribbed corduroy running through Pennsylvania, the accordion-shaped crumple zone of a continental collision millions of years ago. They aren't high, but they are remarkably steep. Though the rail trail was well graded, the mountain pitches on paved roads reach 18 percent. On the

Front Range of the Rockies, by comparison, the grades don't get past 6 percent. For me, the Pennsylvania mountains would be the hardest in the country. The Rockies are bigger climbs in altitude, and some would take two days. But the Alleghenies have straight-up, knee-busting, thousand-foot climbs through the forest, one after the other.

Getting over the steep hills was straightforward: shift into the very low gear and try to set a steady pace, usually with the assistance of a climbing song in the back of my head. "Beast of Burden" was a favorite. It was a matter of punching out a half mile at a time. All too often I simply had to stop and push, remembering what another cross-country cyclist had told me: "Ain't never seen a hill so steep I couldn't walk the bike up it."

Sometimes the hills came with too much warning. When I stopped for morning coffee at a place called the Flying Cow Café, the young lady behind the counter talked about the road ahead.

"Yeah, you're in for lots of climbs, but the real stinker's right after the barbecue stand. You can hear the truck engines screamin' up that one."

I spent much of the day dreading barbecue. Late in the afternoon, the ominous sign appeared: the silhouette of a cowboy leaning on a fence tipping his hat beside the legend HOWDY PARDNER. BARBECUE 1.4 MILES. I didn't partake. A big, juicy sandwich and the nastiest climb of the ride wouldn't mix. A climbing lane for trucks materialized. It wasn't long before I was off the bike, pushing again.

I was far from the first on this road. During the French and Indian War, the British General Edward Braddock, looking to expand an empire, led the greatest army the continent had ever seen through these mountains to attack the French at Fort Duquesne, today's Pittsburgh. His men used block and tackle to haul 2,900-pound cannons and the officers' silver chests over these ridges. One soldier wrote, "I cannot but say the very Face of the Country is enough to strike a Damp in the most resolute Mind."

Perhaps the mountains had beaten Braddock before he even approached Fort Duquesne. His army met an Indian force in broken woodland. To the British, the bullets seemed to come from wraiths in the forest. As their training dictated, the soldiers formed a line of battle and loosed volley after volley into the woods. To an enemy behind trees and rocks, the Redcoats made irresistibly good targets. The lines crumbled and broke as hundreds were lost. Braddock would fall, mortally wounded, and a 23-year-old Virginian, George Washington, would suffer four bullet holes in his clothes yet survive to lead the retreat of the remnants of the army.

Prior to his end, Braddock could not have imagined the riches in these old hard hills, treasure left by ancient seas. The first oil well was drilled in Pennsylvania in 1859, and later coal fueled the steel mills of Pittsburgh. The oil fields and the coal mines have drastically declined in the past century, but much of northern and western Pennsylvania sits atop one of the largest natural gas fields in the world: the Marcellus Shale.[1] In the last decade, the use of hydraulic fracturing—fracking—has made this gas accessible. By tapping into these shale deposits thousands of feet down and injecting water, sand, and chemicals, the drillers released a bonanza.

The 2011 cross-country ride wasn't my only bike trip through Pennsylvania. The following year, I rode from upstate New York to North Carolina, following the Warriors Path, the route of Iroquois raiding parties bound for Cherokee country (see map). That year's ride took me through the intensive fracking region from Towanda through Tunkhannock. Even then, I had been only mildly aware of the shale gas boom in this part of Pennsylvania. My first hint had been on Mother's Day 2011, on my trans-American ride to Oregon. I had expected a quiet Sunday on narrow country roads. The roads were indeed narrow, but they were anything but calm. Water trucks, pipe trucks, pump trucks, and wastewater trucks roared by all day. This was the signature sign of gas drilling, running seven days a week in the Pennsylvania hills.

It was a hot day, and as I was hammering up one of those brutal hills, I looked off to the side, where a man on the stairs of a warehouse building made a motion of lifting a bottle to his lips. I almost fell into the traffic. Of course I wanted a drink. I rolled the bike over to his recycling operation. Over the ecstasy of his office water cooler, we fell into a discussion on the natural gas business in this part of Pennsylvania. Those trucks were all servicing gas drilling rigs, which require large amounts of water and produce similar quantities of waste fluids. My new friend owned twenty acres and expected to be getting $3,000–$20,000 per month from mineral rights.

"A lot of farmers up here are millionaires now," he said. "The groundwater problems are overrated. And if there are problems, they fix 'em."

I tossed my paper cup into the trash can. "How do they do that?"

"They get outside bottled water delivered for life."

Or for the life of the company, I thought. "Who's behind all this?"

"Chesapeake Energy's the big player. Their boss flies around on his own jet, even owns a vineyard in France. Nice work if you can get it."

My friend was right about Aubrey McClendon, cofounder and then-CEO of Chesapeake Energy. In Oklahoma City, his hometown and company headquarters, McClendon was larger than life. Cocky, bold, and indefatigable, with wire-rimmed glasses and a mane of gray hair, he could dominate a conference room. At one point he was the highest-paid CEO of any S&P 500 company.[2] He put enormous amounts of money into Oklahoma City, including creating an Olympic rowing venue steps from downtown. He also co-owned the Oklahoma City Thunder, the National Basketball Association franchise that plays in Chesapeake Energy Arena.

McClendon started as a landman, acquiring mineral rights from landowners. Taking advantage of the emerging hydraulic fracturing technology, he built the company into one of the largest natural gas producers. *Forbes* had a cover profile of McClendon as "American's Most Reckless Billionaire." His tradition is of the wildcat driller from the days of the frontier, the prospector, the risk taker. In many ways he embodies the American dream. He said to *Rolling Stone*:

If you dream of a world where the air is cleaner, where energy is half the price it was before, and we're not exporting a million dollars a minute to OPEC, then you should embrace natural gas.

From thirty thousand feet in a private jet, it all looked good.

McClendon's dream seemed to have come true as I rolled down the last hill of the day into the town of Tunkhannock. Main Street was bustling with new restaurants, bars, and hotels. It reminded me of the California gold rush stories, where the people getting rich weren't just the miners but the storeowners and outfitters as well. A sticker in a convenience store read FRIENDS OF MARCELLUS, referring to the underlying shale deposit. The hotel parking lot was full of trucks with Texas and Oklahoma license plates. Outside the front door was a hedgehog brush to clean off muddy boots. The gas field guys (and they were all guys that I could see) had stacked up cases of beer outside on the hotel gazebo in back. Goatees and tats were much in evidence. I felt I knew them from a long time ago.

Right after college, with a degree in biology, I had driven down to the Louisiana delta, looking for work on the offshore oil rigs. I started knocking on doors of random well supply outfits in the town of Venice (pronounced "Venus"), on the Mississippi River at the very end of Louisiana Route 23. I distinctly remember my first big break. Behind the third door I approached was a man who looked up from his desk and asked, "When can you be ready?"

I hesitated. "Well, I've got my stuff out in the car."

He handed me a form. "Get this done quick. Helicopter's leaving in twenty minutes. Be on it."

In exactly twenty minutes, with a whoosh, my car, Venice, and Louisiana disappeared from under my feet. It was the last I'd see of "the beach" (dry land) for two weeks. Then, as now, offshore oil was a dirty business. The work was hard and dangerous, up on high steel, always with a little oil film underfoot. Giant sunfish would swim in the gulf far below, but if you fell you'd surely bounce off an I-beam before hitting the water. There was a certain fraternity to the men working on the rigs, along with a three-week cycle of life: pure work for two weeks, party in New Orleans the next week, then drag yourself back for the Monday morning crew boat. Once the boat left the dock, some serious poker began. I knew enough not to go anywhere near it. Out on the rig, the crew dispensed plenty of advice for when a newbie ventured back to the local bar in town. One of the chiefs pulled me aside.

"It's a nice, friendly place. Don't even need an extra clip," he nodded. "But watch them pool cues. You're just thinking everything's quiet when you stick your head up from under the table and bang! Pool cue to the back of the head."

So the crew at the hotel in Tunkhannock felt familiar, and I made a mental note to keep an eye out at the bars that night for pool cues.

I went to check in. The least expensive room at the hotel was $180, and I was lucky to find it. The girl at the front desk didn't look to be out of her teens.

"Looks like things are booming around here," I said.

"Yeah, we've been busy for a while," she said in a clipped tone.

"Seems the drilling's been good for the town."

She looked over her shoulder furtively. "There are a lot of problems outside of town. Nasty water turning up all over the place." She shook her head a little and went back to her computer screen.

Despite the views of my friend at the recycling business, the girl at the hotel had a point. Those massive quantities of wastewater generated by fracking include both drilling chemicals and petrochemicals associated with the shale. Chemicals used in the hydraulic fracturing process can include an exotic brew of inorganic acids, petrochemicals, anti-scaling compounds, microbicides, and surfactants. For many years, actual composition was a zealously guarded trade secret. Following legal mandates from state regulators in 2012, drilling companies disclosed what was going into the ground—but only in thousands of well-by-well documents in pdf format, only possible to analyze by hand. For anyone trying to find out the large-scale picture of chemical injections into Pennsylvania's drilling regions, the task was almost impossible.[3] By 2013, the disclosure website was finally upgraded. The process had taken nine years, and the identity of some chemicals still remains proprietary.

Back on the bicycle the next morning, I saw open pits of wastewater, presumably waiting to be hauled off. These waste lagoons were everywhere. Some had fountains spraying the fluids into the air to evaporate them and reduce the volume—and offload some of the chemicals into the air. The lagoons could overflow during storms. There were reports of "midnight dumping" of wastewater on roads. Regardless of the means, the chemicals were getting into the environment.

Near-term effects on people around the drilling operations became clear. Burning eyes, nose, and throat, along with headaches, nosebleeds, and rashes were common complaints to doctors around drilling operations. In feed animals, with more rapid reproductive cycles and typically closer exposure to fracking operations, stillbirths and failures to breed were reported.[4] For people less than a half mile from a well, reported upper respiratory and skin conditions were more common than for those greater than one mile from a well.[5] It's been described as an "uncontrolled health experiment on an enormous scale." A woman named Emily, asthmatic and living near a well, would bring this home to me. More on Emily later.

The continual truck traffic from gas operations was taking a toll as well. I cycled on roads on both sides of the Pennsylvania–West Virginia border. They were in terrible shape, most without shoulders and often crumbling on the outer third. This forced me out toward the middle of the road, and I was listening for trucks coming around every bend. This part of rural Pennsylvania is life in an industrial zone, for better or worse.

Development of shale gas has had implications far beyond Tunkhannock. The United States is now the world's largest gas producer. Natural gas prices have dropped dramatically, and cheaper energy is one of the forces bringing manufacturing back to the United States. From a climate perspective, "clean" natural gas would seem to be a boon. When burned, it releases half the carbon dioxide of coal, and carbon dioxide is the most important heat-trapping, or greenhouse, gas. But in the process of drilling, large amounts of methane, the major component of natural gas, are released into the air. Methane itself is a potent greenhouse gas, over twenty times as powerful as carbon dioxide. Methane leakage of more than 3 percent cancels out any climate benefit from natural gas, and it's not at all clear that this standard is being met. Studies show that official inventories consistently underestimate methane emissions,[6] while US methane emissions increased by over 30 percent from 2002–2014, the same period of rapid increase in US natural gas production.[7] The rollback of regulations designed to limit methane leakage from wells was one of the first acts of the Trump administration.

In the gazebo in back of the Tunkhannock hotel, six-packs were stacked up for the evening, ready for the crews coming back from a day on the rigs. Traffic was brisk, and pickups and gas field service trucks roared through town. I walked to the Walmart that night. The pace of this small town seemed to have sped up. The front half of a deer lay in the road at the turnoff, a puzzled expression frozen on its face.

A little farther down the road, outside of the shale gas belt, is Lewistown. In some ways it's Tunkhannock's counterpart, without the drilling. It still suffers from loss of industry and the closing of its steel mill forty years ago. I went into Lewistown looking for air for my tires after another day fighting the ridges and dodging trucks. It had the only bike shop for miles. The main street had quite a few vacant storefronts and a hotel that didn't look open for business. Halfway up the block, behind a window filled with stickers and skateboards, was Bliss Skate and Bike. I walked my bike in the front door.

A tennis ball rolled across the floor of the shop, followed by a pug that breathlessly returned it to the three old men sitting in the back. A high school girl with jet-black hair and a leather collar stopped by the counter, leaving change for the soda she'd taken out of the cooler. A steady stream of boys carrying skateboards walked through the shop and out the back. Presiding over this world was a solidly built guy with an ex-military air named Bill Shoemaker.

"What's going on in back?" I asked.

"Oh, I've got a little skate park back there. Built it over a couple of years during slow time in the shop. Want to take a look?"

The door opened onto a cinder block room under bright fluorescent lights, filled with plywood platforms and ramps. Graffiti covered the walls. Kids paused at the top of the ramps, waiting for the next one's move. The black-haired girl sat on one of the benches.

"There's not a lot going on in this town, especially for the kids. They need some kind of outlet, some place to go. The grown-ups have got to give them something constructive to do."

The Alleghenies had knocked the legs out of me again, and I still had to find a motel and shower for the night. Bill walked with me to the front door and the deserted main street. The bike shop Prometheus looked back toward the skate park.

"The operation's not exactly about making money. Last week I go down to pay the tax bill, and I'm wondering how we'll get through this next crunch. Next thing there's a couple of big orders for boards that gets things by. Sometimes you just have to have faith that the money will come."

I think a lot about these two towns, Tunkhannock and Lewistown, and making a living in these hard hills. I suspect that the people of Lewistown would gladly trade their main street for the prosperity of Tunkhannock. But sometimes a glimpse of the past can provide a clue to the future. I would find it on another Pennsylvania byway.

I rode down the Youghigheny River toward Pittsburgh. The Yough is an old mining valley with remnants of coke ovens and giant abandoned coal plants now almost covered by forest. Thin coal seams can still be seen in the rock. Wild turkeys ran by, and an enormous owl flew over in gathering dusk. It's a quiet, beautiful valley, but every now and then I could see a red waterfall: acid drainage from mines closed a hundred years ago or more.

Pennsylvania has over seventeen hundred miles of streams with no fish, the legacy of these abandoned mines. The mining companies, of course, are long gone. I wonder if there might be a way to temper the gold rush psychology of today's shale gas boom to leave the next century without the legacy of barren rivers or vast new emissions of greenhouse gases.

But like the old coal barons, Aubrey McClendon moved on. In 2012 he was deposed from Chesapeake Energy for multiple conflicts of interest and for borrowing company money for his personal use. He orchestrated a comeback through a new firm, American Energy Partners, raising over $4 billion for new drilling, principally in Ohio. Back in Pennsylvania, there are now thousands of gas wells, and the percentage that leak range from 5 percent of new wells to over 60 percent of gas wells more than thirty years old. That's on top of an estimated two hundred thousand unaccounted oil and gas wells existing in the state.[8] It's safe to assume that the gas drillers won't be around to clean things up when the gas wells eventually run dry.

I banged through the final accordion hills of the Alleghenies in western Pennsylvania, then across the thin western panhandle of West Virginia. I paused at the top of the last great hill above the Ohio River Valley, sun low in the west. Just a little push, and a sweet, wild 40 MPH descent into Moundsville. I imagined a contrail behind. The sun set over the Ohio River in a waterfront park with a bridge arching over the river.

A young family was fishing. The dad was muttering gently, trying to untangle one boy's line from his brother's. The girl was holding a bright pink fishing pole and pointing to the calm water of the Ohio reflecting a bright golden crescent.

"The moon, Mommy. Look at the moon."

Five years passed since the time of the rides in 2011–12. During that time I kept an eye on the shale gas business in Pennsylvania. The vast amounts of natural gas brought online by hydraulic fracturing, especially in Pennsylvania, had the effect of steadily depressing gas prices. In the spring of 2016, the headlines appeared one after the other. On February 26, Chesapeake Energy, Aubrey McClendon's old firm, announced that it had stopped drilling new wells in both Pennsylvania and Ohio. The same day, the biggest financial backer for McClendon's new company, American Energy Partners, withdrew support. Three days later, a federal grand jury indicted him for allegedly conspiring with a competitor to suppress land prices by rigging bids while leading Chesapeake.

The day after the indictment, Aubrey McClendon's car crashed into a concrete abutment outside of Oklahoma City. He was driving almost 90 MPH on a two-lane road, with no drugs or alcohol in his system and no health trauma. The police captain said, "He pretty much drove straight into the wall." The medical examiner ruled the cause of death accidental.

Indeed, things had changed in Pennsylvania in the four years since my rides. I decided to go back, on four wheels this time, to find out what happened.

Marie Cusick looks deceptively young, but there's a hint of intensity in bright blue eyes. She's a reporter at WITF, the public broadcasting station in Harrisburg, and has been reporting on the gas boom since 2011, winning an Edward R. Murrow Award in the process. A folder with my name on it was on the meeting room table. Marie knew all about the gas bust.

"The boom has left," she said. "Overproduction led to a gas glut, prices plummeted, and most of the drill rigs disappeared." When I rode through in 2012, Pennsylvania had 116 rigs; in 2016 that number was 16. In 2011, *Time* magazine's headline was "Could Shale Gas Power the World?" Back then, for Pennsylvania landowners who leased their mineral rights, like my friend in the recycling business, the phrase was "mailbox money."

On the ground today, changes are not that hard to see. In Towanda, where I had gotten the ominous warning of the big hill after the barbecue stand, drilling and water trucks no longer rumble steadily down Main Street. New hotel rooms are empty. Chesapeake has been hit with lawsuits for allegedly cheating people out of royalty money from gas drilling. And Chesapeake has sent bills to some landowners for overpayment of royalties. So much for "mailbox money."

But gas is still flowing from the wells. There's no question that the Marcellus shale brought money and jobs into Pennsylvania. Besides the individual royalties, drillers paid over $200 million annually to local governments, and employment in the gas industries went from nine thousand in 2007 to thirty-one thousand in 2012. Many of those jobs have been lost in the bust. As one laid-off gas worker put it, "It was a good five-year run."

On the larger scale, gas is often touted as a "bridge fuel," one that can help the planet transition from carbon-intensive fuels like coal and oil to a renewable energy economy. As we were wrapping up, Marie said, "I'm often asked, 'Are we providing the bridge fuel? After all, people need energy. Is this a good thing?' And I don't know the answer."

Leaving Harrisburg, my next stop in Pennsylvania was up on Nimble Hill, looking for an answer to Marie's question. Emily Krafjack lives on this little hilltop west of Tunkhannock. She runs a small nonprofit that's trying to foster better natural gas industry practices and better community engagement. She's a Chesapeake Energy leaseholder. We sat in Emily's kitchen with the gas pad out the window across the road. She's thin and energetic, nervously flicking her long gray hair as she told her story.

We're right in the richest part of Chesapeake's play, and it's a very dry gas that hardly needs any processing. Everybody around us signed leases, and we were one of the last to sign. They would have drilled right up to our property and taken our gas anyway. So we signed. They put [the pad] right next to us.

There was a lot of traffic on our road. For a year, it had holes so big it could swallow your car. Dave went out with spray paint and painted orange circles around the holes. A couple of tanker trucks overturned on our road. Eventually Chesapeake hired contractors to rebuild it. During one of the fracturing operations, we had diesel exhaust in the house. There must have been twenty trucks lined up outside, idling.

The first drilling event went for thirty-four days, 24/7. That kind of intolerable noise is not meant for humans. There were three drilling and two fracking events. If the price of gas goes up, they'll probably be back.

I asked Emily how it had affected her personally.

I was a severe asthmatic pre-Marcellus. Having the well pad this close to our home, five hundred feet away, resulted in greater health challenges. I need to be aware of activity on the well pad, as diesel exhaust is particularly troublesome for any severe asthmatic. My asthma isn't controlled as well as it was pre-Marcellus. I've had numerous exacerbations requiring steroids and even intermittent nebulizer use. I can't enjoy the outdoors, even to just sit on our porch, when they are working near our home. I have to stay inside with all windows closed.

She's not imagining this, and she's not alone. A study by Johns Hopkins of thirty-five thousand Pennsylvania asthma patients revealed that people with asthma who live near bigger or larger numbers of fracked gas wells are 1.5 to 4 times likelier to have asthma attacks than those who live farther away.[9] I asked Emily where things stood now.

Inadequate regulations and inadequate enforcement have let the companies run amok. I've helped people all over a lot, and I've been down to Harrisburg to testify and be on shale gas working groups. I was pretty nervous the first time, but I've gotten used to it. Boil it down, learn to say your piece in two minutes. So we worked pretty hard over the last ten years to get some regulations to make drilling a little more livable. Now the regulations are held hostage by gas-and-oil financed legislators.

My family were coal people. Coal was rough, but it brought a prosperity with it. There was manufacturing, good schools, good colleges. I just don't see the jobs I thought we'd see, the economic development, all the manufacturing that was going to come in from cheap energy. It could have been so much better. It's all pretty disappointing.

I wanted to be in this place in the middle. Shale gas is here, it's not going anywhere, let's make it work. But many companies, they don't care unless they get caught. They're not interested in doing things right. In the beginning, they sold it as this big patriotic thing, all about American energy independence. Now they're looking to build pipelines so they can export it.

As I was driving down off Nimble Hill, I hoped I would have done just what Emily did in her situation: learn all she could, talk to people, and make her voice heard. And I thought back to Marie's question: Was the Pennsylvania gas drilling boom a good thing? Inexpensive and plentiful gas has led to much of the decline of coal, a major source of both of these greenhouse gases. But is this substitution better for the climate? Given the amount of methane leakage from the natural gas system, that's not at all clear. One event, the 2015 gas leak in California's Aliso Canyon, released the equivalent of the yearly greenhouse gas emissions from 572,000 cars.[10] Whether it's better or worse than coal seems beside the point. It is unquestionable that gas drilling leads to the emission of an enormous amount of greenhouse gases, both methane and carbon dioxide. If we are serious about slowing climate change, we need to prevent the vast majority of these greenhouse gases from reaching the atmosphere.

But what of Pennsylvania itself? In 2012, a Pennsylvania legislature sympathetic to the gas industry passed an act that, in part, allowed statewide rules to preempt local zoning on oil and gas development and allowed this development in all municipal zoning areas. The next year, the Pennsylvania Supreme Court overturned this part of the law. The majority opinion was ringing:

> Pennsylvania has a notable history of what appears retrospectively to have been a shortsighted exploitation of its bounteous environment, affecting its mineral, its water, its air, its flora and fauna, and its people. . . . By any responsible account, the exploitation of the Marcellus Shale Formation will produce a detrimental effect on the environment, on the people, their children, and future generations, and potentially on the public purse, perhaps rivaling the environmental effects of coal extraction.[11]

I thought of riding down the Youghigheny, seeing the legacy of coal mines abandoned a hundred years ago and considering the thousands of gas wells operating now. The red waterfalls of the next century are being created today.

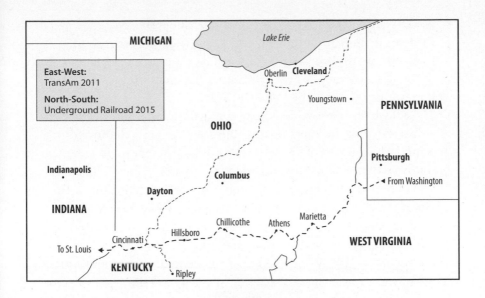

MICHIGAN

Lake Erie

East-West:
TransAm 2011

North-South:
Underground Railroad 2015

Oberlin • Cleveland

Youngstown •

PENNSYLVANIA

OHIO

Pittsburgh
•

Indianapolis
•

Columbus
•

◄ From Washington

Dayton
•

INDIANA

Chillicothe   Athens

Marietta

Hillsboro

Cincinnati

To St. Louis ◄

WEST VIRGINIA

KENTUCKY
• Ripley

OHIO: TIM HORTONS, ARMADILLOS, AND CLIMATE CHANGE

I was near the end of a long, flat beautiful day along the Ohio, spending my afternoon on the river road, racing barges out on the water. Rolling into the town of Marietta, I did a double take: on the roof of a roadside brick fast-food place, there it was in bright red script—Tim Hortons. If you've been to Canada, you've almost certainly seen them. They're cheery coffee-and-doughnut places, pretty well ubiquitous on the Canadian landscape. Not long ago, I was in Penn Station in New York City, and I was surprised as I rushed by a Tim Hortons on the way to a train. Later, a friend told me that they were all over Ohio now. The tendrils of Canadian imperialism have reached into the heartland.

Meanwhile, more ominous news comes from the South. Because of global warming, the range of armadillos is steadily expanding northward. The scratching of their little toenails has been heard in Indiana, southern Illinois, and Missouri. It's only a matter of time until a sure sign of the End of Days: an armadillo is spotted waddling into a Tim Hortons parking lot, eying the drive-through, licking his chops.

Okay, maybe not. At least not the End of Days part. But what's quite clear is that armadillos, as well as a lot of other species, are on the move, largely due to a warming planet. I had an encounter with one of those species. Back in the 1970s, I did a lot of solo backpacking in the Colorado Rockies. I camped out one night at Silver Lake, a ghost town at twelve thousand feet, way above tree line. There was only one building still standing, so it seemed like a good idea to sleep there instead of pitching a tent. When darkness fell, things started to get weird, which I should have expected in a ghost town. The ruins of the town came alive with sound. A scurrying motion was coming from all directions. I cut on the flashlight to see who the company was.

Frozen at the edge of the light were pikas, little brown animals with Mickey Mouse ears. They spent the night running around the room, over my sleeping bag, and even over my head. Fortunately, I had hung my food from a rafter. Unfortunately, I found that in the morning they had climbed down the rope, chewed through the nylon bag, and gnawed into a tube of peanut butter. They made an amazing mess, leaving dozens of peanut buttery paw prints for some future archaeologist to puzzle over.

They were irritating, but I don't hold a grudge. I wouldn't wish on them the problem they now face. Pikas are high-altitude, cold-weather animals, and as climate warms, little of their habitat is left. Roughly one third of the pika populations in the Great Basin, between the

Rockies and the Sierras, have gone extinct in recent decades. Unlike armadillos, if they want to stay in their habitat, pikas have nowhere to go but up. These days there's less and less of their cold, high places.

Luckily, humans have instruments, and we have a good idea of what's been going on with the climate. Some of these have been in place for quite a long time. When I was director of the Global Climate Observing System office in Geneva, my job was to look after all of these disparate measuring systems in many nations and try to keep them running. One of the more fascinating was the Argo system, an array of thousands of ocean instruments that hover more than a mile down. They rise to the surface every ten days to measure temperature and salinity, transmit the data to a satellite, then return to the ocean depths. It gives us a clear picture of where heat is distributed in the upper part of the sea.

On the land and the ocean surface, we have many more instruments that give us a good idea of how the planet's temperature has changed. Here's what the data look like:

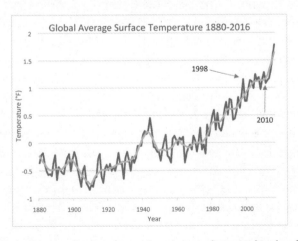

Earth's global average surface temperature has risen, as shown in this plot of combined land and ocean measurements from 1880 to 2016. The light line is the filtered record with 5-year smoothing. The temperature changes are relative to the global average surface temperature of 1951–80. Data from NASA Goddard Institute for Space Studies.[1]

It's a squiggly line. Climate's like that; it will bounce around from one year or even one decade to the next, though the trend has been, with very few exceptions, a steady warming for the last hundred years. The year 2015 was the warmest on record, that is, until 2016 happened. Note that it's possible, if you choose carefully, to pick a stretch of years that start with a warm one and end with a cold one to show that "Global warming has stopped!" For example, if you start with 1998 and end with 2010 (shown above), things might seem to have leveled off. This was even presented in testimony to Congress. Cherry picking is possible, but when you look at the whole record, particularly since 1960, the warming is unmistakable.

So is one cold winter or hot summer proof or disproof of global warming? Consider a cyclist on steroids. Was this particular fast race the result of doping? That question can't be answered. But a pattern of large numbers of fast times from a formerly average rider gets to be serious evidence. So it is with climate, and the clear pattern of warming.

This is all having unprecedented effects on things that live on the planet, and it's not just armadillos and pikas. In some places seasonal behaviors are taking place two or three weeks earlier than they did just a few decades before. Ocean species are moving to deeper depths and toward the poles. And evidence gathered across several continents points to a lengthening of the growing season of ten to twenty days in the last few decades.[2]

Yet climate has changed naturally throughout its history, long before humans entered the scene. For example, in the Eocene epoch, fifty million years ago, the planet was essentially ice free. How do we know that humans have anything to do with the current warming? Gases such as carbon dioxide (CO_2) absorb heat given off from Earth's surface. Increases in concentrations of these gases cause the Earth to warm by trapping more of this heat. Human activities—especially the burning of coal, oil, and natural gas—have increased atmospheric CO_2 concentrations by about 40 percent, with more than half the increase occurring since 1970. The present level of atmospheric CO_2 concentration is unprecedented in the past eight hundred thousand years.

One of the most remarkable records of climate comes from air bubbles trapped in ice in Antarctica, laid down over hundreds of thousands of years. Measurements of these bubbles, shown below, reveal that up until the 20th century, the CO_2 concentration stayed within the range 170 to 300 parts per million, making the recent rapid rise to over 400 particularly remarkable. Measurement of oxygen isotopes in the water provides a measure of temperature (the second graph). CO_2 concentration and temperature have tracked together for the better part of a million years, and the CO_2 is way up now.

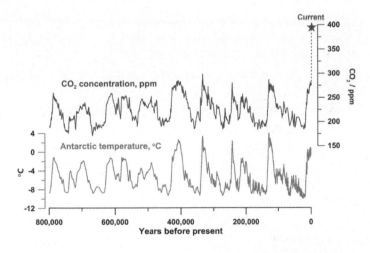

Data from ice cores have been used to reconstruct Antarctic temperatures and atmospheric CO_2 concentrations over the past 800,000 years. Temperature (top graph) is based on measurements of the isotopic content of water, while CO_2 (bottom graph) is measured in air trapped in ice. The current CO_2 concentration in the atmosphere is the star. The recent increase in atmospheric CO_2 concentration is unprecedented in the past 800,000 years.[3]

There's no question that climate changes naturally. It's easy to see in the ice core record above. Most of these fluctuations have to do with changes in the Earth's orbit over thousands of years. Over these long time periods, the Earth wobbles on its axis like a spinning top, changing which parts of the planet receive the most solar radiation. On shorter periods, from one year to the next, the presence or absence of an El Niño—the sloshing of warm water across the Pacific—will have a big effect on global temperature. And volcanic eruptions like 1991's Mount Pinatubo can cool the entire planet for months by injecting ash into the stratosphere. But when it comes to steady, decade-to-decade change, these effects are being dwarfed by what humans are doing. We're creating a new era dominated by man-made climate change. Geologists have a name for it: the Anthropocene. It is important to remember that we're basically on a one-way street. Temperature change due to CO_2 emissions is essentially irreversible for several hundred years, since this CO_2 is removed from the atmosphere only very slowly by natural processes.[4]

These temperature changes don't seem very big. The atmosphere has only warmed about 1.5°F over the last hundred years. When temperatures can swing by 30°F over a day, that doesn't seem like much. But we're really comparing two very different things. The instantaneous temperature is part of weather, which is what's happening right now. Climate, on the other hand, is an average, the mean of what's happened over a season or a year or a millennium. A couple of degrees makes a huge difference. Consider that the change in average temperature between the last Ice Age, when half of North America was buried in ice, and today is just about 9°F. The Intergovernmental Panel on Climate Change (IPCC) states that continuing on a path of rapid increase in atmospheric CO_2 could cause another 4° to 8°F warming before the year 2100.[5] What seem like small increases in average temperature matter.

Global warming has led to shifting rainfall patterns and concentration of rainfall into heavier downpours—critical risk factors for both flooding and drought. Sometimes those big floods get personal. One of those more frequent intense storms cited in the Delaware chapter was Hurricane Sandy, coming up the East Coast in October 2012. As days and hours passed on October 28, it became increasingly clear that Sandy would make landfall near New York. My son Tom and his wife, Missy, lived in lower Manhattan about two blocks from the aptly named Water Street. Based on real-time data from the local tide gauge and storm surge models, it was clear that flooding was likely. My email to Tom that morning said, "Think about a foot of water outside the front door and consider if you want to be there." They rode it out on the second floor, but their block provided one of the iconic Sandy images: cars piled up in the entrance to the underground parking garage next door.

New York is no stranger to powerful storms. The hurricane of 1938 did tremendous damage to New York and New England, including cutting new inlets into Long Island. But like the cyclist on steroids, the odds of enhanced performance are shifting. No single storm can be attributed to climate change, but man-made warming is projected to increase the intensity of both hurricanes and extra-tropical cyclones (e.g., nor'easters) impacting North America.[6]

Over the thirty years I've been working in climate, the facts supporting human-induced climate change have become more and more clear as we've accumulated more research, better measurements, and more powerful computers. Among climate scientists, 97 percent agree that global warming over the past century is likely due to human activities,[7] and the leading scientific organizations worldwide endorse this position. Yet in the US political arena and on news channels, a grand debate still seems to be raging. If you went to one hundred doctors and ninety-seven gave you a cancer diagnosis, would you go back to the three who didn't for second opinions?

Given how slowly climate responds, many of the adverse effects of climate change are already baked into the system. It's like a big ship; it takes time to turn. But the United States is a remarkably resourceful society, and we can make big contributions to the solutions. We've responded to big environmental challenges before, like acid rain and the ozone hole. Innovation for the climate is coming fast, and there's reason for optimism.

So what should we be doing about all this? More on that when I reach Oregon. Time to get back on the bike.

OHIO:
AWAKENINGS

The sunny ride down the Ohio River again brought the comforting sound of chain spinning through sprockets. I zoomed by a mural of a sidewheeler, painted on the side of a barn, that recalled the riverboat days of the 1800s. The Ohio remains the commercial artery of the Midwest, serving the same function as the Rhine River in Europe. The Ohio has the same pleasing dimensions as the Rhine, a similar width and depth, with just as much ship traffic but fewer castles.

Not far down the river is Point Pleasant, West Virginia, where the first NOAA ship I served on was built. During my sea years, we would be thrown around in gales out on the Atlantic, listening to the sound of the hull twisting and creaking. An often-heard line from the crew was "How much do you think those fellas in West Virginia know about building ships?" We weathered every storm, so the answer would be "Enough."

My legs were tired and my knees sore. After 540 miles in ten days across the Appalachians, I was ready for a rest day. Salvation waited at Athens, home to Ohio University and my friends Debb and Mark Thorne. I had met them on my first long ride back in 2000, in the eastern Washington grain town of Garfield. At the end of a seventy-mile day, I had stopped into the only restaurant in town and asked for the number of the town policeman. It was common to camp in the town parks but wise to let the police know you'd be there. After I hung up the phone, the red-haired waitress said, "Why don't you just stay up at our place?" I was floored. No one had ever offered me a place to stay out of the blue.

Debb was that waitress. She was finishing a PhD at Washington State in sociology before doing a postdoc at Harvard with Elizabeth Warren. She went on to a faculty appointment at Ohio University, later moving to the University of Idaho. Debb has a big laugh, offers an opinion (usually considered) on almost everything, and remains a cowgirl at heart. She and Mark, also then on the Ohio faculty, care for their three horses and other miscellaneous animals. On the road I often woke up wondering where I was. At Debb and Mark's I awakened wondering what this cat was doing sitting on my chest.

Debb had a full day off the bike planned for me, setting up an interview on the local public television station, WOUB, as well as a seminar on observing climate change from a platform considerably slower than a satellite. After digging out my only collared shirt and wrinkled long pants from the panniers, I sat nervously across from the interviewer. But the questions were easy. She asked about how climate change was affecting Ohio. I told her that one of the most substantial impacts in the Midwest, outside of the warming temperatures, was the increase in heavy downpours over the last three decades (and especially on my helmet). It's not hard to understand. Warm air holds more water, increasing both evaporation and precipitation. It's like the whole water cycle gets goosed up. A fair amount of that water cycle would be coming down on me shortly, along with wide swaths of other people, businesses, and farms.

At the seminar, the questions were less about climate and more about the cross-country ride and why anyone would do such a thing. Later, Debb talked about her students' views on climate.

"You've got a small group that's active. They tend to self-select and migrate toward environmental science majors. Those are the ones who came to your talk. Then there's a small group that doesn't buy it at all. The largest proportion accepts the fact of climate change. They don't discount that it's occurring, but it's someplace else. Yes, temperatures are up and islands are disappearing, but it doesn't affect them."

That's not an uncommon position. Lots of people see climate change as something happening elsewhere or off in the future. They don't connect the dots of a heat wave this particular summer or a series of springtime downpours to a changing climate.

"Any thoughts about fracking in Ohio?" I asked.

"The local students by and large aren't concerned. This part of Ohio is part of Appalachia, and the coal mines have been around for a while. This is just the next step for the extractive industries."

There may be more to be concerned about these days. As I saw in Pennsylvania, fracking generates large amounts of wastewater. All of those wastewater trucks are going somewhere, typically to wells in Ohio where waste is injected deep into the earth. In 2011, a swarm of over 109 small earthquakes was detected in the Youngstown, Ohio, area, where there were no earthquakes in the recorded past. These were directly tied to a waste injection well.[1]

Oklahoma provides a case study of what happens when this wastewater disposal gets out of hand. Before 2008, Oklahoma averaged two magnitude 3.0 or larger earthquakes per year. In one six-month period in 2014, there were 183. The U.S. Geological Survey (USGS) concluded that deep injection of wastewater is the primary cause of the dramatic rise in detected earthquakes in the central United States. Oklahoma is now more seismically active than California and only behind Alaska in US states.[2]

This matters particularly for preparedness. People in California are used to the ground shaking from time to time, and building codes have evolved to account for seismic activity. But this is quite new for the Great Plains and the Midwest. No one knows the vulnerability of Oklahoma buildings to earthquakes, although building codes designed to help structures resist tornadoes may help.

The oil and gas drillers are not beyond trying to cover their tracks. Much of the research linking fracking wastewater disposal and earthquakes in Oklahoma was done by Oklahoma Geological Survey scientists at the University of Oklahoma. Harold Hamm, president of oil and gas producer Continental Resources and a major donor to the university, requested a meeting with Larry Grillot, dean of the university's College of Earth and Energy in 2014. According to an email from Grillot to colleagues, "Mr. Hamm is very upset at some of the earthquake reporting to the point that he would like to see select OGS staff dismissed."[3] To the university's credit, no actions were taken.

At this writing, things seem to be quieting down in the ground somewhat, both in Youngstown and in Oklahoma. Youngstown has had only five small earthquakes (magnitude 1.5 or greater) in the year preceding September 2016. Oklahoma felt 619 earthquakes of magnitude 2.8 or greater during January–June 2016, versus 701 in the same period of 2015, according to USGS data.[4] Whether this is due to enhanced state regulations or the drilling bust, as seen in Pennsylvania, is open to question. And it should be noted that the strongest earthquake in Oklahoma history took place in September

2016. Regardless, Ohio would be well advised to keep an eye on their deep injection wells.

It was time to leave Athens and familiar faces and head west once again. But there was one more appointment. Out on the road in the heat and the rain, with the nasty taste of warm water from plastic bottles, one gets to wishing for odd things. My dream was focused on finding "the college-town coffee shop." It came true in Athens, no mean feat. My standards were high. First and most important, there needed to be a big soft chair, in sight of where the coffee is poured. No paper cups allowed, only big warm ceramic coffee mugs. A little rich brown dust is in the air from that last bag of fresh-ground Ethiopian beans. Strange music must fill the air, with lots of people talking intently. Such a place, precisely, was Donkey Coffee in Athens. I lingered over a just-baked scone and a cup of big strong dark roast. Yet another Ohio awakening. And then back out into the sunlight.

The road waited outside, suddenly quiet, heat firing up for the day. But the journey wasn't quite so lonely as it might seem. Brief exchanges on the road, just a second or two of conversation, would give me a little boost. A man noticed me as he was walking down his driveway:

"Looks like you're going a ways."

"Oregon."

"God bless and speed you."

Or the flagman on a construction project, waving me by:

"Can't stop you. With that load you might never get started again."

And there was always a little electronic eye in the sky following me. Before leaving, I had activated the Find My iPhone feature. Concetta and her students were tracking my progress day by day. Preparing for her lesson, she checked on me over lunch one day and noticed that the little moving red dot stopped suddenly in the middle of nowhere and moved off-road. Switching to satellite view, she saw the trees and thought, *I know what he's doing.*

The phone rang in my back pocket, out in the woods.

"Could I get a little privacy please?"

"Sorry. Just checking in." I could feel the mischievous smile six hundred miles away.

On the way across southern Ohio, I stopped off in Chillicothe's Hopewell Culture National Historical Park, a well-preserved site from a civilization of mound builders living roughly the same time as the Roman Empire. Huge grassy hills in shapes of squares or circles, used for feasts or funerals, cover the field. The amount of earth moved in the central Ohio region for the Hopewell civilization is about the same as for the Egyptian pyramids.

In the collections of artifacts from the mounds was a shiny black knife made of obsidian, volcanic glass. Bill Huebner, the bookstore manager at the park, was anxious to talk about it.

"That one's a treasure, and we know it's not from around here. By its chemistry, we can trace it back to Yellowstone Park. We think that someone from these cities actually went there and brought this back." I would be passing through Yellowstone in about seventeen hundred miles, which would take me forty-three days on the bike. This traveler would have made the journey on foot.

"How do you know this wasn't passed on from tribe to tribe?" I asked.

"We've got a couple of reasons to think it wasn't traded. Yellowstone was vacant at the time, and we have found no obsidian trade route. If it was a traded good, it should be ubiquitous. But we just found this here."

In the Midwest and South, one encounters tantalizing hints of vast, complex civilizations almost completely lost to us. The site of the largest settlement in North America before Philadelphia was named Cahokia, east of St. Louis, within sight of the Gateway Arch. In its heyday around 1250, the city was larger than London at that time. Like Chillicothe, it was abandoned long before the first contact with Europeans, so Old World disease or conquest were not factors in its disappearance. Its decline is a mystery, although climate change and drought are high on the list of suspected causes.

Artifacts discovered at Cahokia imply trading networks extending to the Gulf of Mexico and beyond. But the obsidian knife at Chillicothe suggested that there might have been a North American Marco Polo on my route, long before Marco Polo.

The rains came back soon enough. Approaching Hillsboro, the Doppler radar showed the thunderheads all dressed up in their finest red and orange, sweeping in from the west. I wasn't sure I could make it to town before they hit. As I pulled over the last hill, I noticed that the far cornfield had vanished into gray, and the near field was rapidly disappearing. Thunder cracked. It was seconds away.

A hundred yards ahead was the tin-roofed picnic shed of the Buckeye Dairy Bar, and I went for it. I had just made it in as water poured out of the sky, and the shed kept me at least partly dry. I poked out from under the shed to talk with a woman parked in her car, waiting for a food order. She was less than optimistic about what lay in store.

"Looks like we're going to get it again tomorrow," she said.

"You can't trust those weather forecasters."

"Yeah, that's what my husband says, too."

A soggy barbecue and fries later, the rain had backed off, but only just. I rode to the motel like a salmon swimming upstream, through torrents running down the shoulder. I found that I had not just a good bike but a good whitewater bike.

The Dairy Bar woman was right. We got it the next day, and the next, and the next. This was the beginning of a new appreciation of heat for me, both on the bike and off. I got into the habit of hugging the World Dryer, the ubiquitous replacement for hand towels at fast-food restaurants. The hugging was less about global oneness than hypothermia. Three days after the rain began, as I rode through Cincinnati and past the Great American Ballpark, where the Reds play, a crowd of little boys waited under an awning. They were clutching their baseball gloves and looking skyward optimistically. Sure enough, within an hour the rain had drifted away and the game was on. The power of prayer.

I would ride into Indiana from Cincinnati. On the TransAm ride, Ohio for me was a big, warm, welcoming place, centered around the friends and coffee shops and bike shops of Ohio University in Athens. But what lingered with me most about this land was the great lost civilization, the Mound Builders, vanished before the Europeans appeared. They had even built a mound shaped like a coiled serpent, visible only from the sky. When I returned to Ohio, the land would tell stories of a more recent time, when white settlers dreamed of Great Awakenings, of new towns on a new frontier with a new moral compass. And of a strong-willed minority who would help the refugees from slavery on their way to freedom.

I would have one more ride through Ohio. In 2015, I rode on a route of the Underground Railroad, beginning in Mississippi, crossing the Ohio River at Augusta, Kentucky, and going up the western side of Ohio to Lake Erie. The trip was about fifteen hundred miles.

In the years before the Civil War, western Ohio was a hotbed of .abolitionism. Kentucky, a slave state, lay just across the river. Ohio was a free state, but gangs of slave hunters roamed the countryside, particularly after passage of the Fugitive Slave Act in 1850. The act compelled citizens to assist in the capture of runaway slaves.

The 2015 ride would bring me another image of the Ohio River. In the town of Ripley, on a high bluff overlooking nine bends of the Ohio, stands a little red brick house where a flinty-eyed Presbyterian minister would look out on the landscape of slavery on the far shore. From 1828 to 1865, Rev. John Rankin and his family kept a light in the window of the house, signaling safe passage for escaping slaves, helping thousands. One night a woman, Eliza, and her baby escaped across the frozen Ohio River with slave hunters in pursuit. Somehow she made it across, up the hundred steps to the Rankin House and, ultimately, freedom. Rankin later told the story to fellow abolitionist Lyman Beecher and his daughter, Harriet Beecher Stowe. The desperate story of Eliza would find its way into Stowe's *Uncle Tom's Cabin*.

Farther north, the 2015 ride brought me to Oberlin, a town where the namesake college was the first in the nation to admit women and lead in the education of African-Americans before the Civil War. It was a hotbed of the abolitionist movement and one of the few places where fugitive slaves could live without fear of re-enslavement. Back in an Oberlin park is a monument to Lewis Sheridan Leary, a young free black man recruited by John Brown for his attack on the Federal Arsenal at Harpers Ferry in 1859, which was Brown's attempt to trigger a slave revolt in the South. Leary stares straight out of a scratched daguerreotype: thin mustache, bow tie and jacket, broad-brimmed hat at an angle. He was killed on the second day at Harpers Ferry.

According to family lore, Leary's blanket shawl was returned to his widow, Mary Patterson. She remarried and, some years later, cared for a baby grandson born into the new century, whom she would wrap in the shawl. The baby was Langston Hughes, who would become the great poet of the Harlem Renaissance. Hughes donated the shawl to the Ohio Historical Society, where it resides today in a nondescript building in Columbus. Last summer the curator unrolled it for me, a physical link to those passionate years. If objects can have power, the shawl certainly does.

As I reflected on the role Ohio played in our nation's great battle over slavery, I encountered some echoes of Ohio's religious past on the Little Miami Trail, a bike path in western Ohio. I came upon a big, strong, young guy pulling a trailer and another older man riding with him. Rich and Adam Hange are father and son. Rich is a retired fireman. Adam's a minister with the United Church of Christ in Shaker Heights, Ohio. They were riding through Ohio from Covington, Kentucky, to Erie, Pennsylvania.

We stopped for a drink on that hot summer day. I was hesitant to ask Adam about his views on climate, as many heartland churches are places where disbelief in man-made climate change runs strong. After asking him, I realized that I needn't have been concerned.

"I like traveling by bike partly because of the low carbon footprint," he said. "We're trying to see if maybe we could make the trip completely car free.

"We believe that faith and science can coexist," he continued. "We've actually been working on divesting our pension funds from fossil fuels. But it's a little different for us than in Catholic or Episcopal churches in that things start in the local congregations and work their way up, rather than having things necessarily handed down from the top."

"We're trying to work on pension divestment from fossil fuels where I live, in Montgomery County, Maryland," I replied. "We get a lot of pushback from the financial people, though. They hate limits on their diversification."

Adam offered a philosophical outlook on divestment. "We believe that a budget is fundamentally a moral document. It shows where your priorities are."

I parted with Adam and Rich after a while, reflecting on the powerful moral and religious subtext to what was going on in Ohio, back when Ohio was the frontier. Many of the people there believed they were part of a moment in history, a new start. Indeed much of the settlement of western Ohio was associated with the Second Great Awakening, a religious revival in the early 19th century. In the 1830s, preachers thundered messages of personal salvation from the pulpit of the cavernous First Church of Oberlin and, thirty years later, announced the signing of the Emancipation Proclamation there. Today, perhaps a bit more quietly, Adam Hange of Shaker Heights speaks of faith and science, of aligning core values with investments, and it's starting from the congregation on up.

Two days after my return from the Underground Railroad ride in 2015, Pope Francis released his encyclical *Laudato Si*, dealing with climate change, the environment, and the poor. A science adviser on the encyclical, Hans Schellnhuber, commented:

The hard lesson scientists have learned in recent years is that presenting the facts and data about global warming and other environmental problems has not been enough to move the public to action. The issues have become so serious that only a broad moral awakening can offer hope of solving them.[5]

I wonder if the kind of long-ago passion, that awakening that was alive in 1840s Ohio, could be turned toward our Earth. No one can make a moral equivalence between the abomination that was slavery and climate change. Yet as Pope Francis notes, we watch as a quarter of the Earth's population living on coastlines are increasingly put into jeopardy as sea level rises. We watch as high mountain forests are lost, oceans acidify, and storms grow more intense by the year. Perhaps it is a time for another awakening, as happened in Ohio a long time ago. In *Laudato Si* the pope calls on us:

Human beings, while capable of the worst, are also capable of rising above themselves, choosing again what is good, and making a new start.

I'm in.

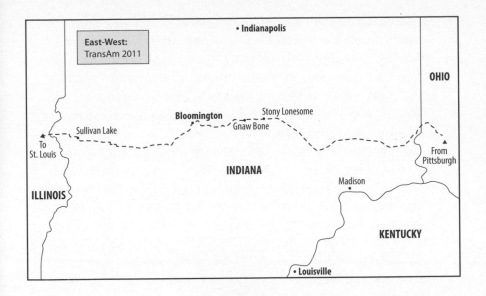

East-West:
TransAm 2011

Indianapolis

OHIO

Stony Lonesome
Bloomington
Gnaw Bone
Sullivan Lake
To
St. Louis

From
Pittsburgh

INDIANA

Madison

ILLINOIS

KENTUCKY

Louisville

INDIANA:
RAIN GAMES

With an occasional break or two, the rains stayed on as I crossed into Indiana, four days after they first began. I was riding through a six-foot layer of spray coming off car and truck tires. I could look up at my helmet cover and watch as a droplet rolled across from left to right, then back again, like a metronome. It's got to fall soon. It's got to. Drip. Then the next one appeared. Drip. The Droplet Theater could be a bit hypnotizing. Keeping focus on that next street, that car pulling out, that gravel patch, was a steady effort mentally, combined with the physical effort of just staying upright amid the spray. In skiing, the worst falls come at the end of the day, the tired falls. As the afternoon turned grayer, I had to find a way to avoid that vault over the handlebars. Asphalt is a lot harder than snow.

Such were the rain games, played with the combination of wet skin under the jacket and warm body core. They worked well enough until the wheels rolled to a halt. Once my feet hit the pavement, the cold would penetrate very quickly. It was this that kept me going more than anything else, but then, suddenly, I found myself contemplating a stop, despite the impending chill. Just before the Indiana border, I saw the sign for William Henry Harrison's grave. Harrison was the hero of the Battle of Tippecanoe and our ninth and briefest president. He caught pneumonia after a too-long inaugural address on a blustery March day. I like to visit quirky historical sites, so I started up the hill to catch a look. Then I heard a voice from old Tippecanoe himself: "Son, get out of the cold." Considering the president's experience with a bad chill, I turned around and retreated to the motel.

There was an awful lot of water in the Midwest that spring. May 2011 brought record rainfall to parts of Indiana and extensive flooding to the state. Out on the road, I had the chance to see most of the cornucopia of roadkill that our nation has to offer. When I started seeing frogs in the mix, that was a good sign that it was getting pretty wet. So it was in Indiana that spring.

I had stopped in at a roadside diner to warm up and dry out just a little. I peeled off the layers, using every chair at the table for a clothesline and getting a few sidelong glances. As I settled into coffee and Danish, a couple of guys in jeans and flannel shirts were talking behind me. One wore a Pioneer seed corn cap.

"Looks like this week's gonna be another washout."

"I got some spots won't dry out for a week even if it stops tomorrow. Which it won't."

"Must be that global warming thing."

"Yeah, that's what they all say. Lotta money in that global warming. Getcha a government grant, you'll be all set."

I bit my lip. The amount of money in that global warming thing is something I know about. I used to run the U.S. Global Change Research Program office, the coordinating body between the various federal agencies involved with climate change research. One of our jobs was to keep track of how much was being spent. In 2011, that was about $2.5 billion, which is not chump change. Though to put it in perspective, oil and gas revenues in the United States in 2011 were $186 billion.

But the basic implication of this overheard exchange is that scientists are on the take in a grand plot to fool the world on climate change. Where did the farmers get this stuff? It's not hard to find. In fact, in some places it's received wisdom. Sen. James Inhofe of Oklahoma wrote a book entitled *The Greatest Hoax: How the Global Warming Conspiracy Threatens Your Future*. People will believe what they want. In thirty years in the field, I've seen empire building and some less-than-wise use of taxpayer dollars. What I've never seen was any hint of a "conspiracy."

Why didn't I engage these farmers in conversation? They're probably driving the pickup trucks that will pass me twenty minutes down the road. It was unlikely to be any kind of a problem. But on the other hand, I'd had some close calls that seemed intentional. One can feel a little vulnerable out there. But in plain truth, at that moment, I was simply too tired.

Indiana had more than a few surprises for me, and one came in a note on the guestbook of my blog. Tom Pritchard, a cyclist in the small town of Madison, had been following me online and saw that I was riding near his home. He posted an invitation for me to stay at his house. That's not so uncommon. There's even an online site called "Warm Showers" for people hosting touring cyclists.

I would spend that night out of the rain, under a big, soft, heavy quilt. Tom's one of those people whom small towns are built around. He's an engineer, woodworker, and Elks Club member.

As a volunteer firefighter, he drives the pump truck and helps pry people out of car wrecks. Cancer surgery in 2008 slowed him down, but not for long. Someday he'll ride across on the TransAm.

His wife, Karen, filled their Madison house with the smell of pork tenderloin that night. Madison is two towns: the downtown, historic riverfront town across from Kentucky, and the Hilltop, the ridge up above town with strip malls fading into farmland. Karen was the Hilltop girl ("We always thought they were a little snooty up there," he says), and Tom was one of those rough downtown boys. They've been married for thirty-six years now. I'm a sucker for sweet old love stories.

That same geography made Madison an Underground Railroad hotbed in the days before the Civil War. The hard part for fugitive slaves escaping across the river was to get past the downtown, where slave hunters roamed the waterfront, and up to the Hilltop, where antislavery towns and churches offered refuge. George DeBaptiste, a downtown African-American barber and conductor, would "borrow" horses overnight from the stable of the local slave-hunting sheriff. They would carry fugitives up the Eagle Hollow ravine from the river to the Hilltop, then return the horses by first light. Eagle Hollow is one of Tom's favorite bike routes.

The next morning, Tom drove me back to North Vernon, where he had picked me up. Unfortunately, he dropped me off a little ways farther down the road. That little stretch of asphalt would become my Missing Mile, the only piece between Atlantic and Pacific that I didn't ride. It provided a good excuse to come back one day.

I'd left the warm cocoon of Tom and Karen's and set back out into the Midwest waterworld. That day I rolled through the towns of Gnaw Bone and, eight miles on, Stony Lonesome. It exactly fit my state of mind. The road was beginning to gnaw, and I had passed well outside of the point where Concetta could easily come bring me home. I had begun to rely more on motels and less on campgrounds for shelter. I had not anticipated the rain chasing me from soggy campgrounds, so my budget often led to lesser-starred establishments in small towns. The idea of a hard, fixed roof as opposed to a nylon sheet sagging with raindrops seemed positively decadent. But as a friend who rode with me on a later trip said, regarding choice of accommodations, "I'm not saying your standards are low. I just haven't been able to detect any."

I opened my eyes those mornings to the sound of rain in the gutters and the view of a riding wardrobe clipped to the plastic curtains above the air conditioner. These were remnants of a desperate overnight battle to dry out. It wasn't an optimistic landscape, and getting out of bed took a little doing. What was the pull? In more than an abstract sense, it was something that had drawn Lewis and Clark, the Oregon Trail pioneers, and Steinbeck: the West. Outside the motel room door, beyond the Mississippi, there was an ocean of grass ahead, lapping at the base of great mountains. It was a feeling not so different from my seagoing days. When a ship gets underway, there is a moment of sheer possibility, when the lines come off the pier and the bow swings out toward the open sea.

Once the wheels started spinning in the morning, everything changed. Out on the road alone, in the long stretches between towns, I could drift off into a different place. It must be something like the state of long-distance runners, but with a lower level of exertion and a higher awareness of the surroundings. I began to listen to red-winged blackbirds and their *conk-la-ree* call. They would be talking about me up on the power lines, giving a *check! check!* alarm before flying off across the fields. They were companions for much of the ride across the center of the country, speaking in a language I could almost understand.

I approached Bloomington, home of Indiana University and the Little 500, the premier college bike race in the country. Back in 1979, it was the setting for the cult cycling film *Breaking Away*, costarring an impossibly young Dennis Quaid. Bloomington's a huge cycling town and the perfect place for a rest day. I found my college-town coffee shop, the unofficial waiting room while the crew at Bikesmiths, the local bike shop, performed neurosurgery on my machine. Any town with this much cycling history is bound to have some good mechanics. Beth, a tiny woman with long brown hair and unmanicured hands, worked over the front and rear brakes together with installing a new drive train. By the time I got back on the road, the bike was spinning magnificently. In my gratitude, I'd have turned around and ridden back to Bloomington to marry Beth, but Concetta would have been upset.

During the following rest day, I'd set up a presentation for Cindy Kvale's physics classes at Bloomington South High School. Her classroom was a showcase of ideas, posters, and physics props. Besides teaching, she found time to sponsor the Solar Racing Team and the Science Olympiad. She showed off the solar-powered bike that her students had been working on. As the bell rang, the first of the students started drifting in.

The class was quite engaged for the presentation. Along with the frequent questions about day-to-day life on a long bike tour, one question stood out:

"Carbon dioxide gets used in plants. Wouldn't more of it in the air be a good thing for them?"

"Very nice," I responded. "You've obviously been hanging out in bio class, too. It's quite true that plants take up carbon dioxide, and all things being equal, increasing CO_2 tends to increase plant growth. If you add CO_2 to a greenhouse, that's what usually happens. But all things aren't equal. Increasing temperature often means increases in insect pests, and that's what's happening in the high forests of the Rockies. And while it's not getting drier here in Indiana, climate change in the Southwest and many other regions is leading to long-term drought and changing the composition of forests. So you have to look at the whole picture rather than just the fertilization effect of CO_2." The kids were pretty quick.

"Are polar bears in trouble because of global warming?" one asked.

"Well, they depend on sea ice in the Arctic to hunt for seals, and Arctic sea ice has certainly been decreasing over the last few decades," I said. "And by the way, don't believe all those cute polar bears you see in commercials. A friend of mine worked on icebreakers in the Arctic, putting instruments out on the ice. Away from the ship, polar bears were what they were most worried about. If you're a black moving speck on the ice, you look like food."

As adults, most of us are wrapped up with the here and now, with what's going to happen today or tomorrow. High school kids seem to be more open to looking at the complete system, to getting an idea of what's going on with the long-term fate of the planet, because that will affect their lives. Subconsciously, adults may be more willing to discount the future in favor of the present.

I finished off at Bloomington South in time for a final stroll around the college town. It would be my last high school talk of the ride, as schools in the Midwest typically close by the end of May, with exams filling the end of the schedule.

The weather was brightening up in Bloomington on the way out. As with anyone wandering the American landscape, I renewed my fascination with road signs. Leaving town, I passed the sign for College Books (Open 24 Hours. Noveltease. XXX Videos), which was certainly catering to some nonacademic endeavors. Farther on, I passed the advertisement for the Friendship Shoot, surely a useful app for Facebook. Okay, so Friendship was the name of the next town to the south. But the sign was matched in barbarity only by the Pennsylvania billboard for the Christian Barbecue.

The most important sign was one right under my nose. Not far outside Bloomington, the bike computer rolled over a thousand miles. Four digits on the odometer felt good, but I wasn't even a quarter of the way across the United States. And the real challenges were still to come.

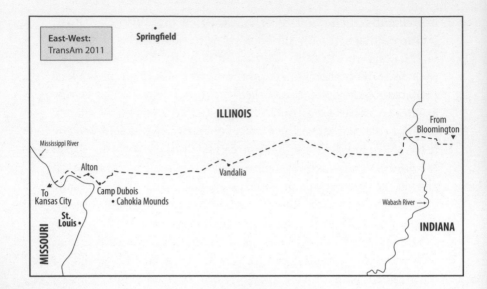

Springfield

ILLINOIS

From Bloomington

Mississippi River

Alton

Vandalia

To Kansas City

Camp Dubois
• Cahokia Mounds

Wabash River →

St. Louis •

MISSOURI

INDIANA

ILLINOIS:
ON MR. JEFFERSON'S ROAD

T he land begins to flatten out in western Indiana, giving the first glimpses of the great land-ocean that is the center of our continent. I spent a pleasant night at Sullivan Lake State Park, near the Illinois border. This was the first time I set up in the ominous-sounding Primitive Area, the space reserved for tent campers. As I drifted off, the tales of Joshua Slocum, author of *Sailing Alone*

Around the World in 1899, came to mind. One night at anchor in the Straits of Magellan, Slocum seeded the deck with carpet tacks to guard against pirates from Tierra del Fuego. He was awakened by their screams as they scrambled to get off his boat. A tip perhaps for campgrounds of darkest Indiana.

The next day's forecast looked good, and I spun west, telephone poles lined up to the horizon. I soon crossed the Wabash River into Illinois, into the first of the prairie country. Slocum wrote of "trade winds, fragrant of the spices" before sighting land in the Indian Ocean. Approaching land and sea is not so different. A lighthouse normally provides first landfall on crossing the ocean. Coming across the prairie, the first sight of a town is usually a water tower, or perhaps a grain elevator, rising above the curve of the Earth.

It was high noon with the pavement shimmering when I stopped for lunch at a small-town ice cream shop. My table was in the midst of a crowd of fourth-graders. The hostess brought water to the table immediately. Guess I looked thirsty. A boy in a Lego T-shirt sat down at my table, his teacher watching from across the room.

"Is that your bike?" he asked.

"Why, yes it is. I'm just riding through town. What's your name?"

"I'm Max. Where are you going?"

"Oregon."

He paused, not quite knowing how to process that. "I have a green bike and a blue bike," he said after a while. "The blue bike doesn't work because the tire has blown up."

"That shouldn't be too hard to fix."

"My grandma died last week. I'm going to have to move. I don't know where."

I caught my breath. That was hard to fix. From the front, a voice: "Come on, Max. Time to line up."

"I gotta go now." And that quickly, he was out the door.

The next day on the Illinois prairie should have been an easy, boring ride down US 40. It was neither. The easy part vanished early. As I turned left onto the road, the wind blasted in my face, enough to keep the flags stretched full out. It was strong enough to keep me down on the drop handlebars, driving into it all day. Every mile came dearly, with crumbling asphalt and the thinnest of shoulders. Much of US 40 is on the route of the National Road, the first federal public works project championed by President Jefferson. He was heavily criticized for it at the time, but it opened up much of the then-frontier territories of Ohio, Indiana, and Illinois.

After a morning of slugging it out on 40, I stopped at the old Illinois capitol building at Vandalia, where Lincoln was a state representative from 1834 to 1839. Just three years before his election, Lincoln had seen the horrors of the slave market in person when he took a flatboat down the Mississippi to New Orleans. In the capitol, stark wooden armchairs were lined against long desks around the Speaker's table. Stephen Douglas was Lincoln's colleague during that time. The gangly Lincoln and Douglas, "the Little Giant," must have made an odd pair. Twenty years later, the same pair would face off on the future of the nation and the issues of slavery and states rights. The Lincoln-Douglas debates would capture the attention of the nation and ultimately propel Lincoln toward the presidency.

The docent at the capitol suggested a stop at the Fayette County Museum next door. I was looking for another excuse to stay out of the wind, and that sounded like a good place to do it. The museum was a single floor, a bit like a rummage sale at an old garage. The curator, Mary, an older lady with a big, easy smile, came up to me.

"When you're done looking around, let me show you a few things from my favorite part of the museum, over in the corner."

I eventually wandered over to her, and she gave me a heavy brass ring, big enough to hold in two hands. "Do you know what this is?"

I turned it over. Engraved on the side was BELLE. J. W. GOSLEY, ANCHORAGE, JEFFERSON COUNTY, KY. "Okay, you've got me."

"That's a slave collar." It brought a vision of sweat, heat, and leg irons in dark wooden rail cars.

"Vandalia was an important stop on the Underground Railroad. That's the name of the slave and master," Mary said, pointing to the two names. "Belle escaped by stowing away in an actual railroad car and finding the safe house in Vandalia. That's where they took the collar off."

Belle would risk everything to go north. I gently laid the collar down. But I would remember the feel of it in my hands.

Mary's next stop was an exhibit of old agricultural implements. She held up what looked like a flat-bladed axe.

"This is called a froe. It was used for cutting shingles." She handed it to me. "Its owner had given it to his old foreman. He said he wouldn't be needing it anymore since he had just been elected to the state legislature." She pointed to the initials carved into the iron: A.L.

There was a time before the marble temple, before the lines went deep on his face. There was a time when he was just Abe, a lanky, funny-looking guy, easy with a smile and a story, restless, done working with his hands, ready for the next chapter. I tried to memorize the feel of the handle, the pattern of the grain on my fingertips, before giving it back. Was it real? Was it authentic? I had no idea, and it's probably impossible to verify. I know that I believed it to be real, and that an out-of-the-way county museum would be just the kind of place to come upon Abraham Lincoln's axe.

As I rode down the highway out of Vandalia, I shook my head in amazement at what had happened. This is a way I've come to love the road. There is a chance for tiny snapshots of people, if only for a moment or two, vivid jolts from lives long past and those yet to be lived. Mary and Max, Belle and Abe all come along with me now.

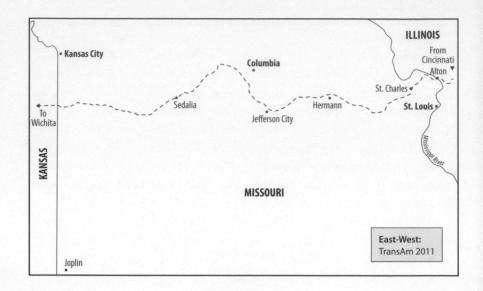

MISSOURI:
THE BEST PLACE IN A TORNADO

Westbound from Vandalia, flying across the flat countryside, I put the last of the southern Illinois prairie behind. I barreled through a construction site, apparently making a little too much noise. A ruffed grouse nesting there gave me a piece of her mind. I was sorry for the disturbance, but I was excited. The gateway to the West, the Mississippi River, was but a few miles away.

The wide-open grassland gave way to the massive oil refinery complex at Hartford, Illinois. Just past the refinery was a historical marker. In the winter before their departure, Lewis and Clark had established Camp Dubois there, the staging ground for their journey to the Pacific. They would become known as the captains, and they would dub their party the Corps of Discovery. From here they would vanish into the west, out of touch for two years.

The road dead-ended at a green, grassy hill, something Easterners like me don't know much about: a levee. I climbed the hill to gaze on tugs and barges laboring on a huge brown expanse: the Father of Waters. A different world would begin with Missouri on the far shore.

I followed the Mississippi north on the Illinois side. On a bright clear day, violent winds were coming off the river. I had to dismount to walk across a rattling, shaking steel footbridge. Swallows soared and corkscrewed in the gale. Something was up. The sky was darkening as I pulled in for dinner in the town of Alton, Illinois. The McDonald's cashier had a blond ponytail sticking out of her baseball cap. She took orders while anxiously keeping half an eye on the TV mounted on the far wall. In the broadcast era where weather forecasters are replaced by Storm Teams and Extreme Weather Centers, a little extra concern was radiating from the screen. Worried voices talking of wall clouds and rotation accompanied sweeping blotches of red and yellow. A knot of customers watched.

"What's going on?" I asked a sturdy guy in overalls.

"Big outbreak across the river. About a dozen funnel clouds already on the ground, trackin' east. They usually fizzle out late at night. Usually. Best stay near a cellar."

On the television, there was first mention of a place called Joplin. The thunderheads were boiling across Missouri that evening.

I finished dinner quickly. Camping was looking less appealing and the nearest motel more so. The one I found was the nastiest of the entire ride, which is saying something. The desk clerk was missing a few teeth, and behind him was a sign: DRUG PARAPHERNALIA FOUND IN THE ROOMS WILL BE REPORTED TO THE POLICE. I asked if he had a basement; he smiled and shook his head. In the room, only one of the lights worked, which might have been a blessing. The floor was gritty and the bed adorned by a well-used spread. The motel had utterly no saving graces but one: it was brick.

The storms blew over the brick motel that night, but the clocks stopped at 5:47 P.M. in Joplin, on the other side of Missouri. High school graduation ceremonies were held at the town auditorium because of the large seating capacity. The students were profoundly lucky. Across town a cafeteria camera recorded their high school being blown apart. It was the nightmare: a direct hit on a city by an EF5 tornado. The storm cut through the middle of town, killing 161 people, the worst in a quarter century. At the high-rise St. Johns Regional Medical Center, the windows were blasted out, sending glass shards through the floors. Doppler radar picked up a debris field a mile in the sky. Later in the ride, I spoke with a lady tending bar who had been there that day. She told me what it was like.

"We heard that freight-train roar they always talk about, then the whole building was shaking. It was over in a minute or two, and then I opened the door. The other side of the street was a big pile of matchsticks."

Big tornado outbreaks seem to be an annual occurrence these days, and one might suspect a link between a warming climate and more tornadoes. Warmer air holds more water, leading to more of the warm rising air that forms summer thunderheads. Indeed, there has been a 37 percent increase in heavy downpours over the Midwest.[1] But other factors affect tornado formation, such as changes in the vertical and horizontal winds. Despite the increase in severe storms, there is no clear trend in the frequency or strength of tornadoes since the 1950s for the United States. Unfortunately, batches of tornadoes would be the rule for my next few days in Missouri.

By the morning, the fierce storms from the night before had scrubbed the atmosphere clean. I rolled up along the Mississippi on the clearest of days. Against the background of a bright blue sky and green cornfields, a shining silver bridge came into view. The Clark Bridge at Alton suspends the roadway from two towers by cables like strands from a spiderweb, in a style known as cable-stayed. The locals call it the Superbridge. It bounced in truck traffic and seemed like a thing alive. I carefully walked the bike across, gripping tightly to the handlebars. My path to the West arched 150 feet over the river. The Mississippi, muddy as in song, was churning and full of debris from the recent storms. Through the slots in the deck I watched a tug and barge pass underneath.

The Katy Trail began about thirty miles from there. It's a rail trail, an old railroad right-of-way converted to a walking/cycling path. The Katy is perhaps the foremost rail trail in the country, rolling 237 miles across most of Missouri. For much of the way it's a dirt-and-gravel tunnel through the forest, with the Missouri River on the left and bluffs on the right. "Katy" is the nickname for the old Missouri-Kansas-Texas Railroad, or K-T. In the years after the Civil War, the train from the east only went as far as Sedalia, Missouri, and cattle drives brought herds from Texas to the rail-head there. These drives were the basis for the *Rawhide* television series, filmed in the early 1960s and starring Clint Eastwood. In the restored Sedalia train station is a photo of a hard-bitten young Eastwood trading a gunfighter stare with a local ten-year-old cowboy.

I had ridden hundreds of miles of highway to reach the Katy Trail. Before me stretched five days of trail riding, with no worries about traffic or shoulders, just the great moving presence of the Missouri off to the left. The dirt would slow me down a little, but mostly it was relaxing, like being back on the Chesapeake & Ohio Canal in Maryland. The obstacles were still to come.

The trail begins just east of St. Charles, Missouri. While Lewis and Clark assembled their expedition at Fort Dubois, this spot, north of St. Louis, was their formal starting point. Their statue, of course, looks west. Sergeant John Ordway wrote in his journal:

May the 14th 1804. Showery day. Capt Clark Set out at 3 oClock P. M. for the western expedition. one Gun fired. a nomber of Citizens see us Start. the party consisted of

3 Sergeants & 38 Good hands, which maned the Batteaux
and two pearogues.

I didn't linger for long with the captains, as the sky was becoming
"showery" for me as well. Lightning and the ragged edge of the
approaching storm chased me into a trailside toolshed. Looking
around at the jumble of axes and shovels and digging bars under the
galvanized steel roof, it occurred to me that this might not be the
safest place. The owner, a middle-aged guy in a ball cap, was looking
down watchfully from the second floor of the house, seated at his
kitchen window. I looked out from an open side of the shed. I had a
three-day beard and mud from the trail covering the front of my legs.

"Mind if I camp out in here for a few minutes while this passes
over?" I asked.

"No problem," he said in a gravelly voice. "And the basement
door is open if things get out of hand."

"Thanks, that's very kind."

"But I might be a little slow getting down there. I'm in a
wheelchair."

"How did that happen?"

"Used to work on the river. Slipped and got my leg caught
between the barge and the dock. Almost got myself a plaque at the
tug company office. But they managed to pull me out."

"That must have been hard."

"Bodies are very fragile things."

Our conversation was interrupted as things began to get a little
out of hand, like he said. Trees were swinging against a dark sky.
Leaves and branches were flying around. The rain front came
roaring through the high oaks. What would a funnel cloud look
like coming through a forest? I passed the time by counting the seconds between lightning and thunder, until they came at the same
time. I was getting ready to make that run for the basement. Then,
remarkably quickly, the lightning passed and the afternoon settled
into a steady rain. I reluctantly slid into clammy raingear and got
back on the bike. The kitchen window reopened.

"Thanks very much for the hospitality," I said.

"You be real careful out there."

I spent the rest of the day dodging puddles, remembering that bodies are indeed fragile things.

Dawn brought another sparkling clear morning and a respite from the storms. Clear sky, no wind, the country's premier bike trail— what's not to like? But the tempests of the last few days had cut a swath, and dozens of trees had fallen across the trail. This led to the cycling equivalent of portages: Stop, take the bags off the bike, haul it through the branches, and reassemble everything on the other side. I would be just up to speed again when I would come across the next downed tree.

These parts of the Katy Trail follow the initial route of Lewis and Clark as they fought their way up the Missouri River. They, too, were on the river in May. It's amazing to think that anyone could pole, sail, or paddle boats upriver against such an incredible torrent. Eddies of debris were carried along in the flood, too, making my stationary fallen trees seem easy compared to a floating tree hurtling down the river.

Another marker caught my eye. In 1804, the Corps of Discovery made one of their last stops before the wilderness at the Boone Settlement, where Daniel Boone, then seventy-two, and his extended family were living along the river. Daniel Boone meets Lewis and Clark! Except he didn't. Despite a meal at the settlement, the meeting between arguably America's most famous explorers and frontiersmen didn't happen. Boone never emerged. One can only speculate why. Were they intruding on the solitude of Boone's wilderness community? Was this the long arm of the government reaching into the frontier? Or maybe he was just an old guy with aches and pains from a lifetime of rugged living keeping him in his bed. For whatever reason, they never got together.

I rolled into the town of Hermann, utterly exhausted from bushwhacking my way across eastern Missouri. By then, the full tragic story of the Joplin tornado had emerged. Given the forecast for another outbreak in Missouri the next day, I could end up with a free ride to the Land of Oz if I stayed on the bike. It seemed like the time and place for a rest day. Hermann is an inviting little town with several wineries. The game plan called for a day of wine tasting, Doppler watching, and waiting for Armageddon.

Tourism has arrived in Hermann, with trains and buses coming in from St. Louis and Kansas City. After a leisurely breakfast, I walked up to the Stone Hill Winery, on a hill a mile outside of town. Missouri had a thriving wine industry up until the 1920s, but Carrie Nation, the temperance crusader who took hatchets to bars in the early 20th century, provokes a scowl even today. With Prohibition, the vineyards were destroyed. Their extensive cellars were converted to mushroom farming. The wine business didn't come back until 1965.

After a decadent steak-and-potatoes lunch complete with samples of the local vintage, I poked my head into the winery office, where the manager was busily tapping away at her keyboard.

"Any tornado warnings up?"

"Oh dear yes. All over the place."

"Um, am I going to die if I walk back into town?"

In a cheery voice, she said, "Let's go check the radar." She peered into her computer screen.

A voice came from another room. "They've got a confirmed touch down in Sedalia."

"Oh, Sedalia's a long ways from here. You'll be fine." I wasn't all that comforted.

It was an uneasy trip back into town. The air was thick, heavy, tropical. Breaks of sunshine made it through, but the afternoon was growing steadily darker. Occasional big drops of rain splatted on the pavement. The sky was almost a greenish color as I walked past the looming structure of Hermann High School, a FOR SALE sign propped in a classroom window. A distant, continuous rumble of thunder came from over the western horizon. The clouds were knotted up in the unusual scalloped form known as mammatocumulus, foretelling severe weather.

The rumbling put a briskness in my step coming into town. The wind had begun to swirl leaves and trash into little dust devils. As I turned onto Main Street, the siren went off. Lots of Midwesterners are used to tornado warnings, but it was a whole new thing for an Easterner, even a bit surreal. No one seemed to know quite what to do. Older people with nametags, presumably tourists, were sitting on the benches, looking around nervously. I caught the attention of one of them.

"Sir, that's the tornado siren," I said. "You might want to get inside." He slowly got up and started for the store.

On a scouting expedition the night before, I had learned that the Hermannhof Winery had the deepest cellars in town. I jogged off in their direction. A busy saleslady with a tight smile was just finishing the last purchase. She motioned to me.

"C'mon down. We've got plenty of room."

We descended into a musty, double-vaulted brick cellar, built 150 years ago. My breathless sprint through the gathering storm had given way to the quiet of the catacombs. Nine strangers had gathered, and I was the only one without a glass. Charlene, the Hermannhof lady, noticed.

"Now that is an emergency. I'll be right back." She disappeared up the stairs and reemerged with stemware and an '08 Chardonnay, dry and fresh and fragrant. It appeared that we would be forced to ride it out there. Despite poor cell reception, Charlene transmitted a few snippets from the outside world:

"The first one picked up but there's another one behind it."

Amid the oak barrels, sheltered from high winds and electronic signals, pours and tales accumulated. Charlene told of the local girl, Pearl White, who left Green Ridge for Hollywood a hundred years ago, becoming the silent film star of *Perils of Pauline*. Glasses raised.

"To the cliffhanger." [clink]

The conversation turned to hometowns. A solidly built, goateed veteran of a Chicago TV newsroom elaborated on secrets of acquiring the incriminating quote.

"To truth and justice." [clink]

I pitched in some well-embellished tales of crossing the Appalachians by bike. They were immediately topped by accounts of the mighty hills of Louisiana.

"Up by Shreveport, they're high enough to make your nose bleed. May you never have to face them." [clink]

Apparently a tornado had been spotted on the ground to the west, then touched down briefly in a cornfield on the other side of town. But Hermann had been spared. We emerged from the cellar after an hour or so, blinking in the sunlight. The town was still standing, as were we. A near thing on both counts.

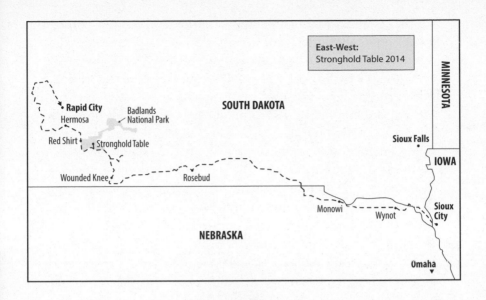

SOUTH DAKOTA:
NIGHT ON STRONGHOLD TABLE

At this point in my TransAmerican ride in Missouri, I stood on the shores of an ocean of grass and made ready to embark at the "gateway to the west." Though I didn't know it at the time, it wouldn't be my last bicycle crossing of the Great Plains. Just three years later, in 2014, I would be led to the Plains by the CIA. No, I'm not an ex-spy, regardless of what my brother-in-law thinks. The

Cowboy-Indian Alliance rode into Washington, D.C., that spring, and I would follow their trail.

It was quite a march. Ranchers and Native Americans came on horseback to the National Mall, setting up tepees and leading one of the great demonstrations against the Keystone Pipeline. The political battle over Keystone, the massive Canada-to-Texas oil project that is on track to be revived, remains one of the epic fights of the environmental movement. For climate activists, Keystone is an abomination, the drain in the bathtub for one of the great carbon reservoirs on the planet, the Canadian Tar Sands. For the riders on the Mall, it was personal. The pipeline route would cross ranches and aquifers, and in particular the Rosebud Indian Reservation of South Dakota. The Rosebud speakers were especially passionate. Inspired, later that spring, I set out to ride across this land. It didn't take that much inspiration, though. There was a place called Stronghold Table that had lived only in my imagination since I was a young man. More in a moment.

South Dakota has a challenging climate, naturally prone to dramatic changes, thanks to its location in the center of the continent, far from the moderating influence of the ocean. With the increasing temperatures, climate models paradoxically project both more frequent, intense droughts and heavier downpours when the rain does come. As the air grows warmer, it holds more water, leading to more evaporation and more rain and snow. The reservations are not wealthy places, with few resources to adapt to a changing climate.

But I had another reason to ride through the Lakota country. Back in 1980, my friend Jan Kublick and I had driven with our new brides from New York across to Wyoming on the quintessential cross-country road trip, detouring for a side trip to Badlands National Park. The Lakota first called this dry, rugged place of barren mesas and deep canyons *mako sica*, or 'land bad.' Later French trappers labeled it *les mauvais terres pour traverser*, or 'bad lands to travel through.'

We had traveled the park's loop road through the eroded alkali landscape and were looking for nothing more than a place to get out of the heat. We pulled into the visitor center. After a soda, I wandered off into a dark back corner where a glass case stood. I remembered some old history, and my jaw dropped a bit. In the case was a shirt of white cotton cloth with loose sleeves, fringed with leather. Faded images of birds and stars covered the front. A Ghost Shirt. The panel said that the person who had worn it, an adherent of the Ghost Dance, believed that the soldiers' bullets could do him no harm.

The Lakota practiced their religion on a mesa far out into the Badlands, a place called Stronghold Table. The Ghost Shirts were worn in an incredible act of faith, or desperation, at Wounded Knee in 1890. After that trip I could never completely put the Ghost Dance story out of my mind. A tattered manila folder labeled BADLANDS, full of maps, would wait in the back of my file cabinet for three decades.

1890

"The old crier told me to move my people who were poorly mounted to the Bad Lands." With these words Short Bull told of how he led a group of Lakota, known to the outside world as Sioux, in the winter of 1890 to a great table mesa, the natural fortress known as the Stronghold. Short Bull was a respected medicine man of the Brulé Lakota, described by the Indian agency physician at Pine Ridge as "an open, generous and kind-hearted man who attends with diligence to his own business . . . His face always wears a smile."

Despite the smile, he had much on his mind. By 1890, the Indian Wars were long past, the Lakota driven from their sacred Black Hills, their Paha Sapa, "the heart of everything that is," and forced onto ever-shrinking reservations on the poorest land. The Black Hills are clearly visible from the Pine Ridge, largest of the Lakota reservations and my destination in 2014.

With the buffalo decimated and the Lakota lacking farming or ranching skills, they were dependent on government rations promised by treaty. But Congress had cut back rations in the 1880s under the slogan of "root, hog, or die"—essentially, fend for yourself. It was not so different from the British attitude toward the Irish people during the Potato Famine in the 1840s. England's man in charge of easing the famine, Sir Charles Trevelyan, declared, "Dependence on charity is not to be made an agreeable mode of life," a sentiment not unknown today.

Disease and starvation followed for the Lakota. The population of the Pine Ridge had dropped from thirty thousand in 1876, the year of the Little Big Horn, to nineteen thousand in 1890. Even worse, in 1890 a great drought spread over the High Plains, and crop failure was widespread. The Lakota were desperate for hope of any kind.

From the West, news of a prophet came by letter and word of mouth. His name was Wovoka, and he spoke of a religion and a dance that would make lost ancestors reappear, the buffalo return, and nonbelievers disappear from the continent. It came to be known as the Ghost Dance. Short Bull was one of those chosen to make a pilgrimage to see the prophet in the Walker Valley of Nevada. In the winter of 1889–90, he traveled fifteen hundred miles from reservation to reservation, through the deep winter snows of the Rockies to the council fires of Wovoka.

In 2014, thirty-five years after our first cross-country trip, Jan and I pulled out of the Flying J truck stop in Hermosa, South Dakota, and headed across the dry, treeless prairie on two fully loaded bicycles. We were carrying all we would need for the next two days in the Badlands and the adjacent Pine Ridge Reservation. Our contingency plan for "what if something happens" was a little sketchy.

I had led him on, pulled by the old manila folder. Somewhere out in the Badlands was the remote, mystical fortress called the Stronghold. It sits on the Pine Ridge, a hard place, now as in 1890. It is still one of the poorest places in the nation. Life expectancy is forty-eight on the reservation, and alcohol and drug problems are severe.

Jan and I had been on many journeys together. Always the sober, analytical one, he retained the angular face and build of the undersized, small-town quarterback. As a lawyer, he spent many days listening to stories of what happens when things go wrong. I believe he was coming along as much to protect me as anything else. Still, this journey would take some convincing. His email came two months before our planned departure: "What indices of safety are you relying on?"

He wasn't the only one with concerns. Over lunch, we mentioned the ride through the Pine Ridge to a waitress in nearby Rapid City. She mumbled, "Like Harlem. Worse than Harlem." I suspected that she hadn't been to either place. Still, it gave me an uneasy feeling that the old manila folder was taking us into a place where we had no idea of what was going to happen.

Yet we soon found ourselves rolling across the grasslands into the heat from Hermosa, leaving traffic, houses, and trees behind. Later Jan would confess, "Never had I looked back with such longing at an air-conditioned interstate truck stop." We were pushing the heaviest bicycles we'd ever ridden. Much of the weight was in five water bottles on each bike, since there was no sure water source until noon the next day. And even then, it still wouldn't be enough, so we had to ration. Getting water from the rivers would be questionable. The early settlers described the sediment-laden streams of the Badlands as "too thick to drink, too thin to plow."

Raptors floated on thermals above the grassland. Temperatures were headed to triple digits with barely a breeze. Sweat started to cake up on my forehead by midmorning.

As we rode, we looked out over a landscape made of great flat-topped mesas known as tables, usually separated by deep ravines.

After twenty-three miles, we crossed the Cheyenne River onto the Pine Ridge Reservation. In the valley between two tables was the settlement of Red Shirt, consisting of a dozen houses and a school. Hoping to top off our already depleted water bottles, we knocked on the school door. A huge Lakota with thick-rimmed glasses, curly black hair, and scraggly beard answered. His appearance was a little intimidating. After we asked about water, he introduced himself as Lance, working security for the school.

"C'mon in out of the sun. Grab all the water you want. Here, I'll show you what we've got. Now's a good time, the kids just went home for the summer yesterday."

A big multicolor WELCOME sign hung inside, not far from the prominently displayed montage of Custer's Last Stand. The library had a full-size tepee in the middle, where the librarian read stories. Hung in the halls were pictures and stories of Lakota veterans. The gym displayed a banner over the back wall: HOME OF THE RED SHIRT RUMBLE. Under a round ceiling, the gym was known, of course, as the Rumble Dome. As we sat down for lunch at an outside table in the shadow of the school, Lance emerged from the building.

"Can you guys fit into these? We've got plenty." He brought out a pair of black T-shirts, emblazoned in red with RUMBLE BASKETBALL and an angry-looking buffalo.

"Perfect. Amazing. Thanks so much." It lives today in a dresser drawer, a talisman.

We'd gotten way too comfortable in the shade, and before long it was back out into the heat of the reservation and the big, hot climb onto Red Shirt Table. The Badlands and the Stronghold lay ahead.

1890

Short Bull stayed for five days in Nevada with the prophet, along with hundreds of Indians from across the West. Wovoka was a young, charismatic Paiute, almost six feet tall. He said, "By means of a dance you will see again those of your relatives who died long ago." He preached that there should be no fights between Indians and whites, that Indian children should go to school, that whites and Indians would become one people. But soon there was to be an end of the world where all nonbelievers, white and Indian, would be covered up. As in many religious faiths, only believers could be saved. Wovoka urged his followers:

> Do not refuse to work for the whites, and do not make any trouble with them until you leave them. When the earth shakes at the coming of the new world, do not be afraid. It will not hurt you.

An important part of the ritual was wearing the Ghost Shirt, a garment decorated with symbols, many inspired by the dancers' visions. The wearers believed that the shirts granted them supernatural protection. They were worn by all, including women and children. Whites took the claims of invulnerability as evidence of hostile intentions by the Lakota, but as one Ghost Dance participant said, "The shirts we wore made us go to Heaven. The dance was not a war dance, for none that went to it were allowed to have one scrap of metal on his body."

When Short Bull returned to the Pine Ridge in the spring, the new religion was sweeping through the Native American communities of the West. As one who had spoken to the prophet, he was a disciple and one of the leaders on the Lakota reservations. The popularity of the Ghost Dance spread across the Pine Ridge and the adjacent Rosebud Reservations. At first, it was a curiosity among the whites, but the policy of the government Indian agents on the reservations soon turned to active suppression of the dance. Reporters arrived, dispatching stories of an impending Indian uprising. The settlers grew increasingly nervous. By fall, the agents were calling for the army, and the first troops arrived by mid-November.

The Lakota grew nervous as well. Short Bull called for a great gathering of Indian peoples to prepare for the coming of the prophet. They began moving to a place to practice the new religion in peace, away from the army. To the Stronghold. In the moonscape of the Badlands, there was a place where Wovoka's prophesy might be fulfilled.

In the north, there was news from one of the greatest of the Indian holy men. Sitting Bull, a Lakota leader at the Little Big Horn, had met with Ghost Dance leaders and was said to be preparing to leave from his home on the Standing Rock Reservation for the Stronghold. Caustic and articulate, Sitting Bull had been a thorn in the side of the federal agent at Standing Rock. A police troop of Lakotas was sent to arrest him in a predawn raid. As his supporters gathered around the house, Sitting Bull refused to leave. The police killed him, along with his son and six others, in a fusillade of gunfire. Left alive at his home was a horse given to him by Buffalo Bill, following Sitting Bull's time in the Wild West Show.

One of the genuine issues of riding on the reservation is that, like in many rural areas, a lot of people have dogs, and they're rarely leashed. Nothing's more exciting for a dog than chasing a bike. As we left Red Shirt, I took up position behind Jan as tail gunner, with my can of pepper spray. Sure enough, a couple of dogs came out of one of the first houses. We managed to outleg them before the pepper spray came out.

We left the pavement and turned east, climbing onto the loose gravel of the Cuny Table Road. Cuny Table is the mesa directly south of Stronghold. Before long, we passed a curious sign: CAUTION: FORMER BOMBING RANGE. More than a third of a million acres of the Pine Ridge, including the Stronghold, was designated as the Badlands Gunnery Range during World War II. US bomber pilots over Germany exercised a certain amount of care to avoid cathedrals, yet there was no such concern over the site of an American religion. The current brochure from Badlands National Park advises, "In addition to empty shells, unexploded ammunition is sometimes found eroding out of buttes. Leave items of this sort in place." As Bill Murray said in *Ghostbusters*, "Important safety tip."

The Stronghold is actually part of Badlands National Park, but it is inaccessible without crossing private land on the Pine Ridge Reservation. With some searching before the ride, I had managed to find the Lakota landowner and ask his permission to cross. He had given it, along with some cryptic directions: "After you pass the grain bins, turn left onto the two-track. Look for the path out after a couple of miles."

The roads grew steadily worse. After a few miles on Cuny Table, we found a two-track dirt road and began riding through fields of winter wheat. There were no trees, scarcely any buildings, and only a few pieces of farm equipment working off in the haze. An occasional prairie dog stuck his head out of a hole and cheeped. Back and neck and legs were beginning to stiffen up. We were already fifty miles in from the nearest town with no sign of the trail to the Stronghold. Had we missed it? Cuny Table doesn't have much, but, amazingly, there was a cell tower. Google Maps satellite view worked perfectly. We were just short. Up ahead, near where a herd of pronghorn antelope was crossing, was the trailhead.

We turned onto the rutted dirt trail and rode for a few minutes. After we'd gotten lulled into a false sense of security, a big pothole appeared, throwing me unceremoniously over the handlebars and into the high grass. The landing was soft, with no damage to body or bike, but the ride was over for the day. I dusted off, and we walked the loaded bikes for several miles. Wheat fields turned to rangeland, and cattle grudgingly moved off at our approach. A few ravines were off to the right, but nothing suggested a great fortress. It had been a long day. The sun was getting low. Then, over a gentle rise, the fields disappeared and the land fell away.

"Jan, look left."

The Badlands stretched for miles to the horizon, a twisted, eroded landscape of creek beds, alkali flats, and layered mesas. They formed a panorama of white and red, with nothing growing but grass on the top of the mesas. It was a vision that had aged for a very long time in the back of my mind. Up ahead, the land formed a great cliff: The Stronghold.

1890

General Nelson Miles, army commander of the Department of the Missouri, gave a description of this land, along with a summary of his problem with the camp on the Stronghold:

> The country appears to have been the result of volcanic action. It was a mass of barren hills, narrow valleys, ravines, canyons, mounds, and buttes, almost devoid of trees and with very little verdure. By following circuitous trails one could ride on horseback over portions of it, but it was wholly impracticable for wagons, and so extensive that it afforded an excellent rendezvous or refuge for hostile Indians. As the Indian supplies were exhausted they could send out in almost any direction and find some game—deer, elk, or domestic cattle—to supply them with food. They were abundantly supplied with horses and well equipped with arms and ammunition.

The Lakota of the Stronghold might not have been quite as well off as Miles portrayed. In early December, winter was closing in, but they were able to survive, if not in comfort. Soldiers were pouring into the Pine Ridge, including the Seventh Cavalry, Custer's old unit from the Little Big Horn. Tensions were high, and the Stronghold might well have been the safest place on the reservation. A conflagration would require only the tiniest of sparks, particularly with the Seventh Cavalry. It speaks to the Lakota state of mind that the most rational thing for them to do was to dig in and wait for the Earth to open up.

Though Miles was receiving relentless pressure from settlers to take action, he wanted to avoid a showdown, and with good reason. His scouts revealed that the Lakota had dug in, with rifle pits across a narrow, fifty-foot-wide neck between two sheer cliffs. It was the only entrance to the Stronghold. He settled into a waiting game, periodically sending "friendly" Lakota into the fortress to try to convince them to come into the Pine Ridge Agency camp, without success.

For the Lakota of the Stronghold, it was a situation like that of the Jews of Masada waiting for the advance of the Romans: barricaded in a mountaintop fortress, vastly outnumbered. In their time, the Lakota danced to bring on their end of the world. Short Bull later described what was happening on top of the mesa:

> First: purification by sweat bath. Clasp hands and circle to the left. Hold hands and sing until a trance is induced, looking up all the time. Brought to a pitch of excitement by singing songs prescribed by the Messiah. Dressed as prescribed. Froth at mouth when in trance. They must keep step with the cadence of the song. They go into trance in from ten minutes to three quarters of an hour. Each one described his vision. Each man, woman and child has a different vision.

Stronghold Table dropped off two hundred feet onto the floor of the Badlands, a fantastic terrain of sharply eroded buttes and spires stretching nearly to the horizon. We set up camp on the narrow neck, that precarious entrance to the Stronghold described by Miles's scouts. Given the unexploded bomb warnings, I let Jan pound in the tent pegs. We cooked up a little freeze-dried something a year past its expiration date and sipped on coffee. Dozens of swifts soared up from nests in the cliffs. Cattle lowed off in the distance, followed later in the evening by yips of coyotes. High grass would be a soft bed for the sleeping bags. As dusk fell onto the colors of the Badlands, the only lights were those of Hermosa, thirty miles out, and our trusty cell tower. The sky turned perfectly clear, and wind rattled the tent flaps.

Today, the National Park Service puts out a brochure on the Stronghold, and one passage stayed with me:

> As you travel on Pine Ridge Reservation, particularly on the South Unit of Badlands National Park, you may find signs of religious worship. These could take the shape of prayer sticks or small bundles tied to branches. It could be simply a piece of brightly colored fabric tied to a shrub. These are signs of traditional worship by Tribal members. Please respect their beliefs and practices and leave these objects . . . Stronghold Table is a favorite site for young Lakota men to go to fast and pray, hoping to have a vision for their future.

A vision quest. After miles of riding and walking in the heat, nursing our precious water, I was not fasting, but somewhere close to it. Sitting at the edge of the cliff, I could understand Short Bull's description of the sweat bath. It was easy to see why the Lakota would come to this place. I could just imagine what a vision might be.

The first sign was the distant lights of Hermosa flickering, then winking out. The horizon was no longer sharp but misty, as though a great wave were coming in from the sea. With a low, deep rumble, tables and towers began to slide into the floor of the Badlands, and the alkali landscape started to swirl and move. The swifts, frightened, poured out of the cliffs and flew away. The Badlands were a whirlpool, eating away at the land.

The Stronghold, where I sat, was safe, untouched, but the whirlpool reached the guy wires to the cell tower. The tower swayed, then fell into the maelstrom. In the distance, the falling land swallowed up the approaching cavalry, like the pharaoh's army in the Red Sea. The land disappeared in slow motion, as Wovoka foretold. I watched from my sky-island as the dust settled below.

The next day, there were still twenty miles of Badlands to ride before the first civilization on the Pine Ridge, with water down to a single water bottle each. After two days riding through a lunar landscape, breakfasting on granola bars and rationing our meager supplies, we were exhausted and ready for anything resembling lunch. The Common Cents was the only store for miles, boxy, almost window-less, with a grated steel front door. It was the Lakota place to be, and they were gassing up, buying food, gossiping. A woman was selling burritos on the hood of her car. Many of the men had long black braids, and lots of people were curious about where we were riding to and from. I mentioned that we were staying at the Lakota Prairie, a motel about ten miles up the road. A Lakota woman immediately piped up.

"Tell them to get new chairs in the restaurant. The chairs are too damn hard! They'll listen to a white man."

Inside, even the mangiest plastic-wrapped sandwich looked like Michelin three-star cuisine, and we bought half the rack. At the checkout counter, Jan asked if there was somewhere to sit in the shade.

"We used to have a tree. They cut it down. Don't know why."

We sat outside in a patch of yellowed grass by the air-conditioning exhaust, watching the Lakota come and go. It was Friday of Memorial Day weekend, and one of the women was preparing to go up to the cemetery.

"The road's pretty well washed out, but we'll find a way to make it. There's a lot of veterans up there, and we want to make sure they're taken care of."

I thought back on a visit to the Museum of the Plains Indian on the Blackfeet Reservation in western Montana. The Blackfeet curator was explaining to visitors about the long history of broken treaty after broken treaty and shrinking reservations, then began talking about the legacy of Native American soldiers in World War II. A visitor with a French accent stopped him.

"You were treated so badly by the white settlers. Why did the Blackfeet fight for them in the war?" The curator paused for a moment.

"You have to understand, it was our country that was attacked as well. Pearl Harbor was a strike on all of us. We were called to defend the country, and we went."

Back at the Common Cents, it was time to roll on down the road. After another ten miles, the Lakota Prairie Ranch offered the decadence of hot showers and a real dinner. The next morning, the real world—a law firm and a family—was calling Jan, and he and I parted ways. Kathy and Rusty, two of the motel managers, gave him a ride in their pickup to Rapid City and his flight back east. They refused payment. Jan later texted, "Rapid City is a lot closer when you're doing 105."

The prairie got a lot quieter after the pickup pulled out. It was a calm Saturday with a couple of beers and the electronic luxuries of telephones, internet, and television. A long stretch of South Dakota lay ahead. I left early Sunday morning for Wounded Knee.

1890

As the Ghost Dancers stayed in their fortress, reporters filed all kinds of stories of armed battles between factions on the Strong-hold, and of battles with the army. These were later shown to be fabrications. Parties of Lakota out foraging at local ranches were greeted with gunfire. Short Bull's nephew was killed. Conflict between groups on the Stronghold was very real, however. At one point, Short Bull told of covering his head because he did not want to see who would kill him. In late December at a council fire, the Lakota decided to leave the Stronghold for the Pine Ridge Agency, to literally come in from the cold. But they would not make it to the agency that morning. As they were on their way in, the sound of cannons and rifles came from the east, from a creek about thirty miles away.

Wounded Knee is one of the darkest episodes in American history. The particulars are well known. On December 28, a band of Lakota led by Chief Big Foot, on its way to join the Ghost Dance, was intercepted by the Seventh Cavalry, arrested, and taken to a camp on Wounded Knee Creek. The cavalry encircled the camp, with Hotchkiss guns—rapid-fire artillery—placed on a hill above.

The following morning, the cavalry insisted on disarming the Lakota. Since hunting was how the band was feeding itself, this led to grumbling within the band. Big Foot, ill with pneumonia, could not stand. One of the Lakota resisted having his rifle taken away, and a shot went off. No one knows who pulled the trigger. The soldiers opened fire from all sides of the encampment. The four Hotchkiss guns, trained on the tepees, each fired at one round per second. Initial survivors took refuge in a ravine near the camp. The artillery found the range on the ravine, and it became a death trap. Bodies were found miles from the site as other survivors were ridden down. As many as three hundred Lakota, including women and children, were killed. Twenty Medals of Honor were later awarded to soldiers involved in the massacre. Pressure to rescind those medals continues to this day.

The site remains today a place where history is laid raw. The mass grave is on the hill where the artillery was placed. A detailed, red historical panel sits by the roadside, with the title board MASSACRE bolted over what was presumably the word *battle*. The panel puts in quotation marks the words *"Messiah Craze"* and *"Ghost Dancing"* but, incredibly, refers to the site as a battlefield, without scare quotes.

On the day of my visit, a young, lean Lakota, long-haired and scarred, spoke to whoever would listen, pronouncing the panel "all lies." It was a hard place to stay. Mental images from the Library of Congress kept recurring, posed photographs of men with handlebar mustaches loading frozen bodies onto wagons in that desperately cold winter of 1890.

Short Bull and the Ghost Dancers stayed out on the Stronghold for another two weeks after Wounded Knee. A December blizzard raged over the South Dakota plains. After many more emissaries from the army came to the Badlands, the band finally surrendered. Short Bull, along with twenty-five others, was sent to prison at Fort Sheridan, Illinois. Salvation would come from an odd source. "Long Hair," Buffalo Bill Cody, needed authentic Plains Indians for his Wild West Show touring in Europe. The government was glad to have the Ghost Dance participants as far away as possible. Cody worked a deal with the authorities to release them to his custody. Short Bull enjoyed the time with the Wild West Show: "It learns us much, we see many people who are all kind to us."

After Wounded Knee, few at Pine Ridge would speak of the Ghost Dance. When asked, one of the Lakota said, "The dance was our religion, but the government sent soldiers to kill us on account of it." Short Bull stayed true to the Ghost Dance throughout his life. For him, it was a form of passive resistance. In an interview sixteen years later, he said, "For the message that I brought was peace. And the message was given by the Father to all the tribes. Who would have thought that dancing could make such trouble?"

That passive resistance found a new voice in 2016 at a place the world would come to know, at Sitting Bull's reservation: Standing Rock. At issue was the Dakota Access Pipeline, under construction to transport oil from the hydraulic fracturing regions of North Dakota to refineries in the Midwest. The pipeline would pass through sacred sites of the Lakota and under Lake Oahe, the principal source of drinking water for the reservation.

For people concerned about climate, the key task of the next decade is to start limiting the amount of carbon dioxide going into the atmosphere. The idea is to start putting the planet on a carbon budget and to set the global economy on a steep path to zero emissions. The pipeline would be another way to bring a new and vast source of carbon out of the ground.

For the Standing Rock Reservation, the problem of their water and their land was closer and more immediate. Their call for help was answered by envoys from around the world, and people from over ninety Native nations came to the Oceti Sakowin, or Seven Fires, camp on the Cannonball River.[1] The camp became vast, a city of tepees and tents, but it was clear who was in charge. The Standing Rock Lakota emphasized nonviolence and prayer to all of their visitors.

Winter approached. To move the protesters, private security brought attack dogs, and police clad in riot gear later sprayed water cannons in subfreezing temperatures. An iconic photograph shows a protester at night covered in ice, kneeling in prayer before the barbed wire. As the North Dakota governor issued a December 5 evacuation order to the camp, a group of over two thousand veterans from across the country, many, if not most, Native American, gathered to serve as human shields for the protesters. As the day of confrontation approached, the amazing happened: The Army Corps of Engineers denied the permit for the Dakota Access Pipeline to pass under Lake Oahe. The following day, as both sides stood down, a blizzard not so different from the one following Wounded Knee swept down out of the north.

Some months later, the new administration reversed the permit decision, and at this writing we are weeks away from the first oil flowing through the pipeline. But something fundamental has changed. The Standing Rock battle has brought the Native Nations together like nothing before. Thousands, from dozens of tribes, came to Washington to march in the snow in support of Standing Rock, chanting, "We're cold. We're wet. We ain't done yet." I saw Native Americans dancing on Pennsylvania Avenue in protest. I thought of my own experience with the Lakota veterans.

I rolled out of Wounded Knee and turned east on US 18, the Oyate Trail, the Trail of Nations. It's the old road between the Pine Ridge, Rosebud, and Yankton Reservations. There were big, sweet lonely stretches of the Plains, just over fifty miles to the nearest store, the Batesland Handi Stop. I took a long rest with an ice-cold soda. Rose, a little Lakota girl at the store, was very curious about the bike.

"How do you stop it?" she asked.

"With these brakes. Want to try them?"

"What's in the bags?"

"All my clothes and stuff to fix the bike."

"Do you see dogs?"

"Yes. Sometimes they chase me."

While I was suitably distracted, her dachshund, Sprite, peed on my tire. Rose waved good-bye as I pedaled back down the road.

I got a late start the next day, Memorial Day. By late afternoon, great thunderheads were sweeping across the prairie. One crossed the road up ahead, lightning flashing from its base. I had finally made it to the Rosebud Reservation. A few miles in, I spotted a chapel high up on a ridgeline, and beside it, American flags. I pushed the bike up the ridge to the chapel, its white paint peeling, now inhabited only by pigeons. The graveyard behind was vacant. Gusts from the approaching storm snapped the flags.

At my feet were the graves of an unbroken line of Lakota veterans from the Two Eagle family: George, born six years after Wounded Knee, with service in World War I; Calvin, a Korean War veteran; and Courtney Lloyd, a sailor in the Vietnam era. Their graves were honored by hands that lashed the flags to three weathered sticks. It seemed remarkable, after the winter of the Ghost Dance and all of the hardship that continues to this day, that Memorial Day would be so celebrated on the reservation. But the warrior tradition of the Lakota remains. I imagine that somewhere in Afghanistan, a Special Forces soldier returns from a mission and removes his body armor, revealing a cotton shirt with images of birds and stars.

NEBRASKA:
THE ONE

turned off South Dakota's Trail of Nations south onto the Outlaw
Trail, which became Route 12 at the Nebraska border. Once
upon a time Jesse James and his gang used to hang out in the
steep bluffs by the Missouri River just off the route. I was bucking
a growing headwind in the haze and heat. After fifty miles or so,
my shoulders tightened up, so I stopped to swing my arms over

my head. A woman in her pickup stopped, turned around, and checked to see if I was okay. Did I mention that Nebraskans are awfully friendly?

Contrary to popular opinion, Nebraska is not flat. In the northeast corner lie hills diabolically spaced for a bicycle, just far enough apart to provide no momentum from one downhill to the next climb. The unholy rollers. The wind, heat, and hills were wearing me down. Up ahead was a simple blue-and-white sign: WELCOME TO WYNOT. WHY NOT STOP? Okay, I'll bite. I rolled a mile off the planned route into downtown Wynot. The town was completely shut down. It was 2:00 P.M., and I rattled the door on the Blue Devil Tavern. Posted hours indicated that it didn't open until 3:00 P.M. After a moment, the door opened, miraculously. The owners, Sandy and Dan, admitted me into the delicious air-conditioning, poured me an iced mug of cold soda (sorry, *pop* around here), and sent me on my way with refilled bottles of ice water.

By 1:00 P.M. the next day, I was back out in the heat and still twenty-six miles from the night's destination. I stopped at a convenience store and asked the clerk if there was any place on the way I could stop for a sit-down lunch.

"You've only got one shot," she said, looking over to a friend. "Think Elsie's open?"

"Yep, think she's open every afternoon these days," her friend replied. The clerk turned back to me.

"Okay, make sure to stop by the Monowi Tavern. Careful, it's easy to miss."

Seven miles later, I saw a sign: MONOWI 1. Something was odd. The town should be right here, not a mile down the road. I came upon a couple of abandoned buildings and a small white structure that wasn't. On the side, a sign proclaimed, WELCOME TO THE WORLD FAMOUS MONOWI TAVERN.

I came into the mercifully cool tavern/restaurant, where a quiet old woman named Elsie took my order and cooked it, while finishing with a group at another table. Fast food it wasn't, though no one was complaining. Another Monowi 1 sign was on the wall.

It gradually dawned on me that Elsie is The One. She is the sole resident of Monowi, the only officially incorporated municipality in the United States with a population of just one. She's the mayor, and she fills out budgets and forms for state funding to keep the streetlights on. She even pays taxes to herself, which has got to go against some conflict-of-interest law somewhere. Once the other group left, Elsie was less quiet as she wiped tables, filled sugar shakers, and brought me lunch.

"After my husband Rudy died in 2004, everybody thought that I should move down to Tucson with my daughter. But who do I know down there? I like seeing all the people, then having a quiet night to myself at the end of the day."

I asked about the newer-looking white prefab building down the street.

"Oh, Rudy had always wanted a library. He had boxes of books stored all over town. So he finally got the building, but he got sick before he could finish it. Later my son and daughter and a couple of nephews came in and put it together. It has over five thousand volumes. People come into the tavern and ask for the key to get books."

Monowi reached its peak in the 1930s, but like many other small towns in the Great Plains, the farming community couldn't keep its young people (including Elsie and Rudy's children), who moved to cities over time in search of jobs. Modern mechanized farming simply doesn't need as many farmers. And as I would discover in Kansas, climate change is one of those stresses that farmers are dealing with. The great Ogallala Aquifer, which covers much of Nebraska as well as Kansas, is used for irrigation in large areas of the two states. Its recharge from rain and snow is well behind the withdrawals from agriculture.

But Elsie stayed, and it turns out that she is something of a rock star. She's had crews from NBC's *Today* show and *CBS Sunday Morning* come by, along with reporters from the *Times* (London) and the *Los Angeles Times*. Larry the Cable Guy had a barbecue for a few hundred people in Monowi. Elsie takes it all in stride. As we were finishing up, she asked me where I was staying that night. I stumbled around:

"A B&B, someplace with a deer name."

"The Whitetail. That's my niece's place."

Of course it was. Everyone knows everyone in this part of Nebraska. It might seem that being the only person in town would be the very definition of loneliness. But it's just the opposite. Many people in cities are far more isolated. For Elsie, all her friends stop by sooner or later. Along with the TV crews and Larry the Cable Guy.

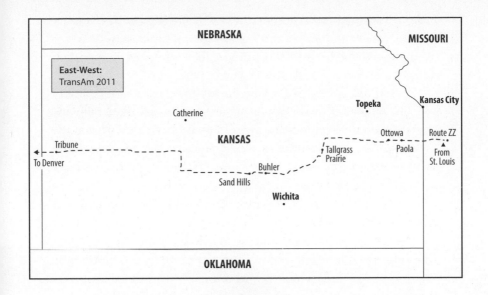

KANSAS:
SMALL HOURS ON THE HIGH PLAINS

he Great Plains have a way of sneaking up on you when you're on a bike. As I continued on my long trek to Oregon, they surprised me in the middle of the night.

Missouri's Katy Trail had eaten me up that day in May, with seventy-four miles of intermittent drizzle along the Missouri River on a day when I'd planned for much less. By the time I was approaching the Kansas border, the trees were beginning to retreat into the creases of the flatland. I was looking forward to a bed for the night, but the only motel near the trail was booked. So I pushed on to Katfish Katy's Campground a dozen miles up the river. Trisha, the host, could tell I'd had a long day by the mud splatters on my legs. She opened the camp store late for me, and I walked out with an armful of canned food. She insisted that she wasn't Katfish Katy.

"We've got some beautiful sites down on the river, but she's rising pretty steady. Supposed to crest tomorrow. I'd camp on the back side of the levee if I were you."

By the time I reached the campground I was fourteen hundred miles in, and the Missouri was at record levels. The surging river was the background score for the night, a low, powerful hum. It was a message from a thousand miles upstream, from the mountains where I was bound, where record snowfall over the winter was melting rapidly. I lay down in the tent, too exhausted to sleep, and listened to a sonata in three movements. The first: about ten o'clock, supercharged pickups, roaring down the river road, g-strings for mufflers. They quieted down after a while, and just as I was drifting off, the second: a distant train from across the river, a whistle at a crossing, fading off into the distance. The third would wake me up from a very deep sleep: yips and squeals and barks, very close. It would take a howl from one for me to recognize the coyotes. Welcome to the West.

Of course, it's been a while since coyotes were just a western species. Originally they were found in prairie and desert areas of the West and Mexico. But coyotes began moving through the Great Lakes region in the first half of the 20th century and into the South and East in the second half, expanding into areas where other carnivores had been removed. As climate changes, species that are the most adaptable will likely expand their range.

Before the cross-country trip, I had debated about whether to bring along a can of pepper spray for dogs. I really like them and wasn't keen on ruining their day. Some folks on the cycling blogs said to simply dismount and put the bike between you and the dog.

That works well for one dog. But a quiet Missouri back road provided a good reason for the spray can. Missouri marks their roads with letters, and I stopped to take a picture of the sign for ROUTE ZZ. Cute. Then I noticed a half dozen dogs accumulating just up the road. They were barking continuously and looked as though they wanted a piece of me, or several. First I decided to wait and let them calm down. The owner would surely come out and get them, yes? No. The next plan involved waiting for a car to come and have it pass me just as I was going past the dogs: sort of an Odysseus and the Cyclops move. Elegant, but one problem: no cars.

The sun was getting low, I still had twenty miles to go, and the mutts weren't going anywhere. Now was the time for the pepper spray. I rode back up the road to get a rolling start, then turned to go by them as fast as I could. They were the most dangerous breed for a cyclist: Uphill Dogs. A bike can fly past dogs on a downhill, but a little climb gives them the chance to catch up. I don't know what it is that dogs like about cyclists—the thigh or the drumstick—but I didn't care to find out.

Sure enough, they were all after me as I went past. The lead dog was off to the left of my rear wheel. A stream of pepper spray took him out, as well as a couple of his friends. But an overachiever was moving up fast on the right. I caught a glance down. The dog was even with my rear pannier. He wasn't barking, but his lips were curled back. I poured it on as I headed up the hill, legs beginning to scream. Adrenaline works even after a day of riding. Gradually, the dog dropped off behind. A burst of energy carried me the rest of the way to the night's campground. I thought of Winston Churchill's quote from his time in the Boer War: "There is nothing so exhilarating than to be shot at without result."

The morning after was clear and bright, calm for a change. I was done with dogs for a while, or at least resolved to keep my habit to a pack a day. I crossed into Kansas, a fluorescent sunflower sign against a deep blue sky. *Enough hills; time to tear into these wide prairies*, I thought to myself. But Kansas would prove to be the hardest state.

Legs spinning and gears whirring after the border, I got a little frisky. There was some traffic at the railroad crossing in Paola. The rules for riding a bike across train tracks are simple: swing wide and go perpendicular to the rails. But, worried about the traffic behind me, I took a shortcut and began to cross the tracks at the same shallow angle as the cars. My front wheel dropped into the gap next to the rail with a thud. I was instantly pitched over the handlebars and onto the jagged gravel of the rail bed.

Dazed, I took stock of the damage. Cycling gloves saved my hands, but blood was starting to fill cuts on my shins. Things began to happen fast. I looked up and saw a pinpoint of light down the tracks. Don't you hate it when that happens? The bell sounded and the crossing gates lowered, shaking me out of my stupor. The pinpoint was now a big yellow ball. The rails next to my hands were singing.

Drivers stopped at the crossing were watching with interest. This could liven up the ride in to work. Cell phone cams began to come on. The whistle on the locomotive blew. Time to move quickly. I dragged the bike, mercifully intact, under the gate in time for the train to pass. A car window rolled down.

"You okay?"

"I guess." I looked down at the blood starting to reach my socks. "I think there's some reassembly required."

Still a bit shaken from the close call, I walked the bike down the street to a nearby convenience store with tables inside. I grabbed a handful of napkins and pulled out my first aid kit to patch up, getting a suspicious look from the clerk. Unsaid: Don't worry, I won't bleed on the linoleum. I pulled out of the lot a little slower, adhesive tape pulling at my knees. I was battered, and felt as though I'd been in the dryer on the tumble cycle.

In planning the ride across Kansas back east at my desk, I had consciously increased the intended mileage per day from sixty to eighty. It's flat, right? I would have reconsidered if I had known the etymology of the word *Kansas*, derived from the namesake Kansa tribe, which comes from the Sioux word meaning "people of the south wind." Writer Timothy Egan describes it as a place "where the wind has its way with anything that dares poke its head out of the ground."[1] For the entire ride across Kansas, crashing and nearly getting run over by a train notwithstanding, I would be battling this wind, whether it was cutting across the road or blasting 30 MPH right in my face. The low point came when I met the hundreds of riders of the Bike Across Kansas tour—headed east, with the wind at their backs. Many waves and comments of "Aren't you going the wrong way?" At that point I silently agreed with them, and cursed the innate romanticism that inspired me to "head west." I responded with a tight smile.

That wind first bit into me near Paola. The initial thirty-mile stretch had no services at all, and in the heat I was using water way faster than I had anticipated. On a rise ten miles in, a crew was servicing a cell tower. I asked if they had water. The boss offered me all I wanted from their cooler. He might have regretted that, as I made two bottles vanish immediately and filled up four others. Their generosity turned the day around for me.

With ten miles left to go until civilization, a strange vision began to appear out of the shiny mirage of asphalt ahead: another cyclist, one laboring to pull a trailer. Slowly I caught up with a young guy in a sweat-stained shirt. In the homemade trailer was a dog, panting heavily. We both pulled off the road.

"You all right?" I asked.

"Yeah, we're fine. It's plain nasty out here today, ain't it?" he said. "This here's Jake and I'm Double D."

"How are you doing on water?"

"Getting a little thin. Figure we'll make it to the next town, though."

I gazed down at my newfound riches. "Look, I'm just restocked. If you need some, I'm good."

"Well, Jake might just appreciate that."

I poured some water into one of my cooking pots while Double D opened up the trailer. Jake quickly had his nose in the pot and lapped it up.

"You're the first one I've met carrying more than me," I said.

Double D had a wistful smile as he scratched the dog's ear. "Yeah, she got most everything in the settlement 'cept Jake. I got family down in Amarillo. Sometimes you just gotta start over."

"You two gonna be okay?"

"Yeah, we always manage to find our way down the road. Thanks for the juice."

I saddled up, and they slowly disappeared back into the heat.

Weather didn't often keep me off the bike. By eastern Kansas I'd ridden in all-day rain, in nor'easter leftovers, even in hail (helmets can be dual purpose). But the winds finally stopped me in Ottawa. With 50 mph gusts predicted, it would be hard enough to stay upright on two feet, let alone on two wheels. So I decided to hole up for the day and sample life in small-town Kansas.

A sunny blond woman at the motel checked me in. It wasn't their busiest day. The loaded bike leaned on the pillar outside.

"Whereabouts you coming from?"

"Delaware. Working my way across to Oregon."

"Have you got people riding with you? Is this some kind of benefit?"

"Nope. On my own. I'm a retired scientist trying to see what climate change looks like across the country. Seems like you folks have got quite a dry spell working."

"Well, I don't know about climate change, but it has been a dry patch. Seems like it's what everybody's talking about."

"From what I see it's even worse down into Texas. Anybody talking about climate?"

"No, not really." She paused. "Do you know Al Gore?"

I answered her question directly. "No, not really. I've heard him speak before and gone to a couple of his hearings when he was in Congress." She finished checking me in and handed me the key, abruptly ending the conversation.

"Now you be safe. Lots of crazy drivers out there."

In fact, I had sat in on a number of hearings, back when he was Senator Gore. Usually it was just Gore with no other senators.

Perhaps the lack of attendance was because he was ahead of his time or he was a bit preachy, or both. The format of the hearings seemed to be testimony from two or three good, enlightened scientists and one bad, unbelieving scientist, with the tacit assumption that the good guys would convince the bad guy by hearing's end. People don't work that way, however. Nevertheless, I carried some of the same naiveté on my trip. I thought that just talking with people could convince them that climate change was a real problem. But if you're not running a hearing, it isn't the kind of topic that springs easily into general conversation with strangers, as I had just seen.

Her question about Al Gore stuck with me, however. He's certainly a polarizing figure and a common demon for those not accepting climate change. Analyzing eight hundred articles skeptical of climate change, environmentalist George Marshall showed that nearly 40 percent mention Gore.[2] I find it hard to criticize Gore, though. Given the array of interests in fossil fuel extraction, any politician bringing up the subject of climate change was bound to be attacked. Although his methods of communication might have been improved, it took courage for him to bring the issue into the political domain, and we owe him a debt of gratitude. Maybe even a prize.

But climate communication is about more than Al Gore. Marshall, from the UK, describes his experience of being in the United States and talking with people about climate: "The native friendliness dissipates the instant the words *climate change* enter the conversation." I've found this to be true. Over and over, across the country, it was something not to be discussed. From beach houses of Delaware to farm fields of Kansas, the answer was "I don't know about that." Yet when you asked specifically about how the sea was advancing or the plants were budding out earlier, heads would nod—and move on. What happened? The Kansas drought was acknowledged as a very real thing, but somehow climate change was politics and hence not a subject for polite conversation. You could talk about the weather, but not the climate.

Eventually the wind backed off enough for me to get back on the road and leave Ottawa behind. There aren't many places in Kansas that I would call luminous. That's not belittling the state. Wonder and awe don't jump out at you on the Plains the way they do in the Rockies. You need to look closely. Early in the morning, as the long shadows cut across the land, there is poetry. And since you're already up early, before the heat comes up, go and catch sight of the Mississippi kites out by an old barn.

I rode onto the Tallgrass on such a morning. The Tallgrass Prairie National Preserve is a remnant of the ecosystem that once covered central North America. Most has been plowed under to where only 4 percent remains, mostly here in eastern Kansas. It's a rich, diverse place, full of bugs and birds, wildflowers and buffalo. In the fall, the grass is so high you can walk in and disappear. One of the grass species, the Big Bluestem, grows to nine feet. Its roots go deeper than that—almost ten feet. Who would imagine that the redwoods of the Plains are right underfoot?

The Tallgrass has burned every few years as far back as we know. After the fires, new growth coming from the giant roots attracted the buffalo. The Kansa knew this; they would deliberately start prairie fires for this reason. Today rangers set controlled springtime burns in the preserve. And the buffalo are back. The National Park Service runs a guided tour of the herd's territory. I joined such a tour group, and we were allowed off the bus to view the herd from a safe distance. A curious calf began to make its way toward the group. The rangers quickly hustled us back in the bus after catching a cow's angry stare.

The wild prairie and the tallgrass may be making a limited comeback. Some Plains farmers are growing prairie strips as an addition to their farms, both to control erosion and as habitat for bees and butterflies, their essential pollinators.[3] Not all the life of the preserve may be so resilient. The aforementioned Mississippi kite, a species of small raptor, is expected to lose 88 percent of its current summer range to climate change by 2080, though it is expected to move northward as temperature rises.[4] The spread of its summer range may cause problems for a species that often nests colonially.

Here at the national preserve, limestone comes close to the surface, making it nearly impossible to plow. It's what saved the Tallgrass and enabled its preservation. The big ranch building on the preserve is made of this limestone, as is the magnificent Chase County Courthouse in the nearby county seat of Cottonwood Falls. A restored cattlemen's palace, the Grand Central Hotel, also graces the cobblestoned main street. Cottonwood Falls is quite a little oasis. I struck up a conversation with a local man down the street from the Grand Central.

"That's quite a beautiful courthouse you have," I said.

"We spend more tax dollars trying to keep that old thing together."

"Well, I'll be headed up to the Tallgrass in the morning."

"Don't know what the big deal is. We used to round up steer there when I was a kid. Can't run them there anymore." Like everywhere else, we don't see the treasures at our feet.

Farther west lies a different kind of preserve, Sand Hills State Park. Like the much larger Nebraska Sand Hills to the north, this park sits not on rock outcrops but on sand. Periodically throughout the modern (Holocene) geological epoch, drought removed the vegetation, and the sand hills became sand dunes. Without grass to anchor them in place, they moved, driven by the wind, like dunes of any desert. Today the Sand Hills are frozen in place by their vegetation. They were not in motion during the worst drought of the last 150 years, the 1930s Dust Bowl. But more severe droughts can be found in the geological record of the last thousand years.[5] It's reasonable to expect such droughts again, and that the Sand Hills would once more be on the move, covering much of the region. In 1821, Zebulon Pike, of Pikes Peak fame, labeled part of the high plains as the "Great American Desert." When the droughts come again, the deep-rooted prairie grasses, not corn or wheat or soybeans, may prove to be the plants most able to withstand them.

Near the town of Hesston, I linked up with the legendary Trans-America Trail, pioneered by the Adventure Cycling Association in 1976. From here to Oregon, the route wouldn't be my improvisation anymore but rather roads taken by many hundreds of cyclists since the bicentennial year. Not that the road was necessarily crowded with cyclists—I'd be lucky to see another long-distance rider during the course of a day. But a loaded touring bike wouldn't be such an unusual sight anymore.

After a day wandering around town, I had a calm start at first light. It didn't last. On the roadside I passed a welded steel sculpture of the Tin Man leaning into the wind, holding his hat with one hand and the mailbox with the other. It was an apt image for the Plains.

I had an appointment that day I wasn't sure I was going to make. More than anything, it required a solid Wi-Fi connection, not always the easiest thing to find in central Kansas. I scanned the road ahead on Google Maps, and then, out of the heat, perfection: the Mustard Seed Deli and Coffee Shop in Buhler. Feed at the Seed: strawberry rhubarb crunch, dark roast coffee, and Wi-Fi almost ringing in my ears. I quickly ordered and opened up Skype. When the waitress reappeared, I showed her the laptop and asked, "Would you like to say hello to my wife's third-grade class in Bethesda, Maryland?"

She backed away a step. The laptop's video was full of kids mugging, laughing, waving. "Uh, hi everybody. Hi from Kansas."

Concetta had the class following the westbound ride. I took them for a tour of the Seed and a look down Main Street in Buhler. A great white wall dominated the horizon.

"Does anybody know what that is? They're all over the place out here."

There was a murmuring on the laptop. From the back of the class, a voice bursting with pride: "That's a grain elevator!"

Somewhere near the coffee shop door, the image froze. The kids' picture hung for a moment or two, and I couldn't get the connection back. As I finished the coffee, I discovered that I had stumbled on one of the magic gathering places of the TransAm. Cindy Kaufman, the owner of the Mustard Seed, showed me her guest book filled with messages from cyclists, both American and international, who had stopped in as they'd been making their way across. It was a milestone. Buhler is not far from the geographic center of the United States and near where my odometer would roll over 2,000 miles. But the moment with the kids was over. The prairie seemed especially wide that day.

On a bike, you can see and hear and smell lots of things that you can't from a car. That's not always a good thing. In western Kansas, I caught a whiff of a particularly nasty something. Maybe it was a question of my citified nose. But I know barnyard; this was beyond barnyard. After a while, the source came into view: a fenced plot of hundreds of cattle standing in dirt, or worse. It was a concentrated animal feeding operation, the kind of place where much of our meat comes from these days. Not surprisingly, livestock raised in these conditions require large doses of antibiotics to keep from getting sick, and more antibiotics are used on animals than humans. I asked a Kansas man with whom I was staying about the feedlots. He smiled wistfully.

"That's the smell of money," he said. I stuck with the pasta that night.

Back into the heat the next morning, I rode past a group of towns with German names, built by people with long experience on hard land. These towns had their origins in Russia, where in the late 1700s the Russian empress Catherine the Great, originally German, decided that the vast Russian steppes of the Volga River needed settlement by her industrious countrymen. In 1763, she granted free land, exemption from military service, and religious freedom for Germans willing to settle on what was seen as barren country. Destitute from the Seven Years War, colonizers came from southern Germany and prospered.[6]

A little over a hundred years later, Czar Alexander II revoked the exemptions. The czar's conscription agents came searching for able-bodied men for the army, and the Volga Germans began searching for a new land. Across the ocean, they found in central

Kansas a land not so different from the steppes, and another great American migration was born.

Sewn into the vest pockets of this wave of immigrants was seed from Eurasia. Turkey Red would be the first winter wheat of the Plains, and its descendants would make Kansas the granary of the nation. An inadvertent passenger might also have hitched a ride: Russian thistle, which would come to be known in the West as tumbleweed.

The Volga Germans would thrive once again in Ellis County, Kansas, starting towns with names like Liebenthal, Herzog, and, of course, Catherine. High wheat prices triggered by World War I were followed by bountiful harvests through the 1920s. Everyone came to plant and turn over the soil. The crash of 1929 found the Plains awash in grain. With neither capital nor a large demand from overseas, buyers disappeared. Then in late 1930, the first dust storm came. In the summer of 1931, the rain stopped. It would not return until almost the end of the decade. The Dust Bowl had begun.

Like the Volga Germans, heat and wind were my constant companions. Every so often I would pick up my head and scan the horizon for windmills, perhaps in the hope that some good would come of this thing that was battering me day by day. I'd expected to see large-scale wind farms everywhere, since Kansas has wind energy potential second only to Texas, but I passed just one in my nine days of riding across the state. Occasionally, though, old-style wind-driven water pumps, one of the iconic images of the Plains, would appear. It was as though Kansas knew how to use the wind once but forgot.

That has changed dramatically since the 2011 ride. Of twenty-one existing Kansas wind farms, eleven have come on line since then, with eight more permitted or under construction.[7] Kansas wind energy production increased by 15 percent from 2013 to 2014.[8] So there would seem to be quite a boom in renewable energy. But not completely. As of September 2016, eleven years after its first proposal, the ironically named Sunflower Electric is still advocating construction of a new coal-fired power plant in Holcomb, in the middle of the windiest part of the state.

Exhausted and dehydrated, I pulled into the tiny town of Tribune in the early afternoon, stopping at the only motel for dozens of miles. The office smelled a bit like the retriever who appeared a few minutes later. The owner hadn't seen a razor for a while. He was quite kind and assured me that the room had Wi-Fi and a hot shower. I rolled the bike around to the back of the motel and kicked the tumbleweed away from the door. There was barely space to get the bike in, with one light for the tiny room. And no signal. I mentioned the Wi-Fi situation at the office. The owner rubbed his chin.

I went back to the room and passed out on the bed into a deep, black sleep. Minutes or hours later, a high-pitched grinding sound right above my head made me jump. It was coming from the next room. From the wall. Something was coming through the wall.

Half groggy, I had no idea where I was. I made a quick inventory of my defenses. I turned to face the wall in my underwear, shoulders clenched, pepper spray and Swiss Army knife in hand. This was not a dream. The grinding was getting louder. A small chunk of plaster flew out of the wall onto the nightstand. The head of a drill emerged from the hole and retreated. Then a wire crawled out of the hole and began to snake down the wall. An Ethernet cable.

A muffled, matter-of-fact voice came through the wall. "That do you okay?"

There's not much going on in Tribune at 4:30 A.M. That was when I walked my bike across Route 96 into the cone of white fluorescent light that was Eagle Travel and Convenience, the only place with a semblance of breakfast across the wide expanse of plains. The heat had forced me into an early start once again. The day before had been the worst yet. Passing the Bike Across Kansas people blissfully heading east, the thermometer had hit 105°F with a hard, steady wind in my face. The only choice was to ball up as low as I could on the bike and drive into it, going pitifully slow and stopping every few miles to drink. Water had been drawn out of my body at frightening speed. I was going through five bottles a day.

This was the epicenter of the Dust Bowl in the 1930s. Then years of drought led to dust storms "black as the inside of a dog," as one farmer put it, and people stuffed wet rags into cracks in the walls to keep the grit out. Many of the Volga Germans were forced off the land, swept westward in the same Depression-era migration that carried Steinbeck's Okies in *The Grapes of Wrath*. Farmers adapt to changing weather. It's what they've always done, except when the Dust Bowl comes. Then, the only choice is to flee. The summer of 2011 was nowhere as severe as the 1930s, but the maps showing drought had a bright red patch stretching down from Kansas into Texas and west into Arizona. And this day, the dry morning sky was brown from the day before—smoke from the huge Wallow fire in Arizona, six hundred miles to the west, with no rain to wash it away.

Over hundreds of years, drought isn't uncommon in the West. Records from tree rings tell us there have been far more severe droughts than the Dust Bowl, well before the era of rapid rise of greenhouse gases. But the unmistakable rise in temperature tilts the odds in favor of drought, like rolling a pair of loaded dice, especially in the southern Plains. The process is straightforward. The same warmer air that holds more water also evaporates more, drying out the land. It also makes for longer and more severe fire seasons in the West. Fire, heat, and drought, all of a piece. A glimpse of the past, intensified in the future.

After battling the shimmering heat the day before, I had resolved to make use of every precious minute of the cool, calm morning hours. Crossing the highway, silhouettes of grain elevators leaned into the starlight. My eyes squinted in the jagged light of the con-venience store. Microwave breakfast burritos were the only selec-tion. One would be plenty. I took my coffee and paper plate to the cashier and paid.

"Any chance of the weather breaking sometime soon?" I asked.

He smiled and shook his head. "You know what they say. Put a twenty-dollar bill under a glass of water on a fence post first thing in the morning. By ten, the water'll be gone."

I found a plastic table behind a couple of men in dungarees wearing baseball caps with the names of farms on the front. Later in the morning these farmers would be in the cabs of combines, moving over the fields like giant bugs. I listened in on the conversation.

"What's the yield looking like for you boys?" one asked.

"Best guess right now is down about thirty percent, and it'll be all we can do to get there."

"I wish I was just down thirty percent. That might just get it done." He paused to look out the window. "They say you gotta get big to survive, but my wife says our bills are twenty thousand dollars this month with fuel and fertilizer and John Deere."

Kansas is a place of tough, hospitable people making a living off a hard land. In a changing climate, it won't get easier. Globally, 2016 was the warmest year on record, and sixteen of the top seventeen warmest years have occurred since 2000. Back in 2011 and 2012, ranchers liquidated large herds because there wasn't enough food or water. From the air, much of Kansas is filled with green circles, the mark of center pivot irrigation. The farmers at Eagle Travel and Convenience pump groundwater from the Ogallala Aquifer for their crops, but it's not clear how long the water will last. In parts of southwest Kansas, the aquifer has been drawn down by over 150 feet since irrigation began.

My stomach was grumbling from the burrito as I went out into the parking lot. I got on the bike and turned west once again, first light to my back, into the hot, dry, blast-furnace wind already spinning up for the day.

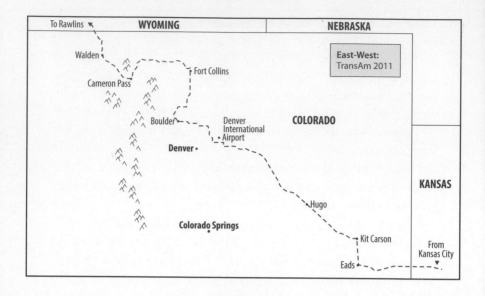

COLORADO:
A VISIT TO THE SCIENCE CITY

As hard as Kansas was, I could begin to sense that the end of the Great Plains was approaching. There's an almost imperceptible incline to Kansas and eastern Colorado, going from nine hundred feet above sea level in Paola in eastern Kansas to mile-high Denver. I could feel the incline in my legs. On some days I could climb a thousand feet in terrain as smooth as a bowling alley. The air on the High Plains was higher, drier, clearer. And emptier.

It had been a thousand miles since the last familiar face, and contact of any sort was precious. Wireless was as vital as water. At the end of the day's ride, I'd find a run-down motel with (nearly) ubiquitous Wi-Fi. Camping wasn't much of an option on the High Plains. The tent stood a good chance of getting blown over, as winds were often in excess of 30 MPH. In the evening I would soak up emails and Facebook, news from home and the East Coast newspapers. I'd write a blog entry to try to crystallize the day. After email grazing, a major part of the evening's routine was washing out clothes and clipping them to the curtains over the air conditioner exhaust. If they weren't dry by the morning, I'd peg them to the panniers for the first part of the day. Sometimes I looked like a rolling clothesline. Staying in one place long enough would probably have been a zoning violation.

I noticed one morning a side effect of the string of lesser accommodations during the last few weeks. On my shoulders, back, and arms, they were unmistakable: bites. That night brought a painful admission in the phone call to Concetta. I had not been sleeping alone, if you count invertebrates. I was looking forward to being able to camp again. Alone.

Up ahead, against the horizon, a cluster of signs came into view. LEAVING KANSAS; COME AGAIN. WELCOME TO COLORFUL COLORADO. And lastly, a thoroughly welcome one: SHARE THE ROAD, with a bicycle symbol. Despite all of Kansas's open spaces, my closest calls with trucks had come there. In separate incidents, a delivery truck and a hay truck had almost blown me off the road. With two-mile sight lines on Kansas's arrow-straight roads, as opposed to the narrow switchbacks of Pennsylvania, there's no excuse for cutting it close. As the panel implied, Colorado would be a much more bike-friendly place. But there are indications that Kansas is coming around. On our trip through the state five years later, signs indicating that traffic should give cyclists a three-foot buffer when passing were visible in Kansas, particularly along the TransAmerica Trail.

The change from Kansas was subtle and anything but colorful. The eastern third of the Centennial State is just as open and treeless, and, if anything, a little drier. Telephone poles still stretched to the horizon. Gradually, sagebrush and yucca started to make their appearance on the land. Then something that hadn't happened for a week: calm, still air. I found my hole in the wind and poured miles into it. Spinning down the road in short shadows and a bright sky, it was high noon on the High Plains.

In the later part of the day, something small crossed the road ahead. At first I thought it was some large rodent, but then I saw the crested head, long tail, and black-and-white striped body: a roadrunner. He darted off into the brush, without even sticking out his tongue or a "meep-meep." Not a half hour later, a tan, bushy-tailed animal was out in the sage. The coyote turned toward me, half-smiling as he panted. Warner Brothers notwithstanding, I'd put my money on the coyote.

Rolling across the plains of eastern Colorado, I was drawn toward the mountains and some old friends. Before the ride started, I had set up a Friday seminar at the NOAA Earth Systems Research Laboratory in Boulder, Colorado. The lab is part of my former outfit, and colleagues abounded. I'd been to many meetings there, including one in 2005 to design one of the climate observing systems that I would later help manage in Geneva. Good attendance at my seminar was virtually guaranteed. Whether the presentation was scintillating or not, everyone would want to relax and sit in on a Friday afternoon talk. But Boulder was still 210 miles away.

When I was a teenager, my dad told me about driving west across the Plains. He was on a last visit home, a calm before the storm, between his graduation from West Point in 1940 and the 1942 American landings in North Africa. He would tell me how, after a twelve-hour drive across Kansas that summer, the mountains first started to rise up from the flat horizon in the distance. Boulder is one of those Colorado cities at the foot of the mountains, right below the spot where the Rockies rise. It's a perfect place to watch the theater of thunderheads sweeping across the Plains. Behind town, the angled stone faces of the Flatirons are the prelude to the Front Range of the Rockies. I have always felt a quickening with the sight of mountains in the distance.

The University of Colorado is in Boulder, as well as the National Center for Atmospheric Research (NCAR). NCAR sits on a mesa above town, just below the Flatirons, in a building designed by I. M. Pei to resemble the Anasazi cliff dwellings at Mesa Verde. Between NCAR, NOAA, and the university, Boulder is home to some of the most prominent US climate scientists, many of whom I came to know well throughout my career, and I was looking forward to seeing them again.

But on a dusty Tuesday evening out on the Plains, arriving in Boulder in time for that Friday seminar was very much in doubt. The big winds across Kansas had slowed me to fifty-mile days, when I had planned on riding eighty to one hundred. Getting to Boulder by Friday midday would now require two seventy-five-mile days on the bike, plus fifty miles before lunch on Friday. If the wind stayed in my face, that wasn't likely.

There was another problem. Somewhere outside of Tribune, an odd rattle started coming from the back of the bike. After six weeks, the sounds of a functioning bike—the purr of a chain, the sing of tire on asphalt—get well imprinted on the inside of one's skull. It took me a while to figure out this new noise. A close examination showed that one of two metal stays holding the rear rack on the bike had broken, the result of weeks of bumps and bounces. If the other one went, fifty pounds of gear would flop off the back of the bike. My laptop, complete with the Boulder presentation, would be skittering along the asphalt, along with a yard sale's worth of clothing and gear.

The nearest bike shop was three days down the road in Boulder. I needed to come up with something to keep the rig together. Fortunately, an auto parts store was within sight, framed by little dust devils in the parking lot. The man behind the counter wasn't busy. He squatted down on his haunches next to the bike, squinting dubiously.

"Dunno what we'd have to help you. Looks like you need to fabricate a piece. They might be able to do something at the garage tomorrow morning."

Losing another day would scrap the Boulder presentation. I hesitated. "Let me take another look at what you have inside."

Right by the register was the second-greatest jury-rigging invention after duct tape: bungee cords. I bought a bright red pair of them and lashed the rear rack to the seat post with all the strength that rubber bands could muster. It was a sketchy repair, and I hoped it would hold out until that bike shop. But it meant another seventy miles under my wheels and another night with the schedule still intact.

I was on the road again before 8:00 A.M. that Wednesday morning. Back when I drove ships for a living, there was a certain comfort in knowing that down below, in the bowels of the ship, an engineer was taking care of all that spinning steel that was keeping us going: a little grease here, a tweak there. On the bike I was engine and engineer, and my body and the bike were all part of the same machine. Chain a little noisy, stop and oil. Hands numbing up, change grips. Knee complaining, drop a gear and spin faster. Rub sunscreen into dried sweat. And always drink, drink, drink. I thought of the entry in every ship's log at the start of a watch: "Underway as before."

The wind was roaring again from the west when I rode out of Eads that morning. I started out of town and could barely stay upright. I decided to retreat back to my breakfast diner for some oatmeal and hold out for the predicted wind shift. It didn't happen. So I tucked my chin down by the handlebar and pedaled back into the torrent of air. Three hours and twenty brutal miles later found me almost wasted in the little town of Kit Carson. Aches stacked up: my back from being bent over, my neck from holding my head up, and my shoulders from clenching into the next gust. But there was a pleasant surprise. Despite the slow going, my legs didn't blow out for the day. In fact, they were pretty strong.

In the town park was a giant, rusting observation tower. On closer inspection, it was made of old steering wheels, fan blades, tractor seats—basically any kind of old steel junk. The internet says that a retired submarine welder built it back in the 1950s. That could have been a red herring. It might as easily have been an obelisk or an alien homing beacon. Whatever it was, it had just enough mojo to back the wind around behind me. By the time I was done with coffee, I barely needed to pedal at all. I was tempted to rig up my tent fly as a spinnaker. It was ecstasy. All my pains vanished. I could pick up a couple of miles per hour just by sticking out my elbows. Seventy miles were behind by day's end.

Like Kansas, many of the towns in eastern Colorado seemed to be just holding on. Making ends meet by farming is challenging, in a business that demands big equipment, major capital expenditures, and few people. An abandoned garage in Hugo lay bleaching in the sun. On the side, in sun-bleached hand letters: WE FIX EVERYTHING. FROM DAYBREAK TO HEARTBREAK. Maybe there was just too much to fix.

I pulled in for Thursday morning's breakfast at a truck stop. Inside was a mammoth spread on the steam table. I sat down at the counter next to a hefty truck driver with a goatee, plaid shirt, and jeans. He had seen the loaded bike leaning against the wall outside.

"Imagine you get up close and personal with some traffic from time to time."

"Well, I've had a few rigs pass a little closer than I'd like. That's a pretty powerful bow wave you gents put out."

"Nah, don't worry. We'd never hit you. Too much paperwork."

"I appreciate that. You just starting out today?"

"Been going since eleven last night."

"You with a company?"

"Independent. Getting harder and harder, though, with maintenance and dispatch and all. They'd just as soon drive us all out of business. And the oil companies are looking at any excuse they can to jack up the price of diesel."

It's not an unusual complaint. People pay a tremendous amount of attention to the price of fuel, and for truckers an increase cuts directly into their livelihood. Virtually any policy approach to climate change involves increasing the cost of fossil fuels, to make their cost bear some relation to the environmental expense of a warming planet. Indeed, the price of gas in Europe is roughly twice what it is in the United States, and their lifestyle is far from crippled. But that's a tough argument to make at a truck stop with an independent driver.

The driver saw that my plate was nearly empty. "Don't be bashful. You know what buffet stands for? Big Ugly Fat Fellows Eating Together."

"Yeah, maybe I'll lay off the second round of Belgian waffles."

With the wind still behind me, I began to think that I might get to the seminar on time. About that time I heard the snap of the rack's second stay breaking. I tightened up the bungee cord, but the rear rack and bags now would swing side to side on turns. I had run out of cute tricks, and there was no telling how long the fix would last. Like a damaged bomber returning to base, I would be coming in for a landing at Boulder trailing black smoke.

Friday morning dawned with fifty miles to go and a choice. Denver International Airport stood between Boulder and me. I could take the road around it to the east, out on the Plains, or the Denver suburbs road to the west. I picked the quieter Plains road. In roughly a mile, a disconcerting sign: PAVEMENT ENDS. With time at a premium and a shaky rear rack, I rode back toward the suburbs. It was a shock to the senses. My last encounter with serious congestion was Cincinnati. After a month of very quiet riding, suddenly I found myself in the middle of rush-hour traffic and no shoulder. There was no problem with riding fast. I was scared to death.

Sometime after rush hour settled down, a more reasonable road with shoulders appeared. At midmorning the clouds opened like curtains on a stage, and my father's mountains filled the western sky. I had hiked all through them in younger days, even working on a logging camp up there. Seeing them, I was exhausted and excited all at once. Focusing on the traffic and that next car coming out of the Burger King was almost impossible. But the elation had just a tinge of unease. I would have to go over those giants on the horizon. Another day.

I floated down the last miles to Boulder and to the lab entrance. Jeanne Waters, administrative officer and fine old friend, met me there with an understandably dainty hug and pointed me toward the showers. There was another guy there. I casually dropped that I had just ridden two thousand miles all the way from Delaware. He just as casually dropped that he was in training for the Death Valley marathon that weekend. My bruised ego and I headed to the shower. Welcome to Boulder.

At the seminar, I was fresh off the Plains and blinking a bit in the fluorescent lights of the conference room. Boulder had always been a business place for me, site of big, dull planning meetings, white-knuckle budget sessions, or intense reviews of science programs. Some of those meetings had taken place in this very room. This was different. The introduction to my talk included a photo from my blog and the realization for me that people were actually reading it. I gave a long pause before starting to speak. After six weeks alone on the road, it was overwhelming to be with so many people who either knew my name or knew me. These were active climate scientists, some of the leaders in the field.

I couldn't tell them much new about climate, and I would be listening to them later. So I talked about getting to Boulder without benefit of airline food, of tire tracks on the Delaware beach, of slave collars and tornado parties. And of the lifestyle on the barrier islands, threatened by rising sea level. The questions were all about people's attitudes on climate, what I had learned so far about this as I rode, and of course how to get across by bike. As I relearned in the locker room, Boulder is full of amazingly fit people as well as scientists, often one and the same. Gearheads all, a bigger crowd gathered around my bike after the seminar than around me.

My host for the weekend was the lab director, A. R. Ravishankara— Ravi—a distinguished atmospheric chemist, who has spent a career on ozone depletion and climate change. He's one of the true gentlemen of the field. Our discussions over the years weren't always the easiest. Budgets and priorities are often the grist of Washington meetings. But the disagreements were never personal.

In Boulder, he told the story of being hit by a car while cycling up Poudre Canyon, the same road I would ascend in a few days. He broke his collarbone and several ribs. The driver later told the judge he was "late for fishing." Ravi was back up on the bike in a few weeks. What I learned from Ravi is that the kindest are often the strongest.

I stayed with Ravi and his wife, Rochelle, in their house with a sunset view in front of the Flatirons. Rochelle has short brown hair and penetrating eyes behind rimless glasses. Her air was of someone comfortable with being in charge, a good thing for an ER doctor. Boulder is home to many pro cycling teams, and she shared some advice garnered from treating cyclists.

"We see them all the time, not so much for crashes as urinary tract infections. Seems like an occupational hazard. Easy to treat with antibiotics, but don't get yourself in the middle of nowhere with no way to take care of it." I would keep that in mind.

As the science of climate change and the ozone hole evolved and became clearer over the last thirty years, it's been my pleasure to know many of the scientists responsible for defining the science. Boulder has a grand collection, though not all were at the seminar. Dan Albritton, Ravi's predecessor as lab director, couldn't make it that afternoon. Now retired, he has an Alabama drawl and a warm smile behind Clark Kent glasses. When the ozone hole was discovered in the late 1980s, Dan's lab was in the middle of the hunt to learn the cause. When chlorofluorocarbons were found to be the heart of the problem, he served as one of the lead science advisors for the Montreal Protocol, the international treaty that phased out chlorofluorocarbon production. We tend to forget that there was a time when the ozone layer, vital for the planet's protection from ultraviolet radiation, was under genuine threat. The global action that wound down this threat is one of the great environmental success stories.

Dan was also one of the best science communicators I've ever encountered. In the era of PowerPoint, he would insist on hand-drawn overheads meticulously drafted in hotel rooms, felt-tip pens on acetate. At NOAA climate meetings, I had occasion to follow him on the agenda, always to my regret. I could never match his eloquence. In 2001, Dan even gave the first climate change briefing to George W. Bush's cabinet ("Most were quite interested, but some less so"). He drew a sharp line between presenting the science and commenting on policy. At a Senate hearing, he was asked his views on nuclear power:

"It gives off no greenhouse gases."

"But Dr. Albritton, what is your opinion?"

"It gives off no greenhouse gases."

Another of the Boulder climate scientists is Kevin Trenberth, a slight, intense, energetic New Zealander who works up on the mesa at NCAR. Kevin was a coordinating lead author on a chapter for the Intergovernmental Panel on Climate Change's Fourth Assessment Report. The IPCC and Al Gore won the Nobel Peace Prize in 2007. He's been an expert on climate observations for many years and one of the most prominent spokesmen for the reality of human-induced climate change. And he doesn't suffer fools. I faced him often on review panels, where distinguished scientists directed sometimes pointed criticisms of the programs of science managers like me. The programs were sharpened through the healthy but often painful process of scientific review.

Kevin became the center of controversy in the faux scandal that would become known as "Climategate." An anonymous person hacked email correspondence from the University of East Anglia in England, including Kevin's, and selectively published it on the web. Imagine if years of your emails could be searched for that intemperate phrase where your finger went too quickly for the Send button. Kevin's cherry-picked quote was "The fact is that we can't account for the lack of warming at the moment, and it is a travesty that we can't."

Surely a smoking gun for the climate conspiracy, yes? Not quite. A significant part of climate science is figuring out where the heat goes. Satellites have long measured increased heat energy coming into the Earth's atmosphere. If the air wasn't warming for a few years, the heat had to be going somewhere, probably into the ocean. Kevin's "travesty" was that we didn't have the observations in place to track the heat going into the ocean. I know this because it's exactly the criticism he leveled at my program in review panels. To this day, we can only sample the deep ocean temperature intermittently—it's simply a hard place to reach—though progress is being made.

But a conspiracy theory is so much more fun. Three separate investigations cleared the University of East Anglia group of any scientific cover-up or misconduct, but it mattered little. As Jonathan Swift said, "Falsehood flies, and the truth comes limping after it." My own reaction to the "scandal" was somewhere close to amazement. Do some climate scientists often have oversize egos and make mistakes? My goodness, yes. Are they frustrated by the snail's pace of global response? Absolutely.

We go to movies and watch people in body armor and tights try to save the world. I've known some people in tweedy jackets who do the same.

Boulder is also full of cyclists. I took my beat-up bike to University Cycles, one of the busiest repair shops in the country. I pointed the mechanic to the broken rear rack.

"Yeah, we've got that piece. And the new one'll be stronger than what you had there."

I looked around at the bikes stacked up for repair. "I'm headed for Oregon. I was kind of hoping to be back on the road tomorrow."

He looked at the bike longingly. "Wish I could go with you. Stop back by in an hour." He had moved me to the front of the line, and after a walk around town, I came back to find the bike ready to go.

After a Saturday night of beers and stretched-out legs, I rode out of town with the weekly Boulder Sunday morning ride. Ravi and Ells Dutton, one of the leading solar radiation experts, rolled with me out of town in the crystal-clear air at the foot of the mountains.

Business was brisk at a roadside prairie dog town. A few miles further was a café with a tire pump and a dozen bikes outside. On

US Cycling Routes: 2000: Fire —— ; 2011: TransAm —— ; 2012: Warriors Path —— ; 2014: Stronghold Table —— ; 2015: Underground Railroad —— ; 2016: Ice ——. *Map by Lara Taber.*

ABOVE: Fowler Beach, as storm surge from Hurricane Sandy recedes, with Prime Hook Beach at upper left. *Photo: Cape Gazette, by permission.* BELOW: Sharps Island Light, Chesapeake Bay. The island was home to a grand hotel in the early 20th century. *Photo copyright © Monnie Ryan.*

ABOVE: Rose Harris and her mom, Beverly Kipe, on opening day at the Desert Rose Café, Williamsport, Maryland. *Photo by author.* BELOW: Emily Krafjack, gas drilling leaseholder, northeast Pennsylvania. *Photo by author.*

A red waterfall, acid mine drainage from an abandoned coal mine from 1900. Great Allegheny Passage, Pennsylvania. *Photo by author.*

ABOVE: Some animals on the move from climate change. Armadillo range is expanding north. Pikas, high-altitude mammals, have nowhere to go but up. *Photo: Tom Friedel, www.birdphotos.com via Wikimedia Commons.* BELOW: The pika. *Photo: Glacier National Park via Wikimedia Commons.*

ABOVE: Garage entrance, South William Street, lower Manhattan, following passage of Hurricane Sandy, October 2012. *Photo: copyright © Associated Press.* BELOW: Slave collar. Fayette County Historical Society, Vandalia, Illinois. *Photo by author.*

Approaching storm, Memorial Day 2014, Sacred Heart Cemetery, Rosebud Reservation, South Dakota. Below the flags are the graves of three Lakota veterans dating back to World War I. *Photo by author.*

Short Bull, a leader of the Ghost Dance on Stronghold Table, South Dakota. *Photo: Herman Heyn via Minnesota Historical Society.*

Stronghold Table, site of the 1890 Ghost Dance, looking out over Badlands National Park, South Dakota. *Photo by author.*

The remarkable Elsie Eiler, mayor, political power broker, and sole resident of Monowi, Nebraska. *Photo by author.*

A pack of dogs gather at a remote Missouri crossroads. This would get interesting. *Photo by the author.*

Buffalo, Tallgrass Prairie National Preserve, Kansas. I think I've seen this look at a parent-teacher conference. *Photo by Concetta Goodrich.*

High country and storms near Split Rock, Wyoming. *Photo by the author.*

ABOVE: Monk King Bird Pottery and my trailer, Jeffrey City, Wyoming. *Photo by the author.* BELOW: Elk in the Bitterroot River, Montana, August 6, 2000. *Photo John McColgan, Bureau of Land Management.*

Heat on the Hi-Line, Havre, Montana. *Photo: Concetta Goodrich.*

ABOVE: Grinnell Glacier, Glacier National Park, 1926. *Photo# 486.IX.11.037, Morton J. Elrod, Archives and Special Collections, Maureen and Mike Mansfield Library, University of Montana–Missoula.* BELOW: Grinnell Glacier, 2008. Besides the retreat of the glacier, note the advance of small trees since 1926. *Photo by Lisa McKeon, US Geological Survey.*

weekends, the Crane Hollow is sort of a biker bar for cyclists, with cappuccinos replacing Jack Daniel's and not much chance of getting hit with a pool cue. The Boulder people pulled up around a table. This was where they'd turn back for home. Ravi warned me again about the Poudre Canyon Road. Ells had some curious advice for camping in the high country.

"A lot of the National Forest campgrounds are closed. There are a lot of dead trees, and they're afraid of them blowing down." Something was going on in the high forests, and I would be seeing it shortly.

Fueled with a double espresso and the good wishes of my Boulder friends, I returned to the bike. It would be another five hundred miles before the next familiar face. Out on the horizon, Longs Peak and the snowcapped Front Range waited: the next challenge, the highest climb of the ride. I took a deep breath.

COLORADO:
THE FORESTS OF CAMERON PASS

A hole in the mountains notched the skyline ahead. On a June morning I leaned the bike up against the Colorado Route 14 sign. The gateway to the Rockies, Cache la Poudre River Canyon—Poudre Canyon to the locals—opened up out of the plains. French trappers had named it back in the 1700s during an early winter snowstorm, when they needed a place to stash their barrels of gunpowder (*poudre*) for the spring. The snow would be waiting for me a bit higher up, at the head of the canyon, Cameron Pass. Starting at an elevation of a mile, I had another vertical mile to climb with a loaded bike, complete with clothes, camping gear, food, and water. At 10,276 feet, Cameron would be the apex of the ride to Oregon.

In many ways, the ride in the Colorado Rockies had a home-coming feel to it. During college, I had taken time off for a three-week backpacking trip into these mountains as part of the Colorado Outward Bound School. Somewhere in my head, the summer high-altitude choreography of bright blue skies and violent midafternoon storms was still around. The ridgeline sequence of quaking aspen followed by ponderosa and lodgepole pine was familiar.

But things had changed in forty years. Like most of the United States, and the world for that matter, the Rockies have experienced a steady warming. There were many swings about the long-term trend, and this year was one of them. Record winter snows had formed extensive snowpack in the mountains, and the passes had only recently opened up. The snowmelt off the Front Range of the Rockies had led to flooding far out onto the flatlands that spring, with rivers carrying a pulse of melted snow toward the Mississippi and ultimately the Gulf of Mexico. Paradoxically the swollen rivers were flowing right through the drought of Kansas. I was more than ready to get out of the hot winds of the Great Plains and tackle the mountains.

By the time I had reached Poudre Canyon, I had been on the road solo for seven weeks. Each day started without a windshield or a roof, readying for what the skies would throw down. For a cyclist, the major obstacles are electrical storms and wind, and neither of these was insurmountable. With well-tested legs and lungs acclimatized to the altitude, I considered myself well prepared for the climb.

But the day before had been a new kind of obstacle. Echoes of the conversation in Boulder with Ravi's wife, Rochelle, were nagging at me. Maybe it was the power of suggestion or maybe she had a sixth sense, but two days after our talk I found myself walking out of the Fort Collins hospital with a pocket full of antibiotics for a UTI. Symptoms were modest, but I had no idea of medical facilities up in the high country where I was headed.

Thus an unscheduled rest day came to pass. It gave me another chance to check out a college-town coffee shop (Fort Collins is home to Colorado State) and to seek out the source of Fat Tire ale—none other than the New Belgium Brewing Company. Somewhere around my second Fat Tire, I happened to look at the list of the antibiotic's side effects. Well down the list: fatigue. That fact disappeared into the blur.

The next morning, my legs were itching to get at it. The base of the climb was a steady, winding grade along the Poudre River, with steep canyon walls on either side. The river was a roaring cascade of rapids, fed by the deep, melting snow up high. But I was focused on a very small place, bounded by my hands on the bars and my legs turning the cranks. My bike has amazingly low gearing for carrying a full load of equipment, allowing a rider to stay upright and move at speeds as low as 4 mph. I needed all those gears. After a while, the climb got to be another world. From the first push-off up a steep grade, I would make a quick move to get balanced and moving on two wheels. The first thirty seconds were always the hardest: heart spinning up, legs complaining then screaming. Sometime after that initial burst, the legs and the body settle in to find a climbing rhythm, a gentle, sustainable pace, roughly in time to Creedence's "Proud Mary." I'd try to hold that pace for a mile or a half mile, whatever the brain could convince the legs to do.

The steep terrain would often break me out of my little climbing world. At low speeds, the bike is less stable and more prone to wander out into traffic. On the twisting road, the shoulder often disappeared, giving drivers little clearance. At one stretch called the Lower Narrows, a truck came within a few inches of me, and the wash as it blew by almost pushed me down the steeply graded shoulder. This was the stretch of road where Ravi had been left with broken ribs from an impatient pickup.

Around a corner, a few hours in, was a mural by the side of the road depicting mountain lion and elk and bighorn sheep crossing the river, proclaiming the Mishawaka Restaurant and Concert Amphitheater. It started as a dance hall almost a hundred years ago. Built along the Poudre River, it's now a sizable concert venue, and playing the Mish has a certain allure for musicians. The restaurant was just opening for lunch that day, and they gave me a prime seat over the rapids and next to the hummingbird feeder. Their celebrity wall is what caught my eye: signed photos of Joan Baez, Arlo Guthrie, John Mayall, and dozens of newer acts. The animals weren't just on the mural. During concerts, elk were often seen on the hillsides.

The summer of 2012, after my ride, would be very different: hot and dry, without the above-average winter snowpack of 2011. The High Park Fire, then the largest in Colorado history, burned almost ninety thousand acres in the Roosevelt National Forest. It roared up Poudre Canyon. The fire departments from the flatlands made a stand at the Mish, setting up on the deck while the flames came within a dozen feet. They left a signed letter on the bar saying "Long Live the Mish."

The Mish survived, though many of the surrounding houses did not. Several Colorado fires have since supplanted the High Park as the state's largest. Back in the '90s, firefighters referred to Colorado as having "asbestos forests," too wet to burn.[1] All that has changed. Across the West, fires have been increasing in size for the last several decades.[2] There would be more changes in the forest going up the canyon, which we will see later.

Bad weather for cyclists tends to happen in the afternoon, and this day proved the rule. The wind picked up from the west, funneling down the canyon into a strong headwind. I got low on the handlebars, trying to create the smallest profile I could, and crawled up the grade. The Poudre Canyon Road has no towns and just a few stores on the way up to Cameron Pass. My target for the night was a campground and restaurant called Glen Echo. Approaching the campground, my legs were jello, and I had very little left in the tank.

A woman was clearing brush along the road to a ranch. Maybe she was curious, or maybe she just thought I looked like death warmed over. As I approached, she tipped up her hat and squinted in the bright afternoon sunshine.

I pulled to a stop in front of her. "Sorry to bother you, but do you know how far up to the campground?"

"It's just over that next rise, not far at all." She looked me up and down. "That's quite a load. You look like you could use some water."

"I could indeed. Be much obliged."

I followed her up the dusty road to where a couple of chairs sat by the riverside. Sara brought out ice water as I took off the cycling gloves. After a few thousand miles, my hands had perfect white imprints of the gloves, down to the holes in the back. Sara's sister Mary arrived to sit with us in the shade, and a breeze came off the river rapids. The sisters, both about my age, lived in California but summered on the ranch, which had been in their family for decades. Water transmuted into margaritas, and we talked of kids and the canyon and road stories, as the chair became ever more comfortable.

"I'd better get up out of here to the campground while I can still move," I said.

"Well, okay," said Sara. "We're headed to the pass ourselves tomorrow, and we'll see you on the way up."

I tottered down the ranch road, grateful that it wasn't more than a mile to the campground. It was the last stop before the snow line. The woman at the camp store checked me in.

"Don't be too surprised if you hear the bear. He comes through just about every night."

I scratched my head as I went to set up camp. I was the only tent in a sea of RVs, the only thing a bear could easily get into. Hmm. I walked back up to the camp store with a bag.

"You mind keeping my food bag up here for the night?" I asked. "Not sure I want to meet your friend this evening."

"No problem. See you in the morning."

Sleep came almost immediately, with sounds of the river in the distance and the sensation of blood pulsing through my legs.

The bear may have come by, but I was hibernating. It's quite possible that the bears may be hibernating a bit less because of climate change. A recent study on grizzlies, which live farther north in the Rockies, found that high berry availability was associated with late entry into their dens for the winter, while low winter precipitation and high spring temperature resulted in getting out of the dens early.[3]

Morning broke clear and relaxed, and I lingered over pancakes at the restaurant. There was three thousand feet of climbing to go over the next twenty-seven miles, and I didn't get the wheels spinning until 8:30 A.M. Late. The weather was bright and perfect moving up the canyon. I was in harness, pulling steady, with only an occasional car passing on the road. Colors began to grow more vivid. Dark green lodgepole pines covered the steep slopes. The sky was turning a deeper blue with increasing altitude and thinning air, somewhere between the light hazy blue of the Plains and the black of space. Back in the woods, patches of white: snow beginning to show itself. The world had turned clear and stark. The strength in my legs was beginning to ebb, a hollowed-out feeling.

Down a slope from the road, there was motion. Two moose were grazing in the willows along the streambed. They looked up at me, vaguely curious.

I pulled over by a roadside waterfall, one of the increasingly frequent stops. Typical of the effects of high elevation is thirst, and I was pouring water down my throat. Like the day before, the headwind was picking up. As I was about to get back on the bike, the ladies of the canyon pulled up.

Sara ambled up from the car. "Sorry about last night. I would have offered you a place to camp, but I would have gotten a lecture from my husband."

"Not a problem. The campground was cozy."

"How are you doing?"

"Well, getting beat up a little, but making my way up. This is a pretty place to stop."

She looked out over the falls. "A kayaker tried to run that a couple of years back. Got stuck in the rocks. They had to shut down the dam to get the body out."

"Okay then. Think I'll stay on the pavement."

"Well, we're going to do some wandering around up on the pass. We'll see you on the way down."

Neither one of us quite picked up that I was getting into trouble. Approaching the next stop at the Big South campground, I was down to half a bottle of water. This campground was supposed to be open despite the heavy snow. As I rode up to the well, I noticed that the pump handle was missing. In the forest, the snow was now everywhere, though the air was still surprisingly warm. Snowmelt runoff was abundant but risky to drink; it would have to be treated. Luckily, at the far end of the campground was a trailer. I was able to fill my water bottles from the campers. The clouds were amazingly close, white wisps spinning above the peaks. Much of the atmosphere was below me. Bright sunlight was everywhere, banging off the snowfields.

It was still ten miles to go and the grade was getting steeper. My heart began to pound in my ears. Sweat poured out and vanished into the dry clear air. I didn't know if it was the altitude or the wind or the infection, but there seemed to be less and less power in my legs. I was running out of gears. The body-bike machine that transformed pancakes into turning wheels seemed to be breaking down. I remembered the warning on the bottom of the antibiotics package: fatigue.

By now I was committed to getting up and over the pass. The snow cover was complete, with nowhere dry to pitch a tent. I found myself getting off the bike and walking it for stretches. This was the time when riding alone was the most difficult. No one was around to encourage, to drag, to give a kick in the butt.

As I came around a bend, a Forest Service truck was stopped by the side of the road, and I pulled up next to him. My appearance must have given away a certain desperation.

"You doing okay?" he asked.

"Yeah, but I'm getting hammered pretty badly. Any chance I could get a ride from you to the top?"

He pursed his lips. "I'm just a volunteer, and I'm not sure they want me giving rides. But I'll tell you what: I've done this ride a long time ago, and it is a bear, especially with all that weight. I'll take your panniers up to the pass and stash them behind the picnic tables. That should give you a little help."

I jumped at the offer to take fifty pounds off the bike. I wanted to make it across to Oregon all on my own power, and this was the only option. It was a kindness, one of many along the road, and my ride would be unbroken. It seemed that an extra gear or two had been added to the chain rings as his truck sped off.

The last miles drifted into a kind of blur, taking out pieces of the steep grade bit by bit as the sun began to drift down. The forests seemed less bright, with patches of dead trees. The snowdrifts grew to over six feet. Before long, the Forest Service truck reappeared coming back down. He pulled over to roll the window down.

"Okay, your bags are up there. You've only got three miles from here, and you look like you're doing okay. The grade flattens out after this rise. You'll be fine."

I was. Around a bend, and a sign in the distance: CAMERON PASS SUMMIT. A bench cleared out from the snow provided a dry place to celebrate with a candy bar from the newly reunited panniers. Not quite all downhill to the Pacific; still, this was as high as I would get. But something was quite unusual about the vista on the other side of the pass. The hillsides were gray. Dead lodgepole pines spread out to the horizon, on one slope after another.

The forests of Cameron Pass were gone. As my breath came back from the climb, there was a slow realization of what had happened. I could remember hiking in the Colorado high country forty years ago, rock and snow and pine up to the tree line. It was our playground, a place to test ourselves, a place to listen to the quiet. Now it was a ghost forest.

I had heard of the culprit for quite a while: the mountain pine beetle. The beetle drills into the thick bark of the older trees, bringing with it a fungus that is typically fatal to the tree. Always present in the pine forests, beetle populations in the mountain West began to explode in the late 1990s. Before, their numbers were typically kept under control by cold winters in the mountains. A week of temperatures well below zero will typically kill off the overwintering larvae. But warming has meant that these deep-cold winters are largely a thing of the past. Even the heavy snows of this last winter did not bring temperatures cold enough for long enough to kill the larvae. Signs of the beetle from a distance are patches of red on the hillsides as the pines are attacked. At Cameron Pass the battle was long over. Red had turned to gray, and a dead forest was what remained.

Cameron Pass is a snapshot of what's happened up the high mountain spine of the continent. Most of the mature lodgepole forests in Colorado and southern Wyoming are gone. About 100,000 beetle-killed trees a day fall in this area of about four million acres, with another area that size in Montana. That's dwarfed by British Columbia and Alberta to the north, where ten times that area is affected. Western US forests are so full of dead trees that some scientists have proposed burning them in power plants instead of coal.[4] The wisdom or practicality of the idea can be debated, but it illustrates the staggering scale of the die-off.

Will the forests return? In many places young pines are growing around the dead trees, and the younger trees are not as susceptible to infestation. And indeed, this is not the first beetle kill in the West, though certainly the largest on record. But the question of the forest's return is intimately tied to the climate. Will the deep-cold winters return? For any climate scientist, the answer is "not likely." So for the high-altitude pines, the beetles will be there when the trees grow large enough. Quite simply, the tall western lodgepole pine forests of my youth are lost for my lifetime, and it's not clear if they will ever be able to come back. The whole face of the Rockies has changed in response to the change in climate. Trees in many campgrounds have been removed, so there is no shade, while remaining trees have been treated with insecticide. The place where I played forty years ago is no more.

I reinstalled the four panniers and pulled out of the parking lot at the pass. My legs were shaky, quivering. It took about two pedal strokes to start into a steep, cold plunge through the snowfields. I dropped a half mile of elevation very quickly, down a switchbacked road through miles of dead trees. Now the challenge was completely opposite from the other side: maintaining alertness and control on a lonely 40 MPH descent. The muscles getting exhausted were those on my forearms, the ones leaning on the brakes. I stopped several times to shake out my arms and convince myself I could still stop. The first campground I found was in the town of Gould. Another dark, exhausted night's sleep awaited.

Though I would find my way to a cold Pacific beach in Oregon about five weeks later, and I would see other fingerprints of climate change, the effects were nowhere as dramatic as in the Rockies. Outside of Gould, salvage logging operations were much in evidence, taking down dead trees before they could fuel another massive fire. Packets of firewood labeled BEETLE KILL were for sale. The real estate industry, ever adaptable, advertised "emerging view lots."

But something's lost. I asked the owner of the campground about the disappearing forest. He looked up from the desk as he was running my card through, a glance out to the horizon.

"The wind seems to blow a bit stronger with the trees gone."

Concetta and I drove back over Cameron Pass five years later, in July of 2016. Things change slowly in the mountains. On that drizzly day, the snowpack so evident in 2011 was gone. Looking up into the hills, the forests, if anything, were more gray. Compared against photographs from five years ago, living trees are far rarer now, present only at the edges of the road and only rarely on the hillsides. It's as though the dead forest is waiting for something.

And that's coming. We drove into Walden, a town in the high country where a big breakfast had helped revive me after the 2011 Cameron climb. The waitress even said that she remembered me, probably a kind sentiment on her part. On the way into town was a familiar sign on the roadside, spray-painted onto plywood: THANK YOU FIREFIGHTERS. I asked the waitress about the fire.

"The Beaver Creek fire's been going for a while now. They can't seem to do anything with it. There's miles and miles of beetle kill up there. The crews won't go into the dead trees. They could go down anytime, and there's a jumble of deadfall underfoot. Can't hardly walk in it if they wanted to."

Two months later, the Beaver Creek fire still burned, blackening over thirty-eight thousand acres. The Forest Service confirmed what the waitress had told me: "The fire is burning in heavy beetle killed timber. The infested trees are subject to blowing over, contributing large amounts of down timber and providing fuel for extreme fire behavior when strong winds and terrain features are in alignment, making the timbered areas unsafe for firefighters."[5]

What Concetta and I saw at Beaver Creek wasn't necessarily representative of western forests generally. Beetle kill does not appear to have a large-scale effect on how much forest ends up burned during fire season.[6] Overall, western forests that have been decimated by the beetles are not necessarily more likely to burn, though there's no question that climate change per se has been making fires worse, as we'll see in Montana and Idaho. Regardless, Colorado mountain pine beetle outbreaks have dropped in recent years, because there's just not that much left to chew on.

In the understory of beetle-killed forests, young trees and bushes are growing as needles have fallen and light has penetrated. Will this ultimately be a new forest of different species or resistant varieties? Or will these trees simply be attacked once more when they grow larger? We don't know the answer, and won't know for many years. For the forests of Cameron Pass, like many of our ecosystems on a warming planet, it's not the end of the world. Rather, it's the entry into a very different one.

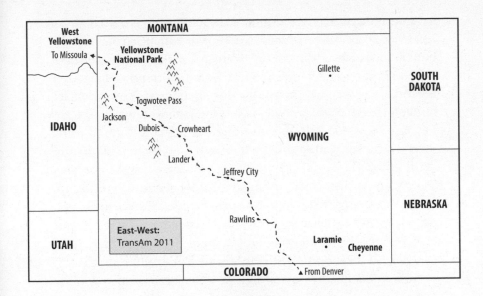

West Yellowstone
Yellowstone National Park
To Missoula
MONTANA
Gillette
SOUTH DAKOTA
Togwotee Pass
Jackson
Dubois — Crowheart
WYOMING
IDAHO
Lander
Jeffrey City
NEBRASKA
Rawlins
East-West: TransAm 2011
UTAH
Laramie
Cheyenne
COLORADO — From Denver

WYOMING: THE POTTERY STUDIO AT THE END OF THE EARTH

C oncetta and I drove through northeast Wyoming in that same summer of 2016. The sign at the entrance to the town of Gillette reads ENERGY CAPITAL OF THE WORLD. It's not difficult to see why. In the mesas around Gillette are several open pit coal mines, great black seams in the earth with orange bulldozers working at their base. Wyoming is one of the leading coal-producing states. It's hard times for the business. A glut of cheap natural gas from fracking has made coal relatively expensive. Federal climate change regulations known as the Clean Power Plan required a 32 percent reduction in greenhouse gases, favoring natural gas-fired power plants over those that run on coal.[1] Even as these regulations are withdrawn, it's unlikely that coal will become more competitive than gas.

These blows have led to plummeting demand, bankrupting several coal companies. Gillette has been hard hit, too, with hundreds of layoffs. Yet change in the energy economy has not been completely negative for Wyoming. In Carbon County to the south, where Wyoming's first coal mine opened a century ago, the largest wind farm in North America is in advanced planning stages. Wind turbines are already spinning prominently along the Interstate 80 corridor, one of the windiest places in the country.

Back on the Energy Capital sign in Gillette is a curious symbol: not a coal mine but an atom. In the early 1950s, prospectors combed Wyoming's hills in search of uranium. They found it in the center of the state, prompting one of the great booms in the middle of the last century. It's where the bicycle would take me on the TransAm ride in June of 2011.

Best be prepared when leaving Rawlins, the seat of Carbon County. I was twenty miles out, looking for the remnants of a town, or at least a bar and grill. A bottle and a half of water sat on the bike frame. Rock and high desert stretched to the horizon. The yellow of my bags provided the only splash of color against the dull green of sagebrush and dark gray of the storm clouds. This day's ride had been on my mental bulletin board for months. Of all the days from Delaware to Oregon, this was the only one where no motel or grocery store was anywhere near the route. In fact, there was very little of anything in the 125 miles to the next town, Lander. In the planning stages of the trip, it was the remoteness of this particular stretch that dictated the need to carry camping gear—tent, sleeping bag, and cook kit—adding substantially to the weight on the bike.

Midway between Rawlins and Lander was a dot on the map: Jeffrey City. This town of five thousand grew on the strength of the nearby uranium mines. The demand for uranium crashed in the wake of the 1979 Three Mile Island nuclear reactor accident, and the town nearly vanished. Now about fifty souls live there. I was prepared to camp and had plenty of food, but I wasn't sure if there even was water. In the high country, it wasn't an idle concern. Yet the clerk at last night's motel had assured me that there was still a restaurant in Jeffrey City, some comfort as Rawlins faded off into the distance.

I was on a gentle climb to the Continental Divide at 7,174 feet in high, crystalline air. It was the first of seven crossings of the Divide on the trip. Painted mesas were the horizon fifty miles out, without a tree in sight. All the bars on the cell phone had disappeared. It was radio silence now. I was well out of my Eastern orbit, completely alone, into those far belts of the solar system where only comets travel.

If there was a word I'd heard more than once about this part of Wyoming, it would be *unforgiving*. Many pioneers on the Oregon and Mormon Trails were lost to Wyoming's October snows. Snow in June, when I was riding, was unlikely but not unknown. With elevations of a mile and a half, the weather was always close and changeable. The forecast that morning seemed reasonable enough for mid-June: scattered showers. I was on the road early, since most thunderstorms boil up in the afternoon. But as I crested the gentle slope on this part of the Divide, the storms were laid out in the treeless basin before me, sweeping across from west to east, waiting. A jagged string of lightning flashed from the dark, flat base of the storm just up the road.

I slowed down. The storm that was so eager to pounce drifted away harmlessly to the east, and I rode into a lighter gray sky behind it. I was congratulating myself on my cleverness and navigational skills without focusing much on the west, on what was coming. It turned out that it was a baby storm that had scooted off to the east. Mama was just behind, and she was angry.

I was rapidly folded up in darkness, gusting winds, and lightning flashes. Shelter was nowhere in sight, not even a ranch house. I stopped to put on foul-weather gear as raindrops began to slap on the pavement. The sky was crackling and electricity very close. There was nothing to do but ball up low on the side of the road, away from the metal bike, and get drenched. The rain front swept across the road, with an occasional hailstone. In the distance cattle were mooing nervously. The crackling was now overhead. A trace of the metallic scent of ozone drifted in the air. Mama was sniffing around, hunting for me. I comforted myself that the steel roadside reflectors were a little higher than me.

She lashed the road with sheets of rain as I tried to tuck my knees up under my jacket. The moments between the flash and the thunder vanished. One thousand one—BAM. I was shivering uncontrollably, watching the water bead up and run down my legs. Finally, she gave up and moved on. Freezing and stiff, I got up from the pavement, shaking off the rain and reconnecting with fingers and toes. I clenched both fists, and a stream of water came out of the bike gloves. There were still forty miles of red mesas and barren mountains before Jeffrey City. Time to spin the wheels again.

There are sights and sounds that a cyclist can pick up that never make it inside a car. Baby snakes sunning on the side of the road. The hiss of a wheat field in a strong wind. And after the storm that day in Wyoming, a sound I'd heard before but never identified: in the middle of the sagebrush, what sounded like the caw of a crow. No birds were anywhere in sight when the caw came again. Then I picked him out: an antelope, warning of an intruder, his tan hide perfectly folded into the landscape.

Up the road two granite shoulders loomed. Split Rock was a landmark on the journey west, where wagon trains would stop along the Sweetwater River. I had come across the Oregon Trail. Intermittently, in the dry country, wagon ruts are still visible. Like those pioneers, I was headed for the Willamette Valley of Oregon; my route would go just a bit farther, to the Pacific to dip my tire.

One of the travelers had written of the area, "This region seems to be the refuses of the world thrown up in utmost confusion." In this most desolate country, the Oregon and Mormon Trails shared nearly the same path. According to the trailside panel, Mormons and non-Mormons were careful to stay on opposite sides of the Sweetwater River. Prejudices and distrust were carried with them across the Plains. The Pony Express had a station at Split Rock where a young Buffalo Bill changed horses as he rode 322 miles in a day. My goal was more modest: ride the last fifteen to Jeffrey City before the next line of storms swept across.

The rains came again, though not with the violence of earlier in the day. As the odometer registered the mileage where Jeffrey City should be, I looked around for signs of civilization: a water tower, houses, anything. I was coming down to the last half-bottle of water. My right knee was getting ominously sore, aching on the climbs. I needed a place to stop.

Gradually coming into view were a few nondescript structures: an abandoned motel, streets lined with vacant trailer pads, some boarded-up sheds off in the distance. A roadside historic panel referred to the demise of the uranium mines—JEFFREY CITY: BIGGEST BUST OF THEM ALL. Emerging from the sagebrush, an oasis: the Split Rock Bar and Café. I weaved between the puddles in the parking lot and leaned the bike next to the door.

On the wall of the bar were mounted antelopes and a row of cowboy hats. A young couple was shooting pool in the next room. A waitress was cleaning tables. Behind the bar was a sturdy, welcoming woman in a blue sweatshirt, polishing the glasses. She was the owner, Vikki. I wasn't the first cyclist she'd seen, but I was the first one to stop that day.

After a long, cool drink, arrangements for the night were on my mind. "I'd like to stop by for dinner later, but do you know if there's any place in town to camp?"

Vikki paused. "Well, I think the trailer's open." She saw the puzzled look on my face. "Why don't you go across and ask Byron?"

At the abandoned gas station across the street, a FULL SERVE sign was half peeled off, ready to fall, and grass was well established in the cracked asphalt. Next to the pumps sat a camping trailer, with a garish scene of dolphins jumping in the sunset. Behind, painted on a white panel: MONK KING BIRD POTTERY. A cloud of mosquitoes gathered as I approached the door.

"Don't let 'em in. I know the Buddhists say you're not supposed to kill anything, but damn . . ." Byron's hands were wet with mud as he sat at the pottery wheel. He had sad blue eyes and a three-day beard. A Lander Bar baseball cap covered a tangle of brown hair.

Byron washed his hands and shut down the wheel. "Here, let me show you around. We don't get all that many visitors. I call my things Red Canyon Ware."

Through the old gas station office and out into the service bays were hundreds of pots, mugs, and dishes, all with intricate red clay layers. On one shelf was a set of angry-looking, almost Polynesian masks. It was less a shop than a jumble, with stained glass, macramé flowerpot holders, and a dartboard set amid the pottery. I gingerly asked about a place to stay.

"Oh, they mentioned the trailer? Sure, you can stay there overnight. There's no water, so you'll have to use the bathroom at the Split Rock. I wouldn't be surprised if you had company tonight. This is a natural stopping place for cyclists between Lander and Rawlins, and we put up all we can."

As the afternoon wore on, cyclists appeared out of the high desert. First Rachel and Jack from Miami, riding the country on a diagonal. Then Daniel and Shirley, lean evangelicals from South Dakota. Vikki set us up on a big round table and brought us out plate after plate of giant burgers and hand-cut fries with homemade gravy. We wolfed it all down as we tried to top each other's road stories.

Daniel was a solidly built man, bald, with an open smile. He was a minister taking time off from his church to ride into Wyoming with his wife, Shirley. They seemed to know what they were doing out on the road. After dinner, Daniel pressed me on my climate mission.

"There's a lot of fuss about climate these days," he said. "But climate's always changed. They've found alligator bones in the Arctic."

"Sure enough," I said. "But alligators in the Arctic are from millions of years ago, when the continents weren't even in the same place they are now. That's hard to compare to today. The planet's way warmer now than it was just a hundred years ago, and I think that's the comparison that matters."

"Maybe it is a little warmer. Up by where we are, we get sixty degree swings in a single day. Changing a couple of degrees doesn't matter much."

This wasn't an uncommon view. "It's a question of averages, not what the temperature is right this second," I said. "The difference in average temperature between the Ice Ages and now is only nine degrees. Put on nine degrees of warming instead of cooling, and it's a really big deal."

"Well, the whole idea of thinking that all the little things we do can make any difference to creation"—he waved his hand out to the prairie—"that just doesn't make any sense to me."

"As a scientist, numbers speak to me. Anyway, might be worth a second look for you sometime."

I'd heard the "awe of creation" argument before. Daniel comes from a place where the land is big and the human landscape seems so small. Looking at a sky stretching out to a distant horizon, it does seem hard to believe that humans can affect it. But we have. U2 pilots flying solo across the Antarctic sky on the edge of the stratosphere detected remains of the chlorine compounds that we used in our refrigerators. Those compounds caused the ozone hole. Now, much closer to home, the increase in carbon dioxide driving climate change can be measured in Maryland, right on people's docks, here in Wyoming, right outside the Split Rock, or anywhere else on the planet.

Implicit in Daniel's way of thinking is "If we can't change anything, then we don't have to change." I thought back to the young people I'd talked with along the ride, the kids in Maryland, the college students in Ohio. Change is harder for adults, but it comes naturally for the young. They inherit this altered world and provide much of the hope for action to begin repairing it.

After dark, we wandered back over to the Monk King Bird. Byron threw some scrap wood into a steel drum and lit it off in a whoosh with gasoline. "Keeps the bugs down," he said. Outside of our firelight, the land was nearly pitch black on a moonless night. The sky was another story. The heavens were lit up with stars in the high, clear air.

Concetta had given me a bottle of Armagnac as a retirement gift for just such an occasion. I broke out the hip flask as we gathered around the fire. Byron took a sip. "That is some smooth stuff. I'm supposed to stay away from this, but I can make an exception."

"How'd you end up out here?" I asked.

"I grew up on a ranch not too far from here. Used to camp in the high country shepherding with my granddad. I knew right then it wasn't for me." He took another swig. "Wandered around a bit. Learned how to throw clay out in California, but I always wanted to come back and make pots that look like the land." He made a wave into the darkness.

There was a scratching sound. Jack from Miami gave a start: "Looks like we've got company." At the edge of our little cone of light, a rattler was coiled up in a pile.

"Yeah, I think the light and noise bother him sometimes." Byron picked up a rock and threw it. "G'won, Ralph, get on out. Find yourself a nice mouse." The rattler struck halfheartedly and slithered off into the dark. A bottle of vodka mysteriously appeared in Byron's hand.

The drum was beginning to burn out, and the Split Rock had closed. We were getting ready to retire to our tents and trailer when a headlight appeared on the horizon.

Byron's widening eyes picked up the firelight as he looked out toward the car. He jumped up. "All right, here we go!" He ran into the studio.

The rest of us looked at each other across the fire and shrugged.

Soon he emerged wearing one of his Polynesian masks and carrying a pitchfork. He ran to the roadside, quivering with anticipation. Out of the darkness, he was silhouetted in the headlights of the approaching car. As the car neared, he jumped up and down, shaking the pitchfork over his head. The car swerved, then the driver gunned the engine. It was still roaring as the taillights disappeared over the far ridge.

Byron grinned as he took the mask off. "And out-of-state plates, too. Damn, that never gets old."

Jack was laughing, with his head in his hands. "I'd say it's time to call it a night. Maybe find someplace to hide."

We stumbled off to our sleeping bags. I made a last visit out into the sagebrush, keeping an eye out with the flashlight for Ralph. Shutting off the switch, I saw the Milky Way arching up through the Northern Cross. The spiral arms of the galaxy reached out into the sky. I was hundreds of miles from anyone I knew, but for a night I had the keys to Jeffrey City.

I woke up early in the trailer, with all problems still intact and a hangover added on. Sixty miles and two thousand feet of climbing to Lander waited outside, and my knee ached. I smelled nasty. Gluey gray mud covered the parking lot on the walk over to the Split Rock, sticking in the cleats on the bottoms of my shoes.

A truck was parked outside, so I knocked at the door. Vikki wasn't necessarily pleased for the company—early morning is her quiet time—but she was kind enough to pour the coffee and make one of her thick, platter-sized pancakes. A few sips helped the hangover cloud begin to burn off. All worth it for a rare banquet of the Order of the TransAm. I was far from the only person to notice the hospitality. Vikki and Byron received the Trail Angel award from the Adventure Cycling Association in 2012.

With the bill paid and good-byes said, I opened the door back out onto the high desert. The buzzing of mosquitoes came up without hesitation. They attacked relentlessly. I looked over to the pottery studio. Byron would be a while sleeping this one off. Time to get back on the bike.

They say Kansas is the center of the country, but looking back, maybe Jeffrey City was the center of it all.

WYOMING:
THE GRAND, STRAIGHT AHEAD

The rain cleared soon after I left Jeffrey City, and the Wind River Range began to take shape on the western horizon. Precious few signs of human habitation appeared between the mesas, absent the occasional steer. Central Wyoming remained the loneliest part of the ride. About twenty miles out, a collection of buildings materialized by the roadside. It turns out that riders on the TransAm weren't the first to haul their gear across this part of Wyoming. The Mormon Handcart Historical Site is a memorial to a desperate time in the history of the West. In 1856, Mormon pilgrims were making their way west to the home of the new religion in Salt Lake City, many coming across from Europe. Few could afford wagons and mule teams, so they built handcarts to pull their belongings across the Plains and the Rockies. Most made it.

In the late summer, though, two handcart parties were delayed and could only leave Iowa in late July. Their leaders said the Lord would provide. The mountain men shook their heads. In mid-October they reached Wyoming, when early snow caught up with them. Wolves took to following the camps, shadows in the distance. About 250 were lost to exposure and starvation, far more than the Donner Party, before the rescuers from Salt Lake reached them. Wyoming is a hard place to make a mistake.

Snow season was still months away, but like the handcart parties, I had few options. My right knee was still painful, and outside of my own propulsion, there was no other way of getting down the road. No buses and few cars passed. My strategy was to slow down, go gently on the knee, and pop ibuprofen. Concetta and our son Andrew were flying into Jackson to meet me in Grand Teton Park, but between us there were 220 miles and another crossing of the Great Divide at ten thousand feet: Togwotee Pass.

"We can come over the pass to get you. You don't have to ride this stretch."

Concetta's voice came through the cell phone as I cupped it in my hands, trying to find a place to talk out of the wind. For each night of the ride, she had been the steady presence, lifeline to a stable world, my brown eyes. Coming on two months on the road, more than anything I wanted to curl up next to her.

"No, it's okay, I think I can manage this. It's probably just old guy aches and pains. I'd really like to get to Grand Teton on my own power."

Before the high climb over the Divide was a long day through the rimrock country along the Wind River, through the Shoshone

Reservation. The river is well named. That morning, packing out of Lander, the Weather Channel said "winds light and variable." Not likely. By 10:00 A.M., they were strong enough to play a note on my open Gatorade bottle. The night's destination, at the end of a long, gradual ascent, was originally named Never Sweat, for the warm, dry winds that dominate this part of Wyoming. They later settled for the more poetic Dubois. The grade, the wind, and the distance combined to make for a twelve-hour day on the road in crystal-clear high altitude. A fluff of cottonwood seeds gathered along the roadside. Cresting the tops of the red-layered mesas were the snowy peaks of the Tetons ahead.

Proust wrote, "It is a curious experience to see in fact places we have known only in imagination." Back in my bedroom, the metric for what to include in my packing centered around Crowheart, perhaps the most out-of-the-way point on the route across the country. It lay astride this day's route. The question back home was: Do you have what you need if something goes wrong in Crowheart?

The real Crowheart was more rich and desolate than anything in my imagination. Rising up out of the sagebrush is a gigantic butte of the same name. At the base of the butte in 1866, a great battle swirled between the Crow and the Shoshone over hunting grounds in the Wind River Basin. The story goes that Washakie, chief of the Shoshone, emerged from the battle with the heart of a Crow opponent on his lance.

When I reached Crowheart, I was simply exhausted. The settlement consisted of a dusty little gas station/convenience store selling all the usual items. There was nowhere to sit, nowhere to simply curl up and lie down. I walked around the building and sat down in the high grass in back, out of the wind. I drank as much as I could, leaned my head back against the vinyl siding, and closed my eyes. Forty-five miles out, and somehow I needed to come up with the energy for the next thirty miles into Dubois.

Somehow I did. Successful long days on the bike consisted of a series of second, third, and fourth winds. The reserves seemed to come through on the road out of Crowheart. And I was helped along by stunningly beautiful country. The river wound through layered red rocks and irrigated green hayfields. Dubois was, to my surprise, a busy, pretty place, one of the gateway towns to Yellowstone. Never Sweat it wasn't. I was almost completely dehydrated by the time I pulled in, after seventy-five miles and four thousand feet of climbing on a fully loaded bike.

After the long day into Dubois, I decided to use the golfing strategy of laying up: I'd get as far toward Togwotee Pass as I could and still have a place to camp, then go after the rest of the climb the next day. I found the perfect stopping point about twenty miles up, a campground/bar called the Lava Mountain Lodge. Trees were starting to thin out in the transition to rock and ice country. I set up the tent in back and proceeded to work my way through their microbrews out on the lodge balcony. A hawk turned over the Wind River, and there was just enough breeze for the chimes hung from the eaves.

Stretching out my legs, I mused on conversations I'd had on the ride across thus far. People seemed to assume that riding across the country is a thoroughly risky endeavor. The discussion at every other convenience store involved "You be careful out there" or "Stay safe." I had even passed a drive-in featuring A Million Ways to Die in the West. Let's see: charging buffalo, rattlesnakes, unexploded bombs, grain trucks, tornadoes, the pie at Sissy's Cafe (it's to die for) . . .

All of the warnings were routine kindnesses, of course, but the long ride wasn't really unsafe. A few trucks passed closer than I'd want, and some weather was iffy and uncomfortable. But people seem to assume, probably based on watching too many Steven Seagal movies, that the world outside the living room is full of terrorists and psychopaths. Despite what's on movies and television, that's not so. In younger days, I hitchhiked across the country three times and learned that most people wanted to help me along. For the bike trip, some were curious about why I was doing such a thing, some were even wistful, but no one was ever hostile. Maybe I was lucky, but I've been doing this for a while. Perhaps naively, I was never afraid of anyone, and, conversely, no one was scared of me.

If I wanted to pull something on the cycling trips, I had the slowest getaway vehicle imaginable.

Sitting on a couch watching the world on TV and waiting for one of our range of sedentary diseases to strike seems vastly riskier. I know that most people don't have the time or opportunity to do something like this, and I'm fortunate. Yet there seems to be an unspoken assumption that It's Dangerous Out There. I'd suggest that the reverse is true: it's dangerous in here.

The morning brought an early start. Concetta and Andrew waited on the other side of the pass, and I almost jumped out of the sleeping bag. Breakfast brought another round of immense pancakes and a surprise: the battery for the cycle computer was dead. Along with a nonexistent cell signal, it meant there'd be no way of figuring out where I was or how far to the top. I'd be switching off the computer and using the Force.

It was a steady, steep climb, with the first dirty snowbanks appearing soon after I started. Babying the knee, I stayed in the lowest gear and stopped every twenty to thirty minutes. The snow grew deeper by the roadside, but working hard under the deep blue sky of high altitude, I was soon stripped down to short sleeves and shorts. There were no buildings and few cars in a world of gray rock castles towering over Ponderosa pines. Sweat dried instantly, caking on my face. With a slow, steady, climbing rhythm, I sold my increasingly skeptical legs on just one more pitch, then the next, and the next.

After a while, the road began to even out through the deep snow, then a little downhill. I swore. The last thing I wanted to do was give up the slightest bit of hard-earned altitude. A little more downhill and around a bend, framed in the distance, was the Grand Teton, America's Matterhorn, the greatest mountain vista on the continent. A sign indicated a 6 percent downhill grade for the next six miles. I was over the top. My scream echoed off the cliffs. I rocketed down the mountain, swinging through banked turns, swimming into the warmth of the valley below. It was a quiet entrance to Grand Teton National Park at Moran Junction, and soon buffalo herds were in view from the road. The traffic picked up going north, with RVs passing close. I could hear a car close behind that wouldn't pass. I motioned to the driver to go around me. A window rolled down.

"Get off the road!"

It was Andrew. He and Concetta parked on the shoulder, and we hugged. The road's not necessarily dangerous, but it does get lonely.

We did all of the tourist things in Grand Teton and Yellowstone: rafting, hiking, grizzly watching. It was pure pleasure. They even carried my bags as I rode over Yellowstone's three crossings of the Divide. Climbing the first pass, a couple of young cyclists on fancy machines blew by. I harrumphed. With three thousand miles behind me, I wasn't going to let that happen. But as I cranked up the speed, an epiphany: all those miles had not transmuted fifty-something legs into twenty-something legs. I dropped away, newly resolved to ride my age.

Along the road in Yellowstone, we came across a sign in front of a rock outcropping: THE OBSIDIAN CLIFFS. Obsidian is black volcanic glass, and we had stumbled on the source of one of the most remarkable artifacts of the ride. Back in Ohio at the Hopewell National Historical Park, seventeen hundred miles back, I had gazed on a black obsidian knife. Chemical analysis indicates that these cliffs are the only possible source. It looks like this is where my Marco Polo had ended up.

I had been to Yellowstone a few years after the 1988 firestorm tore through the park. Back then, the blackened trunks of the trees still covered the land like a gray-black winter coat. Even on this bike ride a quarter century later, only small trees, not much bigger than a man, had grown in. Regrowth is slow in the northern Rockies.

Decades later, a new, slow-motion fire was coming to Yellowstone. As in Colorado, mountain pine beetles were advancing through the conifer forests. Winters are no longer cold enough to kill the beetle larvae, and the red and gray of dying pine trees were becoming increasingly common in the park. It was quite clear on the eastern approach to Togwotee Pass. The lower-elevation pines, Ponderosa and lodgepole, have faced the beetles for thousands of years and have evolved some defenses. It's a new threat for the trees growing up high, especially the whitebark pine, and this species is quite vulnerable. Whitebark are particularly important to grizzly bears, who use their seeds to fatten up before hibernation. Another species with virtually no evolved resistance to the beetles is the jack pine, which covers much of the boreal forest of Canada. And the beetles are moving toward our northern neighbor along with the warming.

It isn't simply the forests of the great parks that are changing. Teton Glacier, the snowfield that frames the iconic view of Grand Teton, has lost 20 percent of its area in the last forty years. For someone of my age, it's as though these great iconic places are fading before my eyes. The loss of snow and ice is similar to what's happened in both Glacier National Park to the north and the Wind River Range to the south. It's not simply a local effect. Glaciers and snowfields provide much of the water for western Wyoming and Idaho, and, to a lesser extent, Utah.

With the declining snowfields, pikas, those small, Mickey Mouse–eared animals, may have a particularly difficult fate. A heavy snowpack insulates the ground, where pikas hibernate from severe cold in the winter, since the temperature under a thick blanket of snow doesn't drop much below freezing. Even in a warming world, Teton winters get seriously cold. With a diminished snowpack, pikas, ironically, may actually freeze to death.

Decreasing snowpack also means less runoff and warmer summer temperatures in the streams. Cutthroat trout, prized by fishermen, thrive in the cold water from spring snowmelt, but in the new conditions, the nonnative rainbow trout are moving upstream from the lower elevations. Heat stress and low water have already caused some fishkills.

Concetta, Andrew, and I parted at West Yellowstone that morning, and I watched them drive south to the airport, just before I turned north into the Lewis and Clark country of Montana. The winds were funneling down the canyons, and I could feel the weight of the next thousand miles.

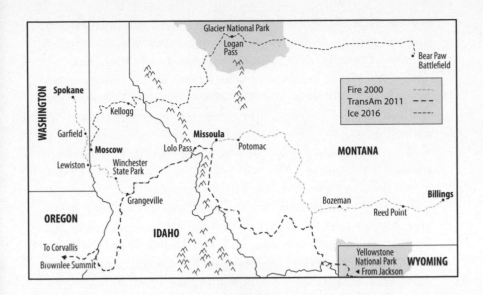

IDAHO–MONTANA PART I: FIRE

God gave Noah the rainbow sign
No more water but fire next time
> From the African-American spiritual
> "Mary Don't You Weep"

C rossing into Montana on the TransAm in 2011 felt like a bit of the past, as I rolled through some familiar places. The northern Rockies were the setting for my very first long ride in August of 2000. That had been a steep learning curve. It was my first tour, and I traveled alone. But the landscape was different indeed. That tour in the summer of the millennium was in the time of fire.

That summer of 2000 I rode east, from Spokane, Washington, across Idaho to Billings, Montana. The national news had plenty of stories on the massive fires in the West that year. When I changed planes in Denver for the flight to Spokane, it got a little more immediate. In the arrival lounge were firefighters in green jumpsuits carrying loaded equipment packs and hard hats. Later at Spokane baggage claim, it seemed that every other duffel bag had an axe handle coming out of it. I realized that I'd been swept up in a grand, haphazard armada of firefighters converging on my destination. Aircraft, heavy equipment, and people were pouring into these mountains from around the country and the world, with teams from as far away as Australia and New Zealand.

On the flight from Denver to Spokane, we flew over much of the northern Rockies. I craned my neck to look out the window toward Montana. A brown haze shaded the mountains below, with pinpoint plumes of smoke pouring off the land, extending out to the horizon. A little unease settled into my stomach. I'd put in the training and the planning. I'd saved up for tickets, a new bike, and, at the time, vacation days. This trip was years in the making. But maybe this wasn't a good time for a bicycle ride through the burning country below.

I was drawn to this country and this ride by an obsession with an old story. I had read the account of the Nez Perce, or Nimiipuu, who were removed from their land in 1877 and led the army on a 1,170-mile chase through the Northwest. An entire tribe—men, women, and children—outran and outmaneuvered the cavalry for five months, fighting repeated battles. They were stopped only forty miles from the Canadian border and exiled to Oklahoma's Indian Territory. I wanted to follow their route. I was also looking for a first long tour after commuting to work by bike for most of a decade. It occurred to me that the Nez Perce Trail might be all paved roads after 123 years. But fire wasn't part of the plan.

Nevertheless, the fires were still a long way from the Spokane airport and western Idaho. I assembled the bike in a motel room and was soon headed across the Washington wheat fields. Late summer was harvest time in the great fertile wheat belt known as the Palouse. Raptors circled over freshly cut fields, where rodents were newly deprived of shelter. I had a close encounter with a giant combine, wide enough to take up both lanes of the road. The combine operator hadn't seen me, and I took a quick detour into the ditch. Dusting off, heart racing, I took a glance up. In the cab was the terrified driver, who looked to be about fourteen. Driving lessons start early out here.

Eastern Washington was where I first met Debb and Mark Thorne in the grain town of Garfield, and it was a treat to see them again in Ohio. But the task after I left them that first time was to get to Idaho. From Garfield, it was a two-thousand-foot descent into the town of Lewiston. The selection of routes was Scylla or Charybdis. One choice was the well-traveled main road, US 95. In the late Friday afternoon sun and howling wind, I decided to avoid the traffic in favor of the Old Spiral Highway. It didn't take long to discover how it got its name. There wasn't another soul on the road, but fourteen hairpin turns were waiting for me. The road repeatedly dove deep into a baked brown hillside, then turned and launched out into space. Only guardrails kept me from the Snake River Valley below. I was spinning down the mountainside, leaning into the wind to keep from getting blown over the edge. Idaho would be quite a ride.

Lewiston and its neighbor Clarkston, Washington, are named for Lewis and Clark, who had a desperate journey through this part of the world. They called the Bitterroots, the closely packed ridges of eastern Idaho and western Montana, "the endless mountains." They emerged half-starved onto the Idaho prairie in 1805. The Nez Perce tribe reprovisioned and traded with the Corps of Discovery, but they probably came to regret their hospitality. Seventy years after this first encounter with the whites, they would be forced from their home.

Like Lewis and Clark, I would come to rely on the hospitality of strangers to get me through a hard land. This part of Idaho is a deeply incised country, where great rivers have carved canyons. The deepest is Hells Canyon at almost eight thousand feet, but there are many others. On the Idaho landscape, the climbs up out of the canyons are known euphemistically as "grades," suggesting something gentle. Not exactly.

That summer of 2000 I had finally made it to the Nez Perce Reservation, a place I had read about for years. Passing the casino at the reservation entrance, I heard a lump-lump coming from the rear tire. A flat, but no ordinary one. I extracted from the tread The Perfect Thorn: one with the ideal dimensions and hardness to puncture a bicycle tire. Looking up the road, thorn bushes turning brown in the summer sun covered the fields, and thistles blew across the highway. I later found that local bike shops knew all about them. They're called goatheads or puncturevine, an invasive species that's the bane of Northwest cyclists. After wrestling the tire back on the rim and reinflating it, I rode gingerly, weaving between thorn branches through the scorched hills. In a half hour, the tire was hissing again.

I made slow progress through the reservation and goathead country, patching tubes again and again, repeatedly pumping the tires up. Finally the thorn bushes were left behind. After the morning's battle, I rewarded myself with a king-sized homemade strawberry milk shake at a roadside diner in the early afternoon. The shake sat a little heavy on the stomach, but I was only twenty miles from my night's destination at Winchester Lake State Park. Behind the counter at the diner was a towering Nez Perce man with long black hair, as taciturn as they come.

"Where you headed?" he asked.

"I'll be camping at Winchester tonight. I hear it's a pretty spot."

"Mm. Nice and cool up there."

Something about his phrasing made me distinctly uneasy. Unknown to me and unmarked on the state highway map, I was perched at the base of the Winchester Grade, a nasty three-thousand-foot climb covering the entire route up to the park. Most people would call that a mountain. Out on the highway, the switchbacks up the grade came one after the other, and I hadn't exactly been fresh to start with. The milk shake proved to be a poor choice. A queasy stomach didn't help heavy, tired legs as I crawled up the hill. I was toasted, and quickly. It was over twenty miles to the nearest motel. A night in a roadside ditch was a very real possibility.

I came upon a long parking lot after one of the turns. At the far end of the lot was a pickup truck, and I could see there was someone in the driver's seat. I approached the truck with a bit of desperation.

"Excuse me, sir? Sir?" I tried plaintively to get his attention. Eyes appeared in the side-view mirror. The door opened and a pair of boots swung out. Shaved head. Handlebar mustache. Tats on hands and neck. Leather jacket with rivets. I flashed to my stereotype image of the Aryan Nations, one of the fringe groups with a presence in Idaho.

"Uh, I was wondering how far it is up to Winchester."

"Well, it's still quite a ways up there, hoss." He eyed me up and down. "You don't look too good. Throw that thing in the back and I'll give you a lift to the top."

I hesitated for a moment—but just a moment. I was caked in sweat with nothing left to get me up the mountain. I thanked him and put the bags and bike into the truck bed.

"Don't suppose you want one of these?" He held out a pack of Camels.

"I think I'll pass this time."

Winchester was indeed another seven miles up the steep grade. I settled into the luxury of a bench seat patched with duct tape, finally catching my breath. Pine trees started to appear on the steep hillsides.

"You been in Idaho long?" I asked.

"On and off. Was down in L.A. for a couple of years."

"What made you come back?"

"Just crazy down there. Nobody looks you in the eye. Been there a month, some yahoo breaks into my place and cleans me out. Couldn't wait to get back."

"You work up in Winchester?"

"Nah, I sell bikes down in town." I was guessing the motorized kind. "I tend a little bar, too. But I've got some land by the park. Need to figure out if I've got to do some kind of goddam forest plan. Government owns two-thirds of the state, and they gotta tell you what to do with the rest."

He pulled into the gravel by the entrance to the park. We shook hands over the stick shift.

"Not sure I would have made it up here on my own steam," I said.

"Yeah, kinda figured that. Take care and get you a good night's sleep."

The tires rolled off the gravel shoulder. With a wave out the driver's window, my rescue truck disappeared up the road. I turned into the state park, registered, and pitched my tent amid a forest of RVs. I was exhausted and dehydrated, struggling to push tent pegs into the stony ground. In the next campsite a family was working on dinner. Their truck pulled a heavily loaded trailer. I was sitting on a log getting my cook kit set up when a dark-haired woman walked up from the campsite.

"We're just getting things going next door, and we were wondering if you'd care to join us for dinner."

I took a quick look down at my mangy freeze-dried package. "That's very kind. I'd love to. It's been a long day."

The campfire was well along as the evening settled in. A thick, rich stew was bubbling on the stove. Diane, who had invited me over, was with Leo, a lean, angular guy in well-worn jeans. His brother Dan was dishing out the stew while his son explored on the outer edges of the firelight.

"You don't look like your average weekend campers," I said.

"No, we're in the middle of a move," Leo said as he took a last drag on his cigarette. "Leaving Eugene, headed up north."

"New job?"

"Kinda. We just needed some room to breathe, that's all. Oregon's got so many damn rules and regulations."

"Like what?" I asked.

Dan smiled. "Well, DWI for one."

Leo flashed him a dirty look. "Aw, you know it's not just that. The schools are a mess. There's speed traps around every corner. The whole place is crowded and falling apart. So we decided to just up and leave. Dan here's got a place up north of Coeur d'Alene. He's gonna let us stay while we build a cabin and find work."

I settled into the stew and stories of the West. After we finished dinner and cleanup, I thanked them and headed back to my tent. It occurred to me that Andrew Jackson would have found himself right at home around their campfire. Frontiersman, war hero, scourge of the Eastern elites, Old Hickory during his presidency was the counterpoint to the aristocratic Virginians and stuffy New Englanders who had run the country up to that point. Jackson would have understood this family on the move, out to build a new life on the frontier. They are the modern-day incarnation of the restless, individualistic, risk-taking part of the American spirit.

This vitality and energy are parts of the best and worst of our country. They gave Meriwether Lewis the courage to say yes when President Thomas Jefferson asked him to explore the lands west of the Mississippi. But add a touch of schizophrenia to that energy and you find yourself in the Unabomber's cabin across the border in Montana, raging against modern technological culture.

The kind truck driver and the Idaho homesteaders are notes in an American tune, but perhaps part of a tragedy as well. At some point they may well watch as their Ponderosa pines go from green to red to gray and their forests burn. Some will shake the hands of the firefighters who saved their home. Others might decry the regulations put into place to try to prevent such fires from raging so uncontrollably in the future.

Yet in the most remote valley or the widest open spaces, climate change is here, now. In Idaho, rising stream temperatures and lower flow threaten the iconic Chinook salmon runs. In the forests of the

Bitterroots, survival rates for the mountain pine beetles are projected to increase by 40 to 100 percent.[1] I would see both Chinook runs and the start of beetle kill on a later ride. There is no place to hide, even in Idaho.

There's not much of Idaho where the terrain could be described as gentle, but the forty miles across the prairie from Winchester to Grangeville ranged from blessedly downhill to level. Sunday was clear and bright and lonely, and I heard church bells in the town of Craigmont in the late morning. I snuck into services at the back of the community church, maybe for the company or perhaps, as W. C. Fields said when he was discovered reading the Bible, "looking for loopholes." I tried to slip out at the end of the service, but it's hard to be inconspicuous in a cycling outfit. As I was walking back to the bike, a meaty hand landed on my shoulder with a gravelly voice behind.

"You look like a traveler. Why don't you join us in the parish hall for a bite to eat?" Brother Ron was the evangelical pastor, relentlessly welcoming, and I was soon at a long table with the congregants and a plate full of spaghetti. I don't know if I was saved—more likely just a day pass—but it was another of the kindnesses along the road in Idaho.

I lingered with Brother Ron and his flock, and the shadows were lengthening as I approached Grangeville. I had been looking forward to Grangeville since leaving the East Coast. A friend of mine, Ed Hillenbrand, had ridden cross-country some years before and had family in town. Unfortunately, I had lost the name and phone number he had given me. I could only remember the occupation: gunsmith. As I rolled into town that Sunday night, it was pretty well closed down, and I was a thousand miles from anyone I knew. The only light in town was at a pizza parlor. I approached the teen-aged girl behind the counter.

"This is kind of a strange request, but I'm trying to find the local gunsmith."

"Oh, you must be Uncle Ed's friend," she said without hesitation. In this tiny Idaho town, I had stumbled into the shop of friends I hadn't met yet.

I found a warm welcome in Grangeville. So far I'd seen few signs of all the fire I'd been hearing about, but that ended quickly. Grangeville was the firefighting base during that very active fire season. Many of the crews I'd seen on the flight to Spokane were camped at the high school football field. Helicopters buzzed in and out of town, fighting fires as far off as the Continental Divide and as close as the hills behind town. They were carrying "Bambi Buckets"— bright orange sacks of water from the local lakes. I rode out to see one of the nearby burns. A woman was sitting in a pop-up canopy tent by the roadside handing out what-to-do pamphlets about the fire burning on the next hillside behind her. It was a little surreal, as though she'd been handing out sale flyers at the supermarket.

Riding out past the Grangeville hills the next morning, I found myself at the head of White Bird Canyon. The wind was blowing a low tune out on the canyon, and raptors were riding the thermals. Out in the distance, fifty miles away, were the snowcapped mountains of the Seven Devils. According to Nez Perce legend, they are the remains of seven giants who would devour the children of the People until Coyote trapped them in great holes. Coyote then struck a gorge at their feet, the place we know as Hell's Canyon. I started down a long, switchbacked, bug-in-the-teeth descent to the floor of White Bird Canyon, with an occasional stop to give my brake hands a rest.

A war started here, almost by accident, as many wars do. In 1877, gold was discovered in the Wallowa Valley homeland of the Nez Perce in Oregon. They were forced to take up residence on a diminished reservation in Idaho. A band of the Nez Perce refused to go to the reservation and camped at White Bird Canyon. A detachment of army soldiers and Grangeville settlers came down the canyon to round them up. Nez Perce riders approached with a white flag. The captain of the volunteers fired two shots. That proved to be a bad idea. They were the first shots in the Battle of White Bird and the Nez Perce War.

The Nez Perce were superb horsemen, the originators of the Appaloosa breed. They were very good shots as well. They circled around both flanks of the approaching line. One Nez Perce described the scene:

> It is a bad mix-up for the soldiers. They do not stand before that sweeping charge and rifle fire of the Indians. Their horses go wild, throwing the riders.[2]

First the volunteers, then the soldiers broke and fled, leaving thirty-four dead. The Nez Perce soon realized that a much larger force would be coming. They broke camp and led the army on an epic chase. Their journey would end at a lonely place in Montana called the Bear Paw, in sight of safety. The Nez Perce would reach the Bear Paw that fall of 1877. After 2000, it would take me sixteen more years to complete their trail.

From Grangeville, I turned east toward Lolo Pass, on the Idaho/Montana border. It was both Lewis and Clark's route west and the Nez Perce route east. It's a two-day climb to Lolo on US 12, along the Clearwater and Lochsa Rivers, with no towns after the first ten miles, scarcely any buildings, and certainly no cell signal. At the far end of the road near the Montana border is a sign that pretty well sums up the Lolo Pass road: WINDING ROAD NEXT 99 MILES. Near the base of the climb was a ranger sitting in her car. I could catch the first whiffs of smoke in the air as I was pulling up next to her.

"Do you know if the road's clear up ahead?" I asked.

She looked a little skeptically down at the loaded bike, then at me. "Well, there's a big team working the fire up there, but they seem to have it under control. The road's open now, but you never can tell. I've seen you guys going up before. You know that's a narrow road with lots of logging trucks, right? Though I suppose there's not much logging happening with all the burns." She paused. "But when you do camp, don't even think about lighting a fire. And keep an eye out. The drought's pushing the big animals down close to the water."

Animals in the water sounded familiar. In the papers just before I left was a photo of fire in Montana's Bitterroot Valley, where I was headed. Two elk were standing in the river with the hillside on fire behind them. It became one of *Time* magazine's Photos of the Year for 2000. I certainly remembered it.

With the ranger's less-than-ringing endorsement, I began the climb to Lolo Pass toward the Bitterroot Valley. Smoke became a continuous presence. I was nervous, not quite sure what "the road's open" meant. It wasn't like I could roll up the windows. Fire stalked the mountains ahead, ready to rise up with a change in the wind.

Before leaving Lowell, the last town on the way up, I called home. Our daughter Laura, sleeping late, had just finished breakfast. It was comforting to catch up on the high school world. In my mind I was saying, *Talk to me about anything. The Pom team. Girlfriends. College essays. The dog. I'm going to be out of touch for a couple of days, and I don't know what I'm riding into.*

As I rode out of Lowell, painted on the side of a store just outside of town was LAST CHANCE. The store appeared to have been closed for some years.

I settled into a steady, gentle climb. The sound track consisted of bicycle tires on pavement, the river, and ospreys. Along the roadside, black-and-white admiral butterflies gathered by the puddles in mating displays. Summer is short; anything living must make the most of time. Occasional suspension footbridges spanned the Lochsa, inviting the traveler into the Selway-Bitterroot Wilderness on the far side. They were wormholes to a parallel universe, from the world of the car and bike to that of the grizzly and mountain lion. I resolved to walk across one of those bridges with a backpack. Someday.

Lodgepole pines lined the river and rapids swirled among the rocks. Coming around a bend, I saw the perfect arc of a fly line in the air. A fisherman was standing in the river. I stopped by the shore and got some lunch from my pack, waiting for him to look up.

"Saw the faculty sticker on your car. Are you at the university?"

"Yep."

"What do you teach?"

"Idiots."

"Isn't the term about to start?"

"Still have a couple of days. I'll take every hour I can get up here." He paused for another cast. "You have a good ride. There's no place else like this."

I finished lunch, watching him drop his fly into the riffles. Later that afternoon I rolled into the Jerry Johnson Campground, beat. The smoke had cleared away for a bit. While I was putting up my tent, the man at the next campsite asked if I knew about the hot springs. My eyes grew wide. Over a beer back east, my friend Ed Hillenbrand had told me about roadside hot springs in Idaho, but I'd long since forgotten. After a sixty-mile climb, nothing sounded more appealing.

I padded off into the woods, towel on my shoulder. Around a bend in the trail there was a giant steaming pool filled with a dozen naked people. Perhaps it was bashfulness, or maybe a concern about polluting their water, but I waved and kept going. Farther up the trail was what appeared to be an empty little pool. A few more steps revealed a woman with her knees drawn up to her chest.

"Uh, sorry, uh, I'll, uh, just be moving on."

Finally, I was able to ease into my own personal bathtub farther up in the woods. The water was almost too hot to stand, but then aching muscles stretched out on the sandy bottom. Absolutely perfect. I remembered the ranger's comment about animals coming down to the water. I scanned the forest around me. Was there something out there looking at me like a steak sandwich? I cut the bath short in the gathering dusk.

The next day's climb brought another smoky morning, with the incline gradually increasing on the approach to Lolo. In one relatively flat stretch, the trees became massive, shaggy giants. I was in the DeVoto Grove, a forest of ancient western red cedars, some one thousand or more years old. It was the frequent haunt of Bernard DeVoto, historian, forester, and conservationist, who was renowned for the championing of public lands just like this. He admonished his readers back in 1951, "The [private] land-grabbers are on the loose again, and they can be stopped only as they were before, by an effective marshalling of public opinion."[3] It's a battle we're destined to fight again.

Foresters say that the trees in DeVoto Grove have scars on their bark from small fires, but the main reason they have survived is that they live in moist areas that repel all but the largest burns. It seemed that they might have just had such a test. Up the road from the grove was a simple yellow triangle sign propped up by sandbags on the shoulder: FOREST FIRE AHEAD. Around the next bend was World War III. The landscape was blackened out to the horizon, with occasional smoldering hot spots. Scattered sections of intact forest were in sight. The fire crews had tried to use the road as a firebreak but failed. The burn had swept across the road up the slope to the pass. The scene looked like a battlefield after the fight had been lost. But one battle was won. Through firefighting or serendipity, the great cedars of the DeVoto Grove still stood. DeVoto would have been pleased.

Another hour of hard climbing through the charred land took me to Lolo Pass, which was a forward base for the crews. Equipment littered a field: pumps, hoses, tents, a small bulldozer. Sitting around a Bambi Bucket were two firefighters relaxing for lunch. They were in hard hats and wore dirty, smoke-stained yellow slickers. One looked like Gary Cooper with ash on his face.

"Anyplace I can fill up on water here?" I asked.

Gary Cooper pointed up the road. "There's a food truck right behind that deuce-and-a-half." Big truck. Two and a half tons. I got it.

"Help yourself to lunch while you're up there."

I brought a sandwich back by the firefighters and sat down in the dry grass.

"Looks like you guys have had quite a job up here."

"Yeah, hopefully the show's over. We're just trying to put the little fires out, keep it from spotting. You know, when the embers get blown on the wind into dry stuff."

"So you think you've got this one under control?"

"Hard to say. In this heat, if the wind picks up in the wrong direction, it all blows up again. It gets up high in the trees and you get a running crown fire, there's nothing we can do."

"'Cept run like hell," said the other one.

"Yeah, if you can run fast enough. Lotsa' times you can't. Seen one crown fire jump across a river just like nothing. But it's pretty quiet today." He looked over at the bike. "You should be fine."

I descended the pass into Montana with more than a little unease. The fires were still all around, and there was no instruction manual for riding through a burning landscape. I was developing a cough from all the smoke. It seemed like each town had its own monster in the hills. They all had names, some straightforward ("Willie," because Willie Nelson had sung the night before the fire started) and some incomprehensible ("Nosebag 22").

I had originally planned to turn south and ride through the Bitterroot Valley into Montana, along the Nez Perce Trail and toward location of the elk photo. It's one of Montana's most beautiful places, with many luxury summer homes tucked up into the hills. My plans changed after I ran into a group of cyclists at the entrance to the Bitterroot. The lead cyclist, lean and dusty with a multiple-day beard, was riding a fine blue Trek 520 just like mine, rigged out with panniers. We stopped on the roadside.

"You folks on a long tour?" I asked.

"Coming across from Virginia," he said. "This last patch was a little dicey."

"That's not surprising. How did it go?"

"Well, they let us through the Bitterroot, but it was a near thing. The fires are getting down near the road. You never really see them, but the smoke is everywhere. It gets tough sucking all that in. But at least I got a souvenir."

He pulled out an I SURVIVED THE BITTERROOT FIRESTORM 2000 T-shirt.

"You know, I just might find myself another route," I said, and opted to go east across central Montana. I wouldn't complete the Nez Perce Trail for another sixteen years.

When I came back across Montana from the east on the 2011 cross-country ride, the Bitterroot Valley was on my list of places to ride through. With the heavy snowpack, the 2011 fire season had been tame. The face of the hills showed how long the forest takes to recover. The 2000 fire had taken out about a fifth of the Bitterroot forest. After eleven years, blackened hillsides with tiny trees remained. Without reforestation efforts, it could take up to thirty years for seed to find its way back into a dry forest site.[4] As I saw in Yellowstone, with just a few months of growing season each year in the northern Rockies, regrowth is measured in decades.

Fire has been a frequent companion to Montana summers over the years. As everywhere, things are changing. In the ten years from 2002 through 2012, large fires (greater than a thousand acres) in the West were six times more frequent than in the 1970s and early 1980s, with the area burned in the northern Rockies increasing by 3,000 percent. While our management of the landscape can influence wildfire, it is a warming climate that is drying out western US forests and leading to more and larger wildfires and a longer wildfire season.[5]

In many ways, the northern Rockies are the epicenter of climate-driven increases in forest fire, and there doesn't appear to be any letup in the future. One model projects a fivefold growth in northern Rockies burned area for each 1.8°F rise in global temperature, making it one of the West's most vulnerable areas to increased fire. In most of the forested western United States, wildfire area burned is best predicted by dry and warm conditions in the seasons immediately preceding the fire.[6]

That was certainly the case in the summer of 2000. Late in the afternoon I pulled into a bar in the town of Potomac, the name reminiscent of home back east. From my barstool, I could see two separate towers of smoke on the horizon. The bartender was a Blackfoot woman talking intently with two men in cowboy hats down by the cooler. She approached as I settled in.

"What's on tap?" I asked.

"Bud or Moose Drool."

"Moose Drool. Absolutely."

She brought the beer and walked back to the conversation. I caught little bits of it as she shook her head. ". . . Not good . . . doesn't look good up there . . ."

I tried to get her attention. "Excuse me. Where are you saying doesn't look good?"

She walked up to the bar and looked me in the eye.

"The way you're headed." She turned to go back. "Want another MD?"

"No, that's okay. I'm good."

This was Blackfoot River country, made famous in *A River Runs Through It*, the film based on the Norman Maclean novella. In that 2000 fire season, Montana was on edge. Any little spark, from a motorcycle exhaust to a lightning strike, could set off a new wind-blown blaze that could take out an entire town. Montana's a place where almost everyone is involved with the outdoors, and when much of that outdoors is off limits or with strict no-fires rules, people get cranky. The equivalent of an occupying army was in charge, with fire crews and National Guard units in place on a normally quiet land.

I stopped in at a roadside bar and grill called Loonie's. In the parking lot I was greeted by a ten-foot sculpture of a Tyrannosaurus with a crazed look. It was welded out of pipe, electrical conduit, and pieces of a transmission, with glass shards for teeth. Inside, above the grill, a sign: WE BUY DEAD STOCK. Just kidding. I hoped. In the bar, a man dressed in full motorcycle regalia was talking animatedly with a companion in dirty jeans. The biker had long, thinning hair and a Harley jacket, and overflowed the barstool.

"Couldn't give a job on the fire line to someone from town, but they're bringing these clowns in from the other side of the world?

They finally offer me one, and now the Forest Service wants me to take a loyalty oath. I ain't taking no goddam loyalty oath."

This was puzzling. As a former government employee, I had a hard time recalling any particular oath, but then it came to me—as a fed, we swore the same oath as the president: to preserve, protect, and defend the Constitution of the United States, words specified in the Constitution itself. Since I suspected that my intervention might not be appreciated, I figured I'd just keep my head down over in this little corner of the bar.

Not far down the road, a sign pointed to the left, to the Bob Marshall Wilderness. It's a legendary place of a million acres of peaks and lakes and waterfalls, one of the most completely preserved mountain ecosystems in the world. I might never get to hike in "The Bob," but like many people, I'm comforted to know that such a place exists.

I turned into the Boulder Valley, a veil of smoke covering the land. It was red and hazy, like the surface of Mars. My legs had nothing left by dinnertime, and I asked a rancher if I could camp next to his corral. He agreed, with a touch of reluctance and a familiar condition: no fires. Since I couldn't light my stove in the tinder-dry conditions, dinner was a grand spread of granola bars. The horses were nervous with the unexpected company, and I heard hooves along the fenceline well into the evening. That night wind blew the smoke away and the sky exploded in stars. The earth turned toward Sagittarius and the center of the galaxy, the brightest part of the Milky Way. I fell asleep listening to coyotes in the draw.

The next morning, I woke to the sound of water on the rain fly. The rancher's dog was peeing on my tent. The day could only get better. As I was washing and packing the tent, a couple of cowboys were getting ready for a rodeo. They were in chaps, and I was in bicycle shorts. They smirked at my outfit. Mamas, don't let your babies grow up to wear spandex.

I rode east into the mesa country that summer and left the forests and the fires behind. One of my last stops before leaving Montana was a little town called Reed Point. I had rolled in the day before the Great Montana Sheep Drive, North America's answer to Pamplona. The main event involves a herd of sheep running through town. There were also floats, covered wagons, a giant hay bale race, and lots of little kids in oversize cowboy hats.

The night before, all the action was at the high school gym and the preseason basketball tournament. I sat behind a family in the stands. The dad had a baseball cap with a ranch name on it. The daughter, who'd been out in the lobby with her friends for most of the first half, had no particular interest in basketball and returned just before halftime. The game was a blowout. Dad stood and hitched up his pants.

"Well, this one's about done with. I've got to be up at four tomorrow, so let's get on the road."

The daughter looked at him frantically. "I know they can come back. I just know it." Over on his other side, Mom was giving him a deadly look. He shook his head.

"Okay, okay, we can finish this one out." The daughter immediately returned to the lobby. When I left, I noticed that, outside of town, there wasn't a light to be seen to the horizon. These are independent people out on the Plains making a difficult living, and the isolation was palpable. The chances to socialize are precious.

I made it to the airport in Billings two days later, pleased to have gotten through the fires pretty much intact. The route I actually rode, as opposed to what I'd planned, consisted of zigs and zags to avoid the different blazes that had popped up all over the state that summer. I needed a week of East Coast humidity to get rid of my hacking cough when I got home, and it would take two trips through the washer to get the smell of smoke out of my clothes.

Fire has been in these mountains as long as there have been forests, and some species of trees have even evolved to disperse seeds even during fire. Lodgepole pines, for example, have heavy resin seals on their pine cone scales that break at high temperatures, leaving large quantities of seeds available after a fire. But things are different now. The science indicates that climate change is increasing the vulnerability of forests, even those that have adapted to fires, to tree mortality through insect infestations, drought, diseases, and, yes, fire, as the fires are now ranging more and more frequently. Today, western US forests are particularly susceptible to increased wildfire and insect outbreaks. Winters don't get as cold now, and insect larvae can overwinter in numbers. This is why the mountain pine beetle that I first saw in Colorado has killed over forty million acres of trees in the United States and Canada. Paradoxically, beetle-killed forests don't necessarily burn that well. A dry, live forest with needles and plenty of understory fuel is more flammable. But that didn't keep the beetle-killed forest outside of Walden, Colorado, from burning.

Climate change is the background music for the growth of fire in the West. Earlier onset of spring, reduced snowpack, and higher temperatures are the major factors leading to increased wildfire. According to the Forest Service, the fire season is now seventy-eight days longer than in 1970.[7] From 1955 to 2015, snowpack decreased by an average of 23 percent over measurement sites in the West.[8] And like almost everywhere else in the world, it's hotter. The vanishing glaciers in nearby Glacier National Park are often cited as a case study of the impacts of warming, as we'll see in the next chapter. It's all led to a mounting fire problem in the West.

All that smoke that I sucked down was a problem, too, but I was rid of my cough before long. The planet doesn't recover quite that quickly. Through photosynthesis, forests keep a huge amount of carbon dioxide out of the atmosphere. When they burn, much of that carbon is released as carbon dioxide. US forests currently take up and store the equivalent of about 16 percent of all carbon dioxide given off by fossil fuel burning in the United States each year. Climate change, combined with current societal trends in land use and forest management, is projected to reduce this rate of forest carbon uptake.[9]

Climate change is far from the only reason for the growth of fire. A policy of trying to put out all fires right away was first instituted back in 1910, after the Great Fire of that year burned an area the size of Connecticut in Washington, Idaho, and Montana. Over time, this policy led to an increase in flammable undergrowth in forests where fire is part of the natural order. This accumulation of fuel primed the system for large fires. The immense Yellowstone firestorm of 1988 underlined the problem and helped institute a change in fire suppression policy. But the increase of total area burned is better explained by change in weather and climate than by fire suppression management, according to many studies.[10]

Controlling fire has come to be a very expensive proposition. The armadas heading into the fire zones that I saw in 2000 are being repeated on a nearly annual basis. In 2015, firefighting consumed $1.2 billion, over 50 percent of the Forest Service's budget.[11] Much of the effort is devoted to defending homes, frequently second homes, of people who have built on the boundaries between forests and towns. This is what's known as the wildland-urban interface—often a place where fire can be expected in the West. It's analogous to what's happened on the coast. People continue to build homes (again, often second homes) and large structures (see Miami Beach towers) on the beach, subsidized by federal flood insurance and oblivious to sea level rise. They then ask the government to fund "beach nourishment" and seawalls to protect against the inevitable, and ask to be made whole when the inevitable happens. The role of the public sector and taxpayers in each place is to subsidize unwise behavior.

In the western forest, people can take measures to protect their homes, like installing fire-resistant roofs and maintaining thirty feet of brush-free area around structures. Most haven't made these preparations and must rely on firefighters to protect their homes. In many of the huge fires in the West, that simply isn't possible. Regardless, even if a home survives a fire, much of the reason for building there—the forest—will be gone.

In 2011, I rode into the Rockies at Poudre Canyon. In 2012, this was where the High Park fire almost took out the Mishawaka concert venue but still burned hundreds of homes. It was all the Denver news stations could talk about. It would be the most destructive fire in Colorado history, until two weeks later, when the Waldo Canyon Fire destroyed half again as many homes near Colorado Springs. They surely won't be the last ones. Large fires are about seven times more common in the United States than they were forty years ago.

"Mary Don't You Weep" gave James Baldwin the title to one of the most influential books of the 1960s. These days, I think of the line in a more literal context: No more water, but fire next time.

IDAHO–MONTANA PART II: ICE

The Ascent

In 2011, as I rolled across Idaho toward the Montana border, I thought about how this particular journey had its roots in a college summer road trip sometime in prehistory, before the Age of Disco. Four of us, including my friend Jan, piled into a couple of decrepit Volkswagens for a ride across the country. The first national park we came to was Glacier. The VWs gasped and wheezed their way up the Going-to-the-Sun Road, a narrow two-laner blasted out of the cliffs. This road tops out at Logan Pass, elevation 6,646 feet, where a giant butte looms over the visitor center. Our friends, who were rock climbers, were anxious to go up the first face they saw, so they headed for the butte while Jan and I relaxed at a picnic table by the parking lot. A couple of rangers came out with a spotting scope, normally used to show tourists mountain goats on the hillsides. Instead, they trained it on our friends. One ranger shook his head.

"Amazing how many people try that. That's just the crumbliest shale there is."

The second ranger nodded. "At least we won't have far to look for the bodies."

Our climbing friends emerged with souls still attached to bodies, but Jan and I came back to Logan Pass in 2016, forty-four years later, for different reasons. This route had not been on my 2011 TransAm ride, but I felt I had to ride it because of this place's particular importance in America's natural landscape. The name Going-to-the-Sun fits in more ways than one. Glacier National Park, known as the Crown of the Continent, is ground zero for climate change in the United States. The namesake ice is disappearing, like most glaciers around the world. Glaciers in the park have gone from roughly 150 in 1850 to 25 today. It's likely that they will all be gone by 2030 and perhaps well before. One motivation for the visit was sort of a morbid fascination: see them before they die. Moreover, the park today is a laboratory for the ways that different species are trying to adapt to the great warming.

The climb would also be a good test for Jan and me. Logan Pass is a steep, eleven-mile ascent looking out over sheer cliff faces. The pass would be a category 1 climb, the second-highest grade if it were on the Tour de France. All that winter and spring, we had the Going-to-the-Sun Road on our mental bulletin boards during training rides and gym time. But we would have a special advantage on this trip: Concetta would be driving support. The road would be a lot less lonely and the panniers a bit lighter.

First we would have to get there. The bike ride in 2016 would be eastbound, Idaho to Montana, in the predominant downwind direction. After a cross-country car ride, we started our bike trip in Moscow, home to the University of Idaho. Our old friend Debb Thorne had recently accepted a professorship at the university, just down the road from where she and Mark had taken me in on my first long bike tour in 2000. Jan and I were headed into mining country, which would provide a distant echo of what I'd seen before in the Marcellus Shale, the Pennsylvania fracking region.

We started north on two wheels from Moscow in big dry heat. After battling trucks and road construction for fifty miles, we picked up the Trail of the Coeur d'Alenes, one of the finest bicycle rail trails in the country. That was a good thing. One of the local guidebooks to the trail describes cycling issues out on Idaho's other roads: "You will find the roads have hardly any shoulders. That's not your fault, but most drivers in rural Idaho will figure there is something wrong with *you* if they have to swerve to get past."[1]

Close calls with vehicles weren't the only issue. The newest addition to my equipment was a small bottle of concentrated electrolyte, for adding to water. Keeping electrolyte balance is a big deal out on the road. Getting out of balance can lead to cramps, nausea, and dizziness. I put the little plastic bottle in my handlebar bag, right next to my eye drops. Of course, when my eyes got dry from all the heat, I reached for the wrong bottle. The first drop was enough to light up my eyeball. After a quick, frantic washout, the eye was a little red but otherwise okay. Riding song of the day: "Tracks of My Tears."

The Trail of the Coeur d'Alenes was worth the wait. We had a sweet seven-mile descent through deep evergreen forest, then another ten miles cruising along the shores of Lake Coeur d'Alene. The trail continues for another fifty-five miles of breathtaking country, through the Silver Valley, site of one of the richest mineral strikes on the planet. There's relatively little mining going on now, but it's very much part of the genesis of the trail. Periodically, HEALTH CONCERNS signs are posted trailside and at rest stops. The asphalt trail and immediately adjoining areas are safe, but the signs warn of heavy metals in the soil and in the wild plants along the way. This contamination is the result of a hundred years of hauling ore on the railroad, with toxic metals leaching out of the rail cars. We would find out that the shimmering, sun-dappled Lake Coeur d'Alene is one of the most contaminated in the country. Following a legal settlement, the rails were removed, the toxic soil covered, and the paved trail installed. We'd have to ride a little farther to see where all the metals came from.

The trail runs through Kellogg, in the middle of the Silver Valley, named for the miner whose burro led him to the silver strikes. Kellogg was the site of the Bunker Hill Mine, at one time one of the world's largest producers of silver, lead, and zinc. Shafts were sunk over a mile down into the earth. The lead for many of the US bullets in World War II came out of the ground in Kellogg and was processed at the smelter there. The company, known to locals as "Uncle Bunker," had a multimillion-dollar payroll and a reputation for generosity in the community. New gymnasiums, band uniforms, and college scholarships were part of its legacy. Families built lives based on good pay from hard, dangerous work in the mines.

Russ Wilbur, a longtime resident of Idaho and owner of the Corskie House B&B in nearby Harrison, went to school in Kellogg during the mine's heyday:

When we came into Kellogg from outside of town to go to high school, we had to take out shirts and put them over our mouth. The smoke over the gulch would burn our lungs. The kids in town, they were all used to it . . . After I graduated, I was over in Vietnam in '68 and '69, in artillery near the DMZ [Demilitarized Zone]. When I got back, I had a job with Bunker Hill almost walking through the door. If you had family that worked there, they'd take you on. It was good pay, union. I worked for a year at the zinc and cadmium plant. They say that the cadmium's worse than some of the other stuff they had there. So it was a dirty job, and I ended up working as a meat cutter instead.

Bunker Hill had other legacies besides generosity and employment. From 1890 to 1968, the company discharged toxic mine waste tailings directly into the Coeur d'Alene River. In 1973, fire destroyed the baghouse, the principal air pollution control system for Bunker Hill's smelter. The smelter continued to process ore without the baghouse for a year and a half, sending lead and sulfur dioxide directly into the air. In 1974, almost two hundred children from the local school were found to have vastly elevated lead levels in their bloodstream. Bunker Hill closed in 1981 and became one of the largest EPA Superfund sites—sites designated for hazardous waste cleanup. About one hundred million tons of contaminated sediment now cover the floodplain of the Coeur d'Alene Basin. Much of it has been capped with clean fill, but cleaning up the mines remains a long-term project.[2] One woman who lived through those days summarized it: "Plenty of poison got pumped out of that mountain. Plenty of jobs, too."[3]

The Kellogg experience reminded me of Pennsylvania and the gas drilling boom and bust. Unlike Bunker Hill, whose management lived nearby, Chesapeake Energy's generosity went back to their hometown, Oklahoma City. The Olympic rowing venue and NBA arena didn't end up in Pennsylvania. But the corporate behavior on pollution was strikingly similar. Gas drilling companies fought hard to avoid disclosure of the composition of drilling compounds they were putting into the ground in the Marcellus Shale. Bunker Hill discharged vast amounts of lead into the air when pollution equipment was down, a fact that did not come to light until years later.

But that decision might have had much to do with distant management. In 1968, five years before the increased discharges, Bunker Hill had been acquired in a hostile takeover by a Houston-based company, Gulf Resources. It must have been easier to keep the plant running when your own kids weren't going to the local elementary school or breathing in leaden air. Regardless, pressure for return on investment is relentless, and sooner or later pollution control is seen as an overhead to be reduced. Or, as Emily Krafjack from Pennsylvania said of the gas drillers next door, "For some companies, they just don't care unless they get caught."

In Kellogg and adjoining Wallace today, we saw something of a rebirth, though nothing can replace the payrolls of mining in its heyday. Kellogg has a ski area, condominium developments, and one of the country's largest Chrysler dealerships. Wallace is taking advantage of its history as a rough-and-tumble mining town with a well-preserved downtown, mine tours, and even a bordello museum. And there's that rail trail. Russ Wilbur says, "I get most of my business from people riding the trail." The Coeur d'Alenes and adjoining trails bring a lot of cyclists to Wallace. In looking for a route, I received some remarkable advice.

When I was planning the ride in wintertime coffee shops, I was trying to figure a way to get from Wallace over the Bitterroot Mountains toward Glacier National Park. From the Trail of the Coeur d'Alenes website I was referred to Jon Ruggles, a gentleman who had done quite a bit of riding in the Bitterroots. Google had directed me to a route over two passes, Dobson and Thompson, and I wondered if this would work. In his reply to my query, Jon mentioned that he'd ridden them:

> Never cycled east of the Rockies, but I know in 2013 I cycled over 200,000 vertical feet here. So we are fairly steep. I beat terminal throat cancer, but the radiation wiped out my jaw. In late summer of 2012, I had my entire jaw replaced with the small bone of my leg. So I had to learn to walk, talk, and ride all over again. I decided the best way to heal was hammering up hills, up that Dobson Pass I was telling you about. I did the pass 103 times that season.

I was awestruck. We had to meet Jon when we came to Wallace. He's rail-thin, with a shock of wavy gray hair. He slurred a little as he talked, not surprisingly. He'd been working on setting up a bike shop in town. "This young tile guy working for me says, 'I wish I had your strength.' I told him I'm sixty-two, which set him back further." Some people are just too tough to kill.

Jan and I started up the pass the next morning. Going up once was plenty for us, let alone a hundred times. We climbed in the early morning, with flashes of sunshine through the trees and rushes of cool air where a stream fell down from the mountain. That day brought the most climbing of the trip, and I was getting jelly legs by the last mile. The name says Dobson Pass, but it's Jon Ruggles Mountain.

We crossed into Montana, taking advantage of an amazing twenty-two-mile descent into the state. The next day was pushing 100°F, and we had another big climb as we headed for Hot Springs. We were taken aback at the sign near the turnoff for the town: WE ARE PROUD OF OUR SAVAGE HEAT. It turned out that this was the high school nickname, rebranded from "Savages" some years back. That wasn't the only quirky thing about the town. A well-stocked organic market is not what we expected after passing the rodeo on our way in. The Symes Hotel, a throwback to the 1930s, was built on the springs. Buses from the mines in Idaho used to bring miners up to the Symes to "take the cure" and try to soak out the toxins their bodies had accumulated. Today Hot Springs, built on the Flathead Reservation, is a mix of Native Americans, cowboys, old hippies, and artists. It wasn't fancy, just welcoming.

We took a couple of days to cycle north to Glacier, taking advantage of the waiting arms of the bike rack to catch a ride with Concetta and avoid the congested parts of the route. All along the ride, National Parks had an upswing in visitor numbers as they celebrated the hundredth birthday of their founding, and the route to Glacier was a prime example. The three of us wandered through the shops and restaurants of Kalispell and West Glacier. Glacier's a stunning place, and we hiked up one of the high mountain valleys to see the waterfalls for which the park is renowned and enjoy a local favorite, huckleberry lemonade, while sitting at the shore of sparkling Lake McDonald. Mostly, we rested up for the big day.

Taking in sunset on the motel porch, we watched Fourth of July fireworks on a darkening vista, knowing that somewhere out on that jagged, snowy horizon was tomorrow's destination.

We were on the road at first light on July 5, temperature in the forties, bound for Logan Pass. Park rules dictated the early start, as cyclists have to be off the Going-to-the-Sun climb before 11:00 A.M. to avoid blocking traffic. I'd ridden this road dozens of times in my mind. On the mapping software, it's a 6 percent grade over ten miles, a bit over thirty-one hundred feet of climbing. I'd studied the (nonexistent) shoulders on Google Street View, cranked up the Stairmaster at the gym, and climbed local D.C. and Maryland hills over and over. But the real thing was all I could handle.

I tried to push the pace on the gently ascending twenty-one-mile approach past a cold Lake McDonald. Still we arrived at the base of the big climb behind schedule. This wouldn't be the leisurely morning looking out over hundred-mile views that we had expected. Before us rose a mountain face with a diagonal slash across it: the summit climb.

Watching the time closely and keeping in mind the impending prohibition on bikes after 11:00 A.M., we'd ridden a little hard on the approach. When I began to sink my teeth into the lower reaches of the climb, the strength in my legs vanished. I was nauseous and having trouble staying with Jan. For the first time, I thought that I might not finish the ride. It was a temptation. Concetta was coming behind us in the car, so bailing out was an option. But in cycling, the road in general, and climbing in particular, is a series of exhaustions and recoveries. I backed off and picked up one of those second and then a third and fourth winds. The pace went back to steady, slow climbing. A bald eagle flew close overhead, which was inspiring, though he might have been investigating future roadkill.

We pushed up, trying to focus on an unwavering, steady line, neither to the right and the cliffs below nor to the left and the cars behind. Somehow I'd found a pace that I could sustain, with my heart no longer jumping out of my chest. Through some of the most spectacular scenery in North America, my gaze centered on the thin black front tire and the next twenty feet of road. Long out of the trees now, we were surrounded by rock castles. We passed a stretch called the Weeping Wall, where waterfalls splashed on the road. Now the last bend and the pass were in sight. The road flattened out, and the butte from forty years ago loomed over us. And a sight for sore eyes: Concetta waited for us at the top.

It was exhilarating, but as on many hikes, the danger lies in the downclimb. In the Tour de France, people stand at the top of passes handing newspapers to riders, who stuff them into their jerseys for insulation on the coming descent. That would have been a good idea for me. Unlike Jan, I sweat a lot, and despite peeling off layers of clothing on the ascent, I was thoroughly soaked by the time we reached Logan Pass. The temperature there was about 50°F with a hard wind. Lunch awaited twelve miles and two thousand feet down.

I was exhausted and chilled as I gave a push out of the Logan parking lot. Immediately my arms began to shake from the cold, as we generated our own wind flying down the mountain. The shaking made the tight line between the cars and the cliff more and more difficult to maintain. I had a feeling of losing control, trying to convince my body to just get me through this stretch. We stopped to pull over at each of the overlooks along the road, and I rubbed my arms intently against my chest. Eventually, I dried out, and the air warmed up as we dropped into the valley below. A hot bowl of soup at the restaurant would be exactly what I needed.

The steep descent transitioned to a gentle glide along Saint Mary Lake. Jan led as we turned into the restaurant parking lot. A crowd of cars was stopped along the road. *Great*, I thought. *A big line for lunch.* A driver stepped out of one of the cars and pointed to the field: a bear. Yellow-brown coat, hump on the back. Yes, that would be a grizzly all right. Jan rode off quickly, correctly surmising that all of these people were in cars and we weren't. I hung around to get a picture of the bear. Jan provided the cycling corollary to the old line "I don't have to ride faster than the bear. I just have to ride faster than you." Fortunately, the bear lumbered off away from the crowd.

That night the three of us went off to find the best dinner we could. Jan and I reminisced about that first summer cross-country trip a long time ago. For this new bike trip, the planning, the travel, the training all worked again. We lifted our glasses to, as Jan put it, putting off growing old for one more year.

The Bear Paw

The next day Jan boarded a plane, homeward bound. Concetta and I would be coming back to Glacier, but I still had a 176-mile journey to finish. Back on the ride in 2000, when I had started following the trail of the Nez Perce, fire had blocked me from the trail in the Bitterroot Valley, but I managed to ride that stretch going cross-country in 2011. The only place I hadn't reached was the Bear Paw Battlefield, in north central Montana. The route to the Bear Paw was dead-straight out on the Montana plains, US Route 2 just south of the Canadian border—the road locally known as "the Hi-Line." It's a crazy, windblown, gently rolling stretch of highway. I asked the local motel owner what the Hi-Line was like. He said, "I don't know why anyone goes. There's nothing out there. It's just empty."

Maybe that's what drew me there. It is indeed a wide-open land, an ocean of grass. Why does one go to sea? To find out what's out there.

I rode across the Blackfeet Reservation, where people were getting ready for their annual powwow. Concetta and I visited the Museum of the Plains Indian in Browning. Coming around a corner, I was stopped in my tracks by an exhibit case: a Ghost Shirt, from the great Ghost Dance revival of 1890, the prelude to Wounded Knee. Another Ghost Shirt in an exhibit case was what had sparked my interest in Stronghold Table and the Lakota almost forty years ago and fueled the South Dakota ride two years before.

Outside the front door, the gift shop cashier was taking a cigarette break.

"It's gorgeous today. How does the museum work during the winter? Do you close down?" I asked.

"We try to stay open, but sometimes we have to close because people can't get in to work."

"Guess you have to enjoy the company of people you're snowed in with."

She laughed and exhaled some smoke. "Well, it doesn't snow so hard that we get snowed in much anymore. And it melts faster. We still have long winters, but they're not as hard."

Rolling out across the prairie, I could look behind at wheat fields with the Rockies in the distance. Amber waves, purple mountains. A roadside wind sock was extended straight out, mercifully a tailwind. Transcontinental railroad tracks run right next to the road, and there were Burlington Northern Santa Fe trains running by all day. A mile-long train came up on me, and I did what any five-year-old would do when a truck passes: make the honk sign. Yep, he blew the whistle for me.

Along with wheat fields, the landscape along the Hi-Line is of giant round bales of hay lined up to a cloudless blue horizon. The Montana Plains seem like a timeless place, but like everywhere else, things are changing. Wade Sikorski's great-grandfather homesteaded in southeast Montana in 1911, and the ranch has been in the family since then. They grow wheat and hay, along with lentils, safflower, peas, canola, and corn. Since they practice no-till farming, they need to do a lot of different crops to keep the weeds under control. Wade's been working the ranch for sixty years. Like the Blackfeet, Wade brought up the cold weather first:

> The winters used to be much tougher, with snow all winter long. Now we go through snows and thaws, and we don't have the big snowdrifts down in the ravines. In the spring, the water doesn't come in a rush anymore. We have dikes and floodgates to flood the land. It's a flood irrigation system. You get one shot in the spring when the snow is melting. After that nothing.
>
> Used to be we could cover sixty acres in a foot or more of water. That was my job when I was a kid. I would walk

the dikes, surrounded by cold, muddy water. In the spring now I can barely get my shoes wet. The dikes are pretty well useless these days, and the yield on hay is about a third.

What surprised me was Wade's take on storms:

We never had any tornadoes when I was young. Then two or three years ago, we had a big one. This June we had a bigger one yet. The fairgrounds in town were full, and we were lucky it didn't go right into them. As it was, three houses were swallowed up. Seems like each year we get more severe weather, as our insurance adjustors tell us.

For farmers, the most damage is from hail. We have an old Quonset hut that's been here for over half a century. Two years ago it got dented up for the first time. We had a whole crop of corn, lentils, and spring wheat wiped out by hail a couple of years back. In town all the roofs had to be replaced. And you could figure out who made the best siding just by looking at who was replacing theirs.

Back on the road early one morning, I saw a black speck on the road ahead, a sign that I wasn't the only cyclist up here. The Hi-Line is on the Northern Tier bike route across the country, as mapped by the Adventure Cycling Association. Occasional through cyclists appeared, loaded just like me when I was on the way to Oregon. Over a half hour, I gradually caught up with the rider, a woman cyclist on a fully loaded bike. I caught up to her quickly so she wouldn't think I was some kind of two-wheeled stalker. I would have offered her something to drink, but as I neared the end of the bike part of the trip, my Gatorade was becoming a witches' brew: Fierce Grape combined with leftover Fruit Punch, with a little Glacier Cherry left in the bottom of the bottle. I suppose Bordeaux is a blend, too.

Danielle from Anchorage was the rider, a teacher eastbound from Anacortes, Washington, to Wisconsin. We were both glad to talk;

the miles flew by on that long, straight road. We shared road stories, then I asked what she saw of climate change in Alaska.

"We haven't had a good hard winter in a long time," she said. "It's been these wet, mushy winters and then a lot of fires in the summer. We have the spruce bark beetle and an awful lot of dead trees."

I'd heard of them. "Same problem in the Rockies," I answered. "No cold winters to kill off the beetles. Do people talk about climate change?"

"They do, and they're aware of it. But a lot of people in Alaska are in the energy industry. I guess they're starting to realize there's a cost to what they do."

After a couple of hours, Danielle rode off. She's younger, stronger, and would make one hundred miles that day. Since I was riding in front, I never really saw her until she left. There is indeed a certain fellowship of the road. When you meet a rider, you talk. The road got a little quieter as she passed again into shimmering asphalt.

In the distance to the north, up by the Canadian border, were the Sweet Grass Hills. In Blackfeet mythology, the hero Kutoyis sought to rid the world of evil in the early days. In the Sweet Grass Hills, Kutoyis defeated Lizard Man after an epic battle that lasted many days. The Blackfeet pay tribute to his memory by naming the hills Kutoysiks. I would find traces of other epic battles on the road ahead.

I turned off the quiet of the Hi-Line to a still quieter route, the road to the Bear Paw National Historical Park, where the Nez Perce Trail ends. On the way out of the last town, Chinook, the sign read NEXT GAS 100 MILES. In 1877, following their removal from their home in the Wallowa Valley, Oregon, after the gold strikes, some of the Nez Perce rebelled. These bands of very skilled horsemen and warriors outmaneuvered and outran the cavalry for several months and 1,170 miles. Exhausted and low on food, the Nez Perce, including their families, stopped to rest at the Bear Paw. At this point, they were far ahead of their original pursuers. They did not realize that another force, under Nelson Miles, was approaching fast from the east. This was the same General Miles who would later go up against the Lakota in 1890, in the campaign that would culminate at Wounded Knee.

The Nez Perce were just forty miles from the border and freedom, with the Canadian hills in sight. One of the warriors, Yellow Wolf, recounted what happened that day:

> From the south came a noise—rumbling like stampeding buffaloes. Hundreds of soldiers charging . . . two wide, circling wings. They were surrounding our camp.

The cavalry had found their position and attacked. In the initial assault, the army succeeded in scattering the Nez Perce herd of horses. The band's mobility was immediately lost. Two waves of charges were repulsed in brutal fights. But there were fewer than a hundred warriors protecting five hundred women, children, and elderly folks against four hundred troops. The army brought up artillery and lay siege to the encampment for five days. One of the women later described the scene: "As cannon scattered shot from bursting shells, people held buffalo hides over themselves."

Some of the Nez Perce slipped through the lines and made it to Canada, but the majority of the survivors, under Chief Joseph, surrendered. An army officer reported that Joseph said at this place:

> My people, some of them have run away to the hills and have no blankets, no food; no one knows where they are, perhaps freezing to death. I want time to look for my children and see how many I can find. Maybe I shall find them among the dead. Hear me my chiefs, I am tired; my heart is sick and sad. From where the sun now stands, I will fight no more forever.

Concetta met me at the Bear Paw. She and I were by ourselves in what might be the loneliest place in the country. A trail leads through the rolling, grassy hills. Small metal markers denote the sites where the chiefs fell. It was reminiscent of the Wall, the

Vietnam Veterans Memorial in Washington, D.C. There people have left everything from a six-pack to a Medal of Honor in memory of those who fell. At the Bear Paw, next to the markers for the chiefs, are artifacts—stones, feathers, coins, a flower vase, antlers, amulets—presumably left by the Nez Perce in the same way. At the spot where Chief Looking Glass was killed were three pairs of glasses. As in Washington, we walked on sacred ground.

The Glaciers

We packed the bike in the car, ending the two-wheel part of the 2016 trip, and turned back west for Glacier. I wanted another look at the park, this time to talk with the people who knew it best: the rangers. The first stop was at Many Glacier Hotel, a giant Swiss chalet–style lodge sitting on the shore of Swiftcurrent Lake with a stunning view of the mountains. Over a hundred years old, it was built by the Great Northern Railroad as a tourist destination. Though still packed with tourists in the summer, the lodge could fit well into a Stephen King novel when it shuts down for the winter.

In the early days, Great Northern also wanted photos of the glaciers to advertise the "natural air-conditioning" for overheated visitors from the East. Those photos would come in handy for tracking what was to come. Many long-term environmental changes are hard to document because of the lack of baseline information, i.e. the original condition before the change occurred. Because of the early photographs of the glaciers, we have that baseline. Since 1997, the U.S. Geological Survey (USGS) has run the Repeat Photography Project, taking modern photos exactly where the early images were made. These comparisons—the dramatic record of glacial retreat—line a hallway of the hotel. In the first photograph, from 1926, a river of ice curves down the mountain with tourists in the foreground. By 2008, small trees have grown where most of the glacier had been. Only a small piece remains in the higher elevation.

Snowfields are also prominent in the park. How are they different from glaciers? Basically, by movement: if ice becomes deep enough, it begins to flow on its own, becoming a river of ice. Using the repeat photographs and more sophisticated instruments, USGS has a very good handle on the shrinking glaciers. One of the most prominent, Grinnell Glacier, has been losing roughly 2.5 acres annually over the last forty years.[4] Glaciers in the park have been retreating since about 1850. That year marks the approximate end of the Little Ice Age, a five-hundred-year cooling period felt primarily in Europe and North America. But because of man-made warming, the retreat that normally happens over thousands of years is happening in less than a century—overnight, in geological terms.

I waited in the grand lobby of the Many Glacier for a presentation by ranger Bob Schuster entitled "Where Have All the Glaciers Gone?" Bob should know; later that week, the other rangers were giving him a party for his fiftieth summer in the park. Outgoing and good-natured, he was a science teacher when he wasn't a ranger.

"I came to the park in 1967, but I really saw the glaciers receding starting in the eighties." He pulled out a pair of comparison pictures of Grinnell Glacier, probably the most photographed in the park, which you can see on the last page of the image insert. The repeat photograph shows not only the dramatic retreat of the glacier but the consistent advance of vegetation up the mountainsides as well. Bob went on:

> Only the north- or east-facing glaciers are left. Also, we used to get these big blows, called east fronts, coming down from Canada during the summer. It would drop the temperature twenty to thirty degrees, sock us in for a week. Haven't seen one of those in some time.
>
> I've been giving this talk for a while. Not as many people are arguing about climate change anymore. But it's harder for them to change the way they live.

Bob's glaciers aren't the only ones retreating. During my time in Switzerland at the climate office, I got to know the Swiss group in Zurich that keeps track of glaciers globally—the World Glacier Monitoring Service. They work with scientists from central Asia to the Andes, Africa to Iceland. In their most recent report, they note that glaciers around the world continue to melt at rapid rates, roughly double the ice loss rates of the 1990s. And since current glaciers are out of balance with the present climate, it's likely that glaciers would continue to shrink even without future warming.[5] Melting is a slow process, and even if global temperatures stayed the same, it would take some years for the ice to "catch up." In the glacial world, things are happening fast.

The retreat of glaciers has impacts far beyond the places where they are found. In central Asia, roughly half a billion people are dependent on meltwater from the Tibetan Plateau glaciers, which are shrinking like almost everywhere else on the planet.[6] The Ganges River in India is one of those glacier-fed rivers. Sometimes the secondary effects of glacial retreat can be quite significant as well. Europe in the summer of 2003, two years before we moved there, experienced a strong heat wave and drought. Among the other effects, navigation was restricted because of low flow in the Rhine River, one of the continent's major commercial arteries. Much of the flow that was present that summer was coming from accelerated glacial melt. As the glaciers of the Alps recede, that melt will be less and less available to make up the flow. A similar drought in the future could have much bigger effects on ship traffic in central Europe.

But in Glacier Park itself, what is happening to the animals as the park warms and the glaciers disappear? There's particularly good information on the white-tailed ptarmigan, a small grouse that lives in alpine areas of Glacier, based on the long-term research of David Benson. David is a professor of biology at Marian University in Indiana during the academic year. In the summer he puts on his ranger hat, leads bird walks, and continues his research on the ptarmigan. He's lean, quiet, and thoughtful, obviously at home in

Glacier's high country. His family comes with him to the park, to a place with no cell, cable, or Wi-Fi, but with a stunning natural theater. David says, "Without Wi-Fi and the tyranny of social media, I get my daughters back for the summer."

David's spent twenty years following a ptarmigan population in the park's Logan Pass. They choose habitat closely associated with snow and water, even in the summer. In the face of changing climate, ptarmigan face the choice of all animals: as David puts it, "Move, adapt, or die." In the two decades of his study, as the snow cover receded, the ptarmigan moved about 1,150 feet up the mountain. They've also changed their habitat by moving away from snow and water. Despite these modifications, populations are roughly half what they were in the 1990s.[7] In other words, the ptarmigan have been moving, adapting, and dying.

Another species challenged by climate change is the snowshoe hare, which changes its fur from brown to white over the course of the year for camouflage. Their fur change is triggered by the amount of daylight, not temperature. If snow comes later or melts earlier, their fur stays white too long, leaving them much more vulnerable to predators. As of now, the hares are experiencing on average about a week of mismatch.[8] That's likely to grow with warming. How much room does a species have to change its behavior? Not all animals can change in response to the climate. For the snowshoe hare, there might be enough genetic variability for the population to evolve the timing of molting.

At David's invitation, I had the chance to speak to other Glacier rangers and their families before I left. The attendance was quite good, but then again, I didn't have to compete with cable or internet. The rangers are quite a varied group, but they're all dedicated to educating and protecting the public. There was some excitement that evening about a report of a nearby mountain lion, and one ranger was quickly on the phone gathering information to confirm the sighting.

The rangers are especially protective of this special place and what lives here. Questions and stories went on into the evening. A young woman ranger recounted a trail encounter earlier that year:

I was hiking on my day off when I ran into some people pointing at a bear about ten feet away. When I took a second look I realized that one of the group was pointing a gun at the bear. I immediately said, "Whoa, you've got a gun! I have bear spray, you're going to be okay!" The look he gave me made me instantly remember that I was out of uniform. I was just some girl yelling at a man pointing a loaded gun. He said, "That bear growled at my son!" I just replied, "Well move, don't just stand there. The bear doesn't know you have a gun." They all backed away.

This situation did nothing to change the bear's behavior. This same bear with two cubs had been seen on the trail multiple times the week before until one day somebody sprayed her with bear spray. After being sprayed, we didn't see her on the trail again.

The bear was able to learn to stay away from people, and thus stay safe from another loaded gun, but the rangers can't protect everything. Bob Schuster, who's seen it all over fifty years, acknowledges that we can't reverse the glacier loss. There are many things that reducing greenhouses gases can do over time, like reducing heat waves, slowing forest loss, and beginning to reverse the loss of coastal land. But we can't put the brakes on fast enough for the glaciers to rebuild. As Concetta and I left Glacier the next day, we stopped at a roadside pullout Bob had recommended. As if orchestrated, the early morning fog and clouds lifted, the sun shone, and we had a last look at the main range that overlooks the Many Glacier Hotel. Grinnell Glacier, once one of the most prominent in the park, was a strip of ice huddled under a ridge. We likely won't see it again. We were looking out on a vanishing world, like the Ghost Dancers on Stronghold Table.

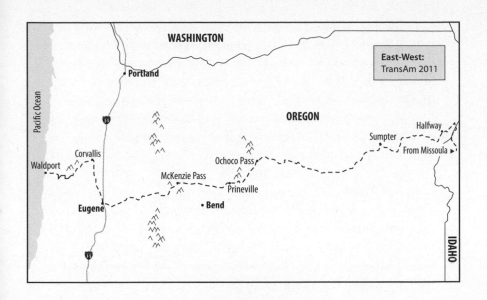

TO OREGON AND THE SEA

The 2016 ride through Glacier and the 2000 ride through the fires were bookends to my TransAmerica ride of 2011. That year, after riding across Montana and Idaho, my final destination was Oregon—and the sea. I had left Concetta and Andrew at West Yellowstone, just over the Montana border, and I had nearly six hundred miles to go before I crossed into Oregon.

The road out into Montana from Yellowstone brought a simple gnawing loneliness. Watching my family disappear into the distance, I started wondering why I was doing this. The notion of that daily adventure, that unexpected thing that would happen in the course of a day, was getting a little threadbare after two months on the road. Still, I had just retired and wanted to prove to myself that I could do this. Besides, I'd backed myself into a corner: I didn't want to give up right in front of my wife and son. Now that they had left, and I was all alone, there really wasn't anyplace to go but west, on two wheels. The odometer rolled over 3,000 miles that day. And I still had 1,200 more to go.

To get away from the empty feelings, I immersed myself in the logistics of cycling across Montana. Fortunately, logistics issues emerged quickly. Not far out of West Yellowstone, I had my first (and luckily only) flat of the cross-country ride, courtesy of an industrial-grade staple that would probably have punctured a Humvee tire. As Steinbeck wrote of a similar situation, "There was nothing to be done but burst into tears and wait for death." Alternatively, I settled into a cloud of therapeutic roadside swearing. Flats are something every cyclist is prepared for, and I'd certainly had practice with goathead thorns back in 2000. I carried spare tubes, a pump, and a patch kit. But riding's still a lot more fun than sitting in the grass, swatting mosquitoes and messing with a tire.

Later that day I was approaching Red Canyon, where an earthquake had created a lake fifty years before. A knee-buckling wind funneled down the canyon straight into my face. Even bent down over the drop handlebars, it was hard to stay upright. I limped into a Forest Service visitor center looking for some kind of shelter. They pointed me to cabins only a mile and a half away. Just as I was approaching the cabins, something amazing happened. The road down the canyon turned, and so did the wind. Suddenly the wind was behind me, sometimes strong enough to blow me up and over hills. It was the biggest tailwind I've ever ridden in. Reenergized and having fun, I flew over the remaining forty miles in a little over two hours.

Some of the most spectacular Montana country is the Big Hole Valley, a land of cattle ranches and haystacks ringed by snowcapped mountains. I stopped at Jackson Hot Springs, a perfect place for tired legs, particularly lured by their steak dinner special. I was dining under the mounted bear trophy and an antler chandelier when I made the mistake of asking where the steak came from.

"Off the Sysco truck," the waitress replied sheepishly.

Seriously? In some of the most stunning cattle country in the world, the steak is shipped in from an indeterminate Somewhere? But it's a globalized food system. In my town back in Maryland, next to the home of the magnificent Chesapeake Bay blue crab, the local supermarket only sells crabmeat from . . . Thailand. Both cases are driven by economy, of course. In Maryland, it's cheaper to pay Thai crab pickers than to pay locals. In the Big Hole, shipping to a central meatpacking facility makes more economic sense than building one in a remote town. All that might change if the true climate costs of all that energy-intensive shipping were part of the bill.

Riding west in 2011, I descended the same "Winding Road Next 99 Miles" that I had ridden up in the smoky summer of 2000. Much of the burn damage from that fire year was still apparent, with young undergrowth starting to cover the hills. Still, US 12 down from Lolo Pass from Montana into Idaho remains one of the most beautiful roads in the country, following the wild Lochsa River.

On the way down that magic winding road, I stopped by a ranger station, one of the few structures of any kind along the river. One of the volunteers had brought in chocolate chip cookies. Munching on a cookie, I buttonholed the ranger, an older man with a face that spoke of a life out-of-doors.

"I saw quite a bit of brown forest on the eastern side of the Divide. Any beetle outbreaks like that over here in Idaho?" I asked.

"Not yet," he said. "We all know about the beetle kills in Montana. There's plenty of dead trees out east in Dillon, where I live. No one would be surprised if they came over the Divide to Idaho. It takes twenty below winters to kill the beetle larvae. Last winter Moscow [Idaho] didn't even get below zero. Think that's climate change?"

"Yes, sir, it is," I said. In 2011, the sense was that for Idaho, dying forests were a matter of when, not if. When Concetta and I would come back across the Lolo Pass road in 2016, we stopped on the Idaho side at the Lochsa Lodge, an immense log cabin restaurant tucked into the woods by the river. Having lunch out on the porch, listening to the sound of the river, I noticed the telltale patches of gray on the opposite hillside. Just five years later, the beetles had arrived.

Back on the bike in 2011, I pushed off again downhill on US 12. Some days the legs scream, but some days they sing. I got into a rhythm swinging through turns down the Lochsa. Out on the river, I glimpsed a kayaker dancing through the whitewater, hanging for a split second on a standing wave, then slaloming through the rapids. I think he saw me, too. We had a little race. When I stopped for lunch, he was off in the distance upriver.

I visited Grangeville again on this trip, staying with my friend's sister Nancy and her husband, Ray. Ray's retired from the lumber industry. They took me for a ride through the forest, up in the hills above town. Ray was on a first-name basis with trees—Doug fir, Pon pine—and we stopped to pick newly ripened huckleberries. He passed on the local feeling about the new automated lumber mill in Grangeville, following the quote by management consultant Warren Bennis:

"The mill has two employees: a man and a dog. The man's job is to feed the dog. The dog's job is to keep the man from touching anything."

Western Idaho in summer is a place of light, with sun streaming down dry canyon walls into raging torrents below. I passed a line of cars parked along the Salmon River. Fishermen lined the riverbank every few feet. I stopped to watch some serious anglers pulling salmon out of the rapids, one by one. As the high water was subsiding, the Chinook were making their run upstream. Those coming from the hatchery outside Riggins were returning to that stream, and the fishermen were returning also. I've never fished much, having the confidence to believe that I'm smarter than a fish and the vanity to avoid being proven otherwise.

My last days in Idaho would bring out an additional reminder of the state's vaunted individualism. Many states have Adopt a Highway signs. Only Idaho has, along the road, ADOPT A HIGHWAY: YAHWEH'S 666 WARNING ASSEMBLY. I couldn't catch a break. After thousands of miles with tornadoes, 40°F rain, and 105°F heat, now I had to get ready for Armageddon? At the very least, I wouldn't litter.

I made the turn toward the Snake River and Oregon. The last state was now in reach. Not far down the road was a café and store, the Gateway to Hells Canyon. Standing in front was a man on the road crew with a stop sign: Charon himself, guarding the passage to Oregon.

There was a ways to go. I started on the hot, dry climb up to Brownlee Summit, not so different from a half dozen others out of Idaho's deep valleys, but this one had a distinction. As I hammered to the top of the climb, my first look at the last state came in view: Oregon's snowcapped Wallowa Mountains were on the horizon. But the journey's end was nowhere near. Oregon's a lumpy place, with no fewer than nine passes yet to climb and 560 miles to the ocean. It wouldn't give up the miles easily.

I took a deep breath at Brownlee and gave the bike a little push to start the descent into Hells Canyon. It was the steepest drop of the trip, and I was feathering the brakes as the speed ticked up over 40 mph. The dry sagebrush hills were a brown blur as I focused every bit of attention on the next hairpin. It felt like I should be wearing a wingsuit. It would be a bad place to make a mistake. I discovered the cycling corollary to Murphy's Law: your nose always itches during the screaming descents.

Down on the canyon floor was a baked, packed-dirt campsite next to dozens of RVs by the calm Snake River. The next morning I was rolling along the river, flanked by huge bluffs. Not far down the road was a nondescript bridge. On the other side of the river was a simple green sign silhouetted against the layered brown hillside: WELCOME TO OREGON. I stopped to take a picture, remembering a conversation back East, repeated many times, when people would see the bike with all the bags on it:

"Whereabouts are you headed?"

"Oregon."

"You're going where?"

I had finally made it to where.

After almost thirty-seven hundred miles, I had been thinking a lot about the smell of the ocean. As Steinbeck approached the West Coast in *Travels with Charley*, he was miles away when he first smelled the salt air. From the other direction, sailors smell land long before they see it. I know this from my time at sea. Land smells rich and fragrant and green coming from the barrenness of the ocean. According to Steinbeck, something similar happens on approaching the ocean from land. On cresting the last Cascade pass in Oregon, would I have my first sense of his "rocks and kelp and the excitement of churning sea water"?

A few days before, in the guestbook on my blog, an invitation appeared to stay overnight at an Oregon town named Halfway. As in Indiana, it seems there are people who read online of cross-country cyclists riding through their towns and volunteer to take them in. I thought for a moment about accepting a random offer from the internet, but not for too long. Media conditions us to assume that there's a Charles Manson lurking behind every bush, but there are simply a lot of kind people out there who'll help you on your way.

I made my way through Halfway. After a long ride on the Cornucopia Highway, the road to an abandoned mining town, strange faces stared at me from over a fence: llamas, chewing sideways like a camel. I knocked at the door of a ranch house with stone pillars, framed by the Wallowas and surrounded by spectacular gardens.

A white-haired lady in a Pine Eagle Basketball shirt appeared at the door. "Oh, you're the biker? Come on in." She motioned toward the fields. "We run a home for wayward llamas. Hope they didn't bother you. I swear they're the most curious animals in creation. They're always craning their necks at me when I'm out in the garden."

Later over coffee, Katy and her husband, Whitey, told me they are retired teachers from Alaska. They own a little piece of paradise.

Katy is a restless gardener and Whitey a restless builder, and their home blooms and grows. Great baskets of flowers hang off the front porch. Out in back Whitey had built a climbing wall for the grandchildren on the barn. They took me for a tour of Halfway that night.

"It's half redneck and half hippie," Whitey said, "but they all seem to get along."

The smell of Katy's pancakes woke me the next morning. I lingered over strawberries and coffee and stories of Cornucopia, the ghost town just up the road, once one of the largest mining operations in the country, the gold now long played out. But before too long I needed to get back into the dry sagebrush country. I was far from the first to pass this way. Wagon ruts from the 1840s are still visible along the Oregon Trail here.

The next day, thunderheads boiling up over the mountains ahead convinced me to stop early in the town of Sumpter. It's an old gold rush boomtown, taken to the extreme. In the river next to town, the miners had assembled a ship in a tiny pond. The ship, known as the Sumpter Dredge, would chew up the riverbed in front, pick out the gold, and deposit the tailings in back. It mowed back and forth in the valley for twenty years, recovering roughly a cubic yard of gold before shutting down in 1954. The lawnmower-like swaths are still clearly visible from space, as are the huge tailings piles from shore.

I don't understand gold. It's just shiny yellow stuff. Basically, it was the reason for the Nez Perce War in the 1870s. After gold was discovered on the Nez Perce reservation in the Wallowa Valley, a new treaty was needed to force them out of the Wallowas into someplace more desolate. Now, after all the gold is gone, there is a movement to purchase back pieces of the Wallowa as the Nez Perce homeland. So much damage done chasing after rocks. But it's not a new sentiment. Virgil said, "Curst greed of gold, what crimes thy tyrant power has caused?"

Riding days weren't always solitary. On a steep climb I was caught by a young French Canadian named Maxim: wiry, red-bearded, cheerful, pure strength and energy in a jet-black shirt. He had ridden across from Quebec. His English was shaky, so we stumbled along just a little better in French. His equipment had seen better days. All of his possessions were tucked into garbage bags and bungee-corded to the back of the bike. He was kind enough to let me draft behind him the next day. As with any proper knight-errant, his destination involved a lady. His Dulcinea lived with her two kids in Redmond, Washington. The next day, on the long, steep climb up to Ochoco Pass, he apologized and began to pull away from the old guy.

He turned and smiled over his shoulder. "See you in heaven above . . . or with devil . . . in earth."

The weight of the miles caught up with me soon after Maxim left. There was scarcely a car on the road. I was suddenly very alone and struggling to reach the pass. Once again I pulled out my mental playlist to try to get into a climbing rhythm, with legs and chain and gears and wheels all part of one machine. But "Beast of Burden" wasn't doing it for me that day. I was slugging out the ascent in one- and two-mile chunks, my knees starting to ache.

Sagebrush turned to deep pine forest. The altitude and the weather changed quickly, and driving rain swept in as I approached the summit. I pulled over and threw on raingear as fast as I could. Sweat soaked the inside of the jacket, and rain did the job on the outside. The wet sucked heat out of my body. I began to shake uncontrollably in the wind of the descent.

I was exhausted and on my own. I needed shelter, a building, something. A Forest Service outhouse came into view, and I went inside to take out every last piece of warm clothing and put it on. It wasn't enough. It wouldn't be the first or last time I'd been on the edge of hypothermia, but I was particularly vulnerable on the road down from Ochoco. I was up in the high evergreen woods on a nearly deserted road, disoriented and without a lot of options.

The storm showed no signs of stopping as I left the dry outhouse, still shivering. Pulling out of the parking lot, I just wanted to move, to spin my legs, to do anything to generate heat. I had to center my attention on the road, on that patch of asphalt ahead of the water spinning off my tire. It would be difficult to recover from a skid on the winding, rain-slicked descent. Tearing down through the rain, I could feel my fingers starting to stiffen. Eventually, I rode out of the storm into the dry plains outside of Prineville. The afternoon ended with almost every item of clothing I had carried across the continent in a soggy, wet pile next to a motel bed.

The next day's riding was a bit gentler, across valleys and grasslands. Stopping for lunch at an isolated bar, I noticed another bicycle in the parking lot, loaded with bags for touring. Inside was another guy in bike shorts waiting for a table. We circled each other warily like gunslingers before deciding to have lunch together. Kyle was a twenty-something, sporting several days of road-beard, rail-thin, with an angled face. He was on a Fort Collins to Portland ride. But he'd done a bit more, namely Singapore to Cairo on a bike, including northern India, "the Stans," and the Karakorum Highway to China. He called it "the KKH." I'm always impressed by name-droppers. He found the Pakistanis to be quite friendly, and security conscious, too. At his "campground" courtyard in Islamabad, the host kept a floor-mounted machine gun pointed at the door all night. Luckily for me, Whitey's llamas were more easily diverted with an apple.

I rode with Kyle for an hour or so before he made his way off into the distance. A day later I had to smile when I got a text from him that he was riding with Maxim. There is a certain fraternity out here: Kyle and Maxim, Katfish Katie from the Missouri campground, Jake and Double D from Kansas, Danielle from Montana. Kerouac's grandchildren are out on the road to this day.

The great volcanic cones of the Cascades were coming into view. The Cascades separate the wet coastal Northwest from the dry East, scraping water out of the moist Pacific air and turning it into giant snowfields. In the summer, the snowmelt provides water for much of the agriculture and municipal water supplies on both sides of the mountains. The snowfields on the horizon are reservoirs in the sky for the people of the flatlands. But less so these days.

The warming climate has had a particularly strong effect on these reservoirs in the sky. The higher temperatures mean that more precipitation falls as rain rather than snow, and rain falling on snow is really effective at melting it. Spring snowpack in the Cascades has declined by about a quarter since 1930, and no one expects that trend to be reversed. Summer flows are dramatically reduced in snow-fed rivers, with peak runoff edging toward late winter rather than spring.

Battles over water, always a feature of the dry West, have become more intense in what Easterners always envision as the wet Pacific Northwest. Irrigated agriculture requires more water, not less, in the hotter summers. But summer flow in the rivers is also needed for hydropower, the source of two thirds of the electricity in the region. Keeping enough water in the rivers is also vital for the iconic salmon runs of the Northwest. Salmon have another climate problem. Sockeye salmon in the Columbia migrate upstream ten days earlier in the 2000s than in the 1940s, corresponding with a 5°F increase in water temperatures.[1] The competition for water between cities, farms, fish, and dams will only become more intense. And with drier conditions, longer, more active fire seasons have arrived, here as well as in the Rockies. In the same way as the rest of the country, climate change isn't just an issue for the next generation. We are dealing with it now.

The road up to the Cascades summit at McKenzie Pass presented dramatic changes on the approach to the land of volcanoes. Advancing toward the summit, the road broke out of the Ponderosa pines into a landscape of black basalt, left from eruptions only fifteen hundred years ago. Wildflowers struggled in small patches of soil between rock and snow. At the pass, the Cascades opened up under a deep azure sky. Snowcapped Mounts Jefferson, Washington, and Hood were in sight to the north, as were the Three Sisters to the south.

I strained to catch that first whiff of the ocean. Perhaps I lacked Steinbeck's literary nostrils. Perhaps it was just wishful thinking. I was still 150 miles from the sea, where I'd spent much of my career. The ocean is seeing its own effects of climate change, in a very different way from the mountains. As described earlier, the oceans are becoming more acidic as more carbon dioxide is dissolved. This causes problems for animals that grow shells, in the same way that an egg placed in soda will have its shell dissolved overnight. The effect is particularly apparent on the Oregon coast. Shellfish farmers there find that young oysters grow poorly when more acidic water is coming in from offshore, and they have changed their production methods to respond to the increased acidification.[2] Since so many marine animals depend on growing shells, this is a huge issue for the oceans globally.

Another scent, quite different from that of the ocean, filled the air: evergreens. The descent from the bare black rockpiles of McKenzie Pass passed into the dark, wet forest of the coastal Northwest. It was populated by giants, huge Douglas firs with their tops towering out of sight. The road down was exquisite: hairpin turns, miles and miles of them. No need to worry about that pickup truck behind, because on this road a bike can actually go faster than a car. I banked into turns so steep I could almost reach out and touch the road. The sunlight flashed like a strobe through the trees as I spun through the shadows of the ancient forest.

The morning brought a run for the great valley, the Willamette. I was headed for Corvallis, where my college roommate Michael and his wife, Paula, lived. They would be my first familiar faces since Idaho. On the road at first light, I was anxious to see them and resolved to cram two days of riding into one. It would be a hundred-mile shot, flying out of the Cascades.

At midday, I rode below a nondescript overpass: the I-5. I was officially on the West Coast. Without stepping off a jetway, thin spinning wheels powered by legs had gotten me to the destination of the Oregon Trail pioneers.

Late Saturday afternoon, long shadows fell across the Corvallis fountain, and little kids danced in the water. The bike, with four bags and a tent, was a conversation starter. I was holding court among the moms. Funny you should ask, why yes, I did just ride in from Delaware. Michael, a man of few words, appeared on his bike, shook hands, and said, "Follow me."

Forty years ago, he was tall, bolt upright, with blue eyes and straw hair, looking every bit the downhill ski racer that he was. He hadn't changed much. Back then, women were attracted to him like moths to a flame. I would hide in the shadows, hoping to bask in his glow. At the Corvallis fountain, I was finally doing okay on my own, however briefly. Crestfallen, I looked out upon my audience, shrugged, and rode away.

The year before, Michael's paraglider had corkscrewed into a boulder field, leaving him with a shattered spine. Rapid, competent first aid from Paula and some sophisticated orthopedics meant that he would be able to walk again, if a little more upright than before. Even better: that weekend in Corvallis would be his first time on a bike since the accident. We made our way up to the house, where Paula had an amazing dinner of steamer clams and Oregon Pinot waiting for us.

One day remained: up into the mist and over the Coast Range. The climb was not hard by Oregon standards, but it would be Michael's big test. With three mountain ranges on my legs, I waltzed up the pass with Michael gasping behind. At the top of the pass, it was another story. The downhill racer emerged, and I couldn't keep up with him. As he disappeared down the hill, I yelled, "If you crash, Paula's gonna be really pissed . . ."

The land flattened out, and the river we were following went from rapids to a wide, flat bay. Then it was so: you can always smell the sea before it comes into view. This time I surged ahead past Michael. Around a curve and over a seawall: surf. I stopped to look. In my pocket I found my talisman: a Lewis and Clark bicentennial nickel from 2005. On the back was Clark's journal entry: "Ocean in view. O! The joy!" Or, as Dean Moriarty yelled on seeing the Pacific in *On the Road*, "We can't go any further 'cause there ain't no more land!"

I was both elated and bone weary. I was as strong as I'd ever been, yet the worse for wear, with scars from a Kansas railroad bed still apparent on the outside and a persistent sore knee from Wyoming mountains on the inside. The rhythm of the road ended that day. From now on I would not scan the weather each and every morning, gaming the wind shifts and sprinting to shelter before the approaching storms. I wouldn't need to check the next town on the phone for a campground or motel, hoping there was room. I was ready for this three-month stint of homelessness to be over.

Despite the weariness, it was a thing done, a dream realized. In my mind I had a high-definition video of passes and plains, faces and forests, that would unroll over and over as I would drift off to sleep in the coming years.

The Pacific was just over the dunes, limitless, the edge of the water planet. From the distance came an occasional thump of breakers. On a bright, clear day, haze from the spray hovered over the nearly empty beach. I would not be mistaken for a surfer. I took off my shoes and socks to walk the bike out to the water with Mike and Paula. My feet were bright white against the brown of my legs. The water, as any visitor to the Northwest will attest, was stunningly and deliciously cold. I reached into my handlebar bag to find the little shell that Concetta had put there in Delaware, dropped it, then watched it roll around in the surf.

The three-month ride in 2011 came to an end on that beach in Waldport, Oregon. After a visit to a seaside bar inventorying the full range of Rogue Farms ales, Mike and Paula whisked me away to Paula's home in Portland, where they were finishing preparations for their long-delayed wedding reception. My son Tom flew up from Los Angeles for the celebrations. He arranged flowers in the basement while Mike and I went out shopping for beer. The party was pure Portlandia and pure joy. Twenty-four hours later I got on an eastbound plane back to Concetta. The lonely days were over.

On the flight back, I began the process of taking inventory of what I'd seen and what had happened. I looked out on the ranges I'd climbed, on the Cascades and the Rockies and the Alleghenies, as well as all the other sneaky hills in places like Indiana and Ohio. Before the ride, I thought that I'd get used to all that climbing, or perhaps even that I'd come to love hills. Not so much. The professional cyclists say, "It doesn't get easier, you just get faster." I never even got faster, but after a while I was able to sustain climbing for fairly long periods. For the serious climbs, it served well to break them up into bite-sized pieces, as is true for mortgages or banana splits.

The ride reshaped my body, but I only lost about ten pounds. Walking up a hill with friends after the ride, I noticed that I didn't get winded. Overall, the effect was kind of like a sauna for the inside: I felt cleaned out. But exercise still left joints and muscles creaking afterwards. And no matter how much I rode, I never developed the legs of a twenty-year-old.

The year 2011, when I went across, seemed to be about the time that television screens started appearing in virtually every restaurant. As a nation, we seem to want to stay indoors, to surround ourselves with video screens, and to need bigger and bigger engines to interact with the outdoors when we do go out. All those Vs have proliferated: SUVs, RVs, ATVs, snowmobiles. It's possible to hear the whispering sound that a wheat field makes in the wind or the crowlike warning that an antelope gives, but not when engines are running. There is much to be gained from walking and riding and listening. The land will show—and tell—you a lot.

CLIMATE AND THE FUTURE

My object in living is to unite
My avocation and my vocation
As my two eyes make one in sight.
Only where love and need are one,
And the work is play for mortal stakes,
Is the deed ever really done
For Heaven and the future's sakes.
　　　　　　—Robert Frost, "Two Tramps in Mud Time"

A s you've probably gathered by now, I like to ride my bike. Unlike most children, I never learned to ride in grade school. That remained the case until college, when several ambitious young ladies decided it was a skill I needed to have and undertook the task to teach me. Once I mastered two wheels, the bike was my go-to mode of transportation. I even brought it along when I worked on the NOAA ships. I began commuting in earnest in the early '90s, riding the thirteen miles into work at NOAA. As I approached retirement, the notion of combining what I did in the mornings and evenings with what I'd learned in my day job was entrancing. To my mind, then and now, there was no issue more important than climate. It seemed quite natural to follow Frost's advice.

I make no claims to working for Heaven's sake, though, or to being an especially great scientist for that matter. What I will assert is that I come by my views on climate honestly. During my career I've had a front-row seat as the national and international science communities have come together on man-made climate change. I had the chance to witness two of the great scientific quests in earth science: finding the cause of the ozone hole and developing the capability to predict El Niños. So a few stops along the way influenced my thinking.

Not long after I came to Washington in 1985, I had the chance to attend a meeting of the American Geophysical Union, the foremost earth science organization in the United States. The presentation took place in a giant, crowded meeting room, and it was given by a British scientist by the name of Joseph Farman. He wasn't much of a speaker, obviously uneasy being in the spotlight before such a large audience. That was understandable. He hailed from one of the most isolated places on the planet, the Halley Bay research station in Antarctica. He had come to tell the audience about the ozone hole.

Loss of ozone in the stratosphere is a pretty big deal. The ozone layer protects the planet from harmful ultraviolet radiation, which can cause skin cancer, injure eyes, and upset the balance of ecosystems. Farman and his colleagues' lonely observations, based on an instrument wrapped in a quilt, rocked the scientific world. Farman's team measured and remeasured the dramatic drop in ozone levels over Halley Bay, finally publishing their results in 1985. Satellite data later showed that what Farman saw in Halley Bay was merely a glimpse at a depleted ozone region roughly the size of the continental United States.

Research teams, including those from the NOAA labs in Boulder, rapidly deployed to the Antarctic. They returned with conclusive evidence that the ozone hole was caused by man-made compounds, chlorofluorocarbons (CFCs), used primarily in refrigeration systems. A global agreement in 1987, the Montreal Protocol on Substances that Deplete the Ozone Layer, led to the phaseout of these compounds. As a result of this agreement and those that followed, the ozone layer is now slowly reestablishing itself and is on track for recovery to pre-1980 levels by midcentury.[1] What Joseph Farman and the scientists that followed him demonstrated was that humans can damage the planet in fundamental ways, but human efforts can fix it as well.

At about the same time as the ozone hole drama was unfolding, my office in NOAA was involved in a different scientific hunt. We were supporting, along with NASA and the National Science Foundation, a program to investigate the El Niño phenomenon. Every few years, at irregular intervals, warm water shifts from the western to the eastern Pacific, carrying with it the great tropical thunderstorms that are the boiler room of the planet's climate system. These El Niños have ripple effects around the world, influencing everything from Indonesian droughts to California rains to Atlantic hurricanes.

Even before the huge El Niño of 1982–3, scientists at university and government laboratories believed that these events could be foreseen. In the year following that event, NOAA began deployment of a network of buoys across the Pacific to monitor the status of El Niño. In 1986, Columbia University scientists Mark Cane and Steve Zebiak made the first successful prediction.[2] From such boldness, progress springs. The 1982–3 El Niño was a surprise, but not so the great 1997–8 and 2015–6 events, and other smaller ones in between. The science community had demonstrated that, with proper observing systems and robust computer modeling, climate prediction was possible. Larger climate models would have their successes on the issue of greenhouse warming and global climate change.

Government agencies had worked together informally on issues like the ozone hole and El Niño, but this same period of scientific ferment also gave rise to an interagency glasnost of sorts with the passage of the Global Change Research Act of 1990, leading to the formation of the U.S. Global Change Research Program. I served as director from 1998 to 1999. The program is more of an Articles of Confederation arrangement than a Constitution—there is no climate change czar in the federal government—but agencies from 1990 on submitted coordinated budgets and worked out who was responsible for what on climate matters.

On climate change as well as many other issues, it's important to have well-developed scientific opinion independent of the government. Abraham Lincoln in 1863, who had a few other things on his mind, still found time to charter the National Academy of Sciences to accomplish precisely this. The academy has been intimately involved in assessment of climate science for many years. I staffed for an academy climate committee in the mid-nineties and can testify to the power of smart, busy people around a table volunteering to come up with the best scientific judgment on an issue.

When the George W. Bush administration took office in 2001, one of their first questions to the academy was, essentially, is this global warming thing for real? It's a question that keeps getting asked, not necessarily for reasons involving the search for truth. The fog of uncertainty is a good excuse for inaction, and there is no lack of fog generators. The academy's response was

> Greenhouse gases are accumulating in Earth's atmosphere as
> a result of human activities, causing surface air temperatures

and subsurface ocean temperatures to rise. Temperatures are, in fact, rising.[3]

That was a pretty direct answer. Man-made climate change has been accepted science in the United States for decades now, partly because our scientists were in the forefront of many of the discoveries. But a consensus from US scientists regarding a global issue doesn't count for much. In parallel, an organization called the Intergovernmental Panel on Climate Change, or IPCC, had been working on developing international consensus statements since 1988. The IPCC office was one floor above mine when I worked at the World Meteorological Organization in Geneva.

In 2007, the IPCC, along with Al Gore, received the Nobel Peace Prize for its work on climate. The task of bringing the Nobel medal home to Geneva from Oslo was given to a staff member at IPCC. Unsurprisingly, she chose not to put it in checked baggage. The large metal object drew the attention of airport security.

"What's this?" they asked.

"It's the Nobel Prize," she answered.

The guard must have been thinking, *Yeah, and I'm the queen of England*. But after inspecting it and determining that it probably wouldn't explode, they let it pass.

In my own mind, the case for man-made climate change has followed these threads from my career. From the search for the cause of the ozone hole and the international agreements that followed, we've learned that humans can change the atmosphere, and that with concerted global action we can change it back. From the burst of progress on El Niño, we've learned that climate prediction is possible, given proper observing systems. From the U.S. Global Change Research Program, we've learned that this hulking body known as the US government can, on occasion, work in a coordinated way on an important problem. In the United States, experts reached past their own parochial research interests to form a consensus on climate change through the National Academy of Sciences. And through international groups, notably IPCC, a global consensus was reached. The last IPCC Assessment Report, in 2013, made this statement:

> It is *extremely likely* [emphasis theirs] that human influence has been the dominant cause of the observed warming since the mid-20th century. Continued emissions of greenhouse gases will cause further warming and changes in all components of the climate system. Limiting climate change will require substantial and sustained reductions of greenhouse gas emissions.[4]

I'm good with that. So for my retirement in 2011, my colleagues gave me a Gore-Tex jacket instead of a gold watch. A month later I was on the road to see what those changes in the climate system looked like on the ground.

Connecting the Dots

> All there is to thinking is seeing something noticeable which makes you see something you weren't noticing which makes you see something that isn't even visible.
> —Norman Maclean, *A River Runs Through It*

These days I think a lot about the visible and invisible changes I've seen as I've ridden around the country. My career gives me some insight into what's behind many of them. The immediate future is not that hard to see. It doesn't require computer models, though what we see developing is largely what they predicted in such publications as the IPCC assessments and the US National Climate Assessments. Regardless, we can combine what we see with our eyes today with what we have measured with instruments over many decades. It's possible to connect the dots across the country.

We can start on the abandoned Fowler Beach in Delaware, near where the ride to Oregon began. Concetta and I returned to Fowler in the spring of 2015, four years later. The road out to the beach was firmly blocked to cars by a fence and sand piles, so we walked out on the remains of the causeway. We crossed a couple of new, deep trenches to get out to where we thought we were in 2011.

There was no parking lot or guardrail left. Little bits of asphalt could be seen in the surf, but a large chunk of the island had been washed away. Out in the water was a square concrete foundation. I asked Annie Larsen, the Prime Hook biologist, what it was.

"That was an old World War Two observation tower where they used to look for submarines. An eight-foot dune and a sandy beach were in front of it just twenty-five years ago. People used to drive around it." I thought of the high-rise towers of Miami Beach.

Out before the road to Fowler, homeowners had put up a sign: FIX THE BREACHES. STOP THE FLOODING. Annie's comment: "I wanted to put up my own sign: Fix the Clouds. Stop the Rain."

As kids, most of us have had the experience of building sand castles on a rising tide. We built bigger moats and higher walls, then came back in an hour or so to see our castles as lumps in the sand. After seawalls, jetties, and beach nourishment, the ultimate answer on low barrier islands is the same: the ocean will win.

What does this mean for low barrier islands of the East and Gulf Coasts? Fowler Beach points out what is happening to them: fragmentation. New inlets will create a series of smaller and more isolated islands. Sea level rise has been, and will continue to be, relentless. The planet is warming, melting glaciers and ice sheets, and that water going into the ocean raises sea level. Seawater itself expands as the temperature climbs. As a result of these two processes, sea level is going up virtually everywhere in the world. The most recent studies indicate that the rate of sea level rise from 1990 to the present is roughly double that of 1900–90.[5] As the ocean creeps up the shore, each new hurricane or winter storm has an easier job punching through the islands. The boxcar-sized waves I saw out at sea will be back.

The choice for people living on barrier islands, increasingly breached by storms, will be to pile up more sand and build seawalls, at great expense, or to retreat from the coast. Ultimately the former strategy works about as well as it does for a sand castle. As sea level rises, enclaves of high-value real estate will be protected—think lower Manhattan and Palm Beach—but it is simply not feasible to protect more than a small fraction of the coast. Major property losses are inevitable, most backed by taxpayers through government flood insurance. A retreat from the coast will happen, accompanied by loss of life and property. One major question is who picks up the tab for the next Hurricane Sandy or Katrina.

For places like Prime Hook and Smith Island, the words *managed retreat* need to come into the vocabulary. With 5 million people and 2.6 million homes in the United States within four feet of high tide,[6] it simply won't be possible to raise or armor or protect all of these homes. *Climate refugees* is not just a phrase for low islands in the Pacific.

In central Maryland, where I live, one of the biggest climate impacts is the increase in heavy downpours. In July 2016, a flash flood devastated the historic town of Ellicott City after thunderstorms dropped over six inches of rain in two hours on the town's immediate watershed. The National Weather Service said that, based on historical statistics, such an event should occur roughly once in a thousand years.[7] There's a problem with relying on history, though, as climate is changing the rules. Katharine Hayhoe, a climate scientist at Texas Tech, highlighted the problem in the context of floods later that summer in Louisiana:

> We design our infrastructure and plan our society looking backwards, assuming that the past is a reliable predictor for the future. And looking backwards does keep us safe, when climate is relatively stable, as it has been over much of the history of human civilization on this planet. When climate is changing, though, relying on the past to predict the future will give us the wrong answer—and not just a wrong answer, but a potentially dangerous one. We buy a house outside the 100-year flood zone, believing that means we're safe;

we expect our storm sewer drains and our levees to protect us from all but the rarest extremes, failing to account for how these extremes are rapidly becoming more frequent in a changing climate.[8]

For inland Maryland as well as for the coast, climate is changing the rules and loading the dice.

Flooding is less of a problem in Kansas, where the ocean receded about seventy million years ago. Climate makes its mark here in different ways. I remember the farmers in the predawn fluorescent light of the Tribune convenience store, talking about crop yields:

"I wish I was just down thirty percent. That might just get it done."

It gives a reminder of the potency of drought, and of how much agriculture there depends on irrigation from groundwater. My ride across Kansas was marked by scorching heat, the middle of a vast drought in the southern Plains.

Intermittent drought has been a characteristic of life on the Plains since long before the era of elevated greenhouse gases. The historical and geological records suggest that another event of Dust Bowl or greater proportions is simply a matter of time. Greenhouse warming tips the scales more in favor of drought, particularly in the southern Plains. Rainfall is critical to recharging the Ogallala Aquifer, the enormous groundwater deposit beneath much of the Plains. But even in times of relative water abundance, withdrawals from the aquifer have far exceeded its recharge. I rode by hundreds of fields with great rotating sprinklers, those green circles visible from the air over Kansas. They are the mark of center pivot irrigation. It's not hard to imagine them gradually disappearing.

Connecting the dots in the Rockies requires less imagination, because in many ways climate and its impacts have already connected. In much of the eastern Rockies, the high forests have been lost to pine beetles, no longer killed by cold winters. The landscape near tree line where I hiked forty years ago has changed from green to gray. This story has gotten virtually no attention back east. I suspect that if such a huge swath of forests had died over the course of a summer, it would have made front pages globally. But since it has unfolded over the course of many years, it moves into the background, happening almost invisibly. But the end result is starkly visible nonetheless.

Beetles and vanishing glaciers aren't the only climate issues in the Rockies. Riding around the corner in Idaho and seeing the yellow triangular FOREST FIRE AHEAD sign was about more than the smoking battlefield scene I encountered. Projected climate changes suggest that large fires will occur more frequently in the forests of the West. This effect is compounded by a legacy of fire suppression that has resulted in many US forests becoming increasingly dense.[9] Projections of increased fire extent in the greater Yellowstone area suggest that the current suite of conifer species may not survive.[10]

In Glacier Park, David Benson spent much of his career documenting how ptarmigan are reacting to the warming temperatures and receding glaciers. There may be some lessons for humans there. As fires grow more frequent and intense in the dry West, homes in the fire-prone forest will either become fire-resistant or burn. There won't be enough fire crews to protect them all. In an analogous situation, people with homes on the coast near sea level will face a choice: retreat, build walls, elevate, or watch them wash away. David's summary of the ptarmigan's choices was "move, adapt, or die." It remains to be seen if humans are as adaptable as ptarmigan.

Eastern Oregon is a dry place, in the rain shadow of the Cascades. I rode by miles of lush green irrigated pastures in the river valleys, just down from dry sagebrush hills. I caught my first glimpse of the white cones of the Cascades in the pastures outside of Redmond. These shrinking white cones are one of the major ways that climate change reveals itself in the Northwest. They are the source for much of that irrigation. The snowpack is down, but the major issue is the timing of the snowmelt. With earlier spring, peak runoff happens when rain falls on the snow, and these days that's happening more in late winter, leaving summer flows dropping in the great rivers like the Columbia. The future holds hard choices between water for irrigated agriculture, for hydropower, for preserving salmon runs, or for municipal supplies.

In parts of the media, discussion of climate impacts invokes a certain eyeball rolling: "Isn't this tiresome? Everything is about climate change." Well, yes, it kind of is. All of the major global environmental changes, and most of the events, have a man-made component. Looking at fires or hurricane damage, forest loss or acidifying oceans without considering climate change is like trying to understand biology without evolution. It's a fundamental underlying principle, and nothing makes sense without it.

The changes I saw across the country are all pieces of a greater whole, unfolding over years and out of sync with the news cycle. There are many more impacts of climate change than can be documented by a guy on a bike in our little corner of the globe. Are these impacts catastrophic? If they had happened overnight, they surely would be perceived as such. It's said that a frog tossed into boiling water would certainly jump out, but not if the pot were gradually heated. I've never tried to boil a frog, nor do I wish to do so, but I get the general idea. Except in our case, we're both the frog and the cook.

Humans caused these changes. Some changes, like the glacier loss in Glacier National Park, are too far along to reverse. But for many, humans can begin reversing them, though it will take a long time. What to do?

Turning the Ship

Changing the composition of the atmosphere has been likened to turning a great ship. Put on a couple of degrees change in the rudder angle, and gradually, after seconds, the bow begins to swing and the gyrocompass starts to click. It doesn't happen fast, and you need to know what the new course will be before you begin to turn the wheel. What should this course look like for the Earth's climate?

By far the biggest contribution to climate change has been the burning of fossil fuels: coal, oil, and natural gas. This combustion has driven levels of carbon dioxide, the most important greenhouse gas, to levels not seen on the planet for at least eight hundred thousand years. Most of this increase has happened since 1970, about the time global energy consumption began to accelerate.[11]

Looking forward, sailing on without a course correction—"business as usual"—leads us toward more warming, more sea level rise, more Dust Bowls. Though plenty of damage has already been done, nations have committed under the Framework Convention on Climate Change to limit global temperature rise to 3.6°F. As has been well documented by prominent environmentalist Bill McKibben,[12] we have roughly five times the proven coal, oil, and gas reserves in the ground necessary for this amount of warming. In light of what we know about climate change, burning it all, or even a significant fraction, is simply foolish.

Yet left to their own devices, fossil fuel companies will extract and sell it all. Christophe de Margerie, late chairman of Total, the French oil company, once gave a terse and candid response to the question of what to keep in the ground: "I am not in charge of the planet."[13] But someone had better be. Fossil fuel companies are going to continue doing what they do: relentlessly explore for more oil and gas.

So to slow down global warming, fossil fuel companies must keep 80 percent of their product in the ground, something they surely won't do voluntarily. The size of the problem is highlighted in a historical parallel drawn to the Abolition movement by Christopher Hayes.[14] Adjusted for inflation, the value of slaves held just before the Civil War was about $10 trillion, roughly the same as the current value of known oil, coal, and gas reserves. As stated back in Ohio, no one argues a moral equivalence between slavery and fossil fuel extraction. But weaning the world from fossil fuels would involve the same sort of economic impact as having slaveholders free their slaves. And that took the worst war in our nation's history to accomplish.

It would seem an impossible task. Yet as Hayes points out, there is a solution. Fossil fuel extraction requires enormous amounts of capital, with the industry spending $1.8 billion a day on exploration. If people begin using less energy and governments begin putting a price on carbon emissions, this capital becomes more and more difficult to raise, and the value of the carbon in the ground declines. There's a phrase for this: *stranded assets*. Exploration for oil and gas needs to become a bad investment, and divestment from fossil fuels a moral imperative. Substituting for fossil fuels and developing sources of renewable energy is a case Pope Francis makes in *Laudato Si.*

But wait: I make the case against fossil fuels and for raising their cost, but I fly on airplanes, heat my house, and drive a car. Isn't that hypocritical? I'm not arguing to cut fossil fuels out entirely, just to cut way back and develop alternatives. In the United States, we use about twice as much energy per capita as people in either Europe or China.[15] Having lived in Europe, it's very hard to make the case that their standard of living is lower. I'm trying to get my family's carbon footprint on a par with that of the Europeans, or a bit less. We have a single hybrid car, use public transit when possible, make rare use of air-conditioning and go gently with the heat. And I ride my bike a lot.

Isn't this "imposing a lifestyle"? Something that flies in the face of the treasured individualism I saw so much of on my ride? Again, no. People should be free to drive whatever they choose or live however they choose. But those choices involve costs: the seawalls in New York, the dead forests in the Rockies, the drying rivers in the West. Taxpayers are liable for the cost of rebuilding homes, roads, and culverts after the floods, fires, and droughts. If the price of gas were increased to $8 a gallon, it would still be cheap compared to the cost of adapting to this new world of altered climate. We who use fossil fuels should pay the cost of adaptation.

A Case for Hope

It's clear that many of the impacts of climate change are already baked into the system. If carbon dioxide emissions stopped tomorrow, the rising temperature and sea levels would continue for many years. The ship has a lot of momentum. But there are reasons to believe that a course change is possible.

One involves a story from my days in Geneva. I was running the UN office charged with supporting the global network of observations tracking climate change. I attended a number of the international negotiations under the UN Framework Convention on Climate Change from 2005 to 2009. It was always fascinating to watch the behavior of the US and Chinese delegations, since they represented the two countries with the largest emissions of carbon dioxide. I initially thought that there would be diplomatically expressed tension between the two. There was none; in fact, their positions in those days were often mirror images. It was tacitly acknowledged that if one side did nothing on emissions, the other side would feel no pressure to take action. Any pressure from the United States would be met with "So the country of SUVs is telling the country of bicycles to reduce its energy consumption?"

Things change. China is less and less the country of bicycles, and the amount of carbon per person that China puts into the atmosphere is going up rapidly. The Chinese people are driving more cars and using more energy. Because of auto traffic and the extensive use of coal, air quality in Chinese cities is some of the world's worst. Their people protest against this pollution. Chinese leadership recognizes the need to do something on emissions, and they are planning a market for carbon permits.[16] It was against this background that the climate accord between President Obama and President Xi in November 2014 came about. The United States agreed to double its carbon dioxide reductions, while China committed to peak carbon dioxide emissions by 2030. There are justifiable questions as to whether what was agreed to is enough. But what it really meant is that the old position of "if they won't, we won't" has crumbled.

The agreement between the top two emitters of greenhouse gases, the United States and China, paved the way for the Paris Agreement in December 2015. In Paris, 195 nations agreed to hold the increase in the global average temperature to less than 3.6°F above preindustrial levels and to pursue efforts to limit the temperature increase to 2.7°F. Most nations submitted plans for how they would reduce greenhouse gases to help meet these goals. From the US side, the accord with China and the Paris Agreement were based on domestic actions, the most important of which are the new rules to cut back on carbon pollution from new and existing power plants, a major source of carbon dioxide. The change in US leadership doesn't necessarily mean that US emissions are destined to rise; more on that in a moment. All of the nations' plans are to be revisited periodically, presumably with collective ambition ratcheted up over time. The agreement comes in for criticism in that the sum of emissions reductions don't nearly add up to the temperature increase goals, and that the commitments aren't binding. After seeing this process for some years, I find the notion that 195 nations can agree on *anything* to be remarkable. It's not a solution, but a start. And after decades of false starts, it's genuine progress.

Saying that the international climate community did well is a long way from saying that they did enough. Paris represents a common way for nations to come together, but the stated actions still represent nibbling around the edges of the problem. To actually turn the ship requires a fundamental change in how we generate and use energy. The word that's used is *mobilization*. More on that later.

The 2017 change in US leadership will likely undermine federal government support for the Paris Agreement, but that's not necessarily crippling for the future of the global climate. Domestically, regardless of the fate of regulations mandating reductions in greenhouse gases, reversing the decline in coal production will be difficult for economic reasons alone. Natural gas is simply less expensive, as are wind and solar power in large swaths of the United States.

And climate is, of course, a global issue, and other nations will have something to say. Europe has long been a leader in clean energy and reduced emissions. Considering the air quality issues in Chinese cities, China has a powerful and enduring motivation to reduce dependence on coal, and the same can be said for India. China also has a rapidly expanding solar industry, and they would be more than pleased to have a greater global market share. Renewable energy has a certain momentum of its own now. As always, US actions will influence, but not determine, the global response to climate change.

Hope also comes from the streets. Demonstrations led to cancellation of the Keystone Pipeline, which would facilitate some of the world's dirtiest carbon extraction, the Canadian tar sands. Demonstrations and legal battles may yet prevent its return. The remarkable gathering of Native Nations and environmentalists at the Standing Rock Reservation in the approaching North Dakota winter slowed, for the moment at least, the construction of a pipeline through their water supply. There's also a growing movement in local governments and on college campuses to divest portfolios from investments in coal, oil, and gas companies. The group founded by Bill McKibben, 350.org, has divestment as one of its primary goals. (The number 350 represents a "safe" level of carbon dioxide in the atmosphere; current levels recently went over 400.) This larger international organization has spawned dozens of local groups, including my chapter, dedicated to divestment in Montgomery County, Maryland. At my alma mater, Dartmouth College, a remarkable group of students and alumni is working for divestment of the college endowment. And regional climate groups such as Chesapeake Climate Action Network have had notable wins in advancing wind power and helping pass state legislation on greenhouse gas reduction.

Reducing use of fossil fuels implies that there's a reasonable way to replace them. There's reason for optimism here as well; a global industry for renewable energy is maturing rapidly. The cost of solar photovoltaic systems dropped 57 percent from 2009 to 2013, while onshore wind costs went down 15 percent over the same period.[17] Of course, the wind doesn't blow and the sun doesn't shine all the time. Here's where some Yankee ingenuity is coming into play. Storage battery technology, exemplified by Elon Musk's Tesla Motors, is expanding rapidly, both on household and project scales.[18] For the long term, what this means is that non-fossil-fuel electricity will be increasingly available in times of no wind or sun. Regardless, there's lots of room to expand. I've ridden across the Great Plains twice now, and trust me, there's plenty of wind. Globally, costs for renewable energy, without subsidies, are now at or below the cost of fossil fuel energy in thirty countries, according to the World Economic Forum.[19]

So there are lots of reasons to believe that we can and should change the climate future. But it's not a small job. McKibben has likened the transformation of the energy system to the industrial mobilization that occurred at the start of World War II.[20] The production of wind turbines and solar panels needs to scale up rapidly to replace the infrastructure of fossil fuels, and a transportation system that relies on electricity rather than the burning of fossil fuels must come into being. A Stanford study has laid out in detail state-by-state prospects for 80 percent renewable energy by 2030 and 100 percent by 2050.[21] It's daunting but doable, particularly in the context of what the United States has done before. And, as a by-product, it would bring an industrial renaissance.

How could this happen, and how could it be financed? As at the start of World War II, the private sector is a vital partner. Promotion of government incentives that support clean energy and elimination of subsidies for carbon-based energy could unlock the global abundance of private capital.[22] Given proper incentives, the prospect of making money while slowing climate change would be irresistible.

Profiting while helping the environment has happened before. In the 1970s, DuPont was the largest manufacturer of chlorofluorocarbons, or CFCs, the compounds responsible for atmospheric ozone loss. Before the discovery of the ozone hole, DuPont lobbied heavily against regulation of these compounds, but also sponsored a substantial research program to examine the science. After the ozone hole was found, DuPont's decision to support international regulation via the Montreal Protocol was the critical moment in the more than decade-long ozone depletion controversy.[23] Environmental groups applied political pressure for industry to phase out CFCs. DuPont's decision was driven by the alignment of these political values, emerging scientific knowledge, and economic incentives. DuPont realized that not only was stopping CFC production the responsible thing to do, but they could also make lots of money on CFC replacements. The actions on ozone depletion aren't necessarily a model for the climate change issue. The costs of slowing climate change will be concentrated, while the benefits will be widely dispersed. But dialogue with industry will be essential in making these course changes.

To be sure, restructuring the energy economy is a heavy lift. In the grand debate on climate change, the true opposition is what I would call the "Whaddaya gonna do" caucus: the people who find reasons why it's too hard to change. In 1988, when James Hansen of NASA brought the issue of climate change to the attention of Congress, the consensus was: "It's too soon." At this writing in 2017, what's often heard is: "It's too late." This is the position of climate despair, that we really can't do anything serious about the problem. And of course, this position helps rationalize fossil fuel profits in the near term. It amounts to shrugging and shifting our problem to the next generation.

In September of 2014, four hundred thousand people marched through the streets of Manhattan for action on climate change, to help preserve the places I've seen changing before my eyes. With them, I choose to fight for those places, this planet, now.

It's been six years since I turned left out of my driveway with a loaded bike to ride to Oregon. The hours on the ride were sometimes hard but always vivid, and years later I can remember each day and each small town. In winters I still spend time in coffee shops dreaming of the road. It's led to more than a few big rides: down the Appalachians on the route of an old Indian trail, then later through the Black Hills and Badlands of South Dakota. The spring of 2013 brought a ride across El Camino de Santiago, a medieval pilgrimage route in Spain. That slave collar in Illinois seemed to burn into my hands and into the back of my head: it led to an Underground Railroad route from Mississippi to Canada in 2015. Planning for springtime rides forces old legs to stay in shape. There is a simple mantra since the ride across: read and write and ride.

I still talk with groups about climate change, with a bit less emphasis on its reality and a bit more on what we can do. The numbers are there, the graphs and maps all support the case. But what I've found always works best are the land stories, the sea stories, the tales of dogs and tornadoes, grizzlies and rogue waves. Yes, they all happened, and maybe the details amplify in the retelling. But we humans are wired to communicate this way. The conservationist Jane Goodall now travels three hundred days a year, telling of her days with chimpanzees in East Africa. She says, "The only way I've found to change people's minds is to tell them stories."[24] For me, the bike is a story machine. I turn the crank and things happen.

Since the trip, I've also found myself contributing to larger things, notably organizations dedicated to keeping carbon in the ground. It might seem quixotic, but the past gives reason for optimism. With the publication of *Silent Spring* in 1962, the environmental movement began here in the United States, with the awareness that people were being sickened by the consequences of unregulated pollution in the air and water by industries that had no responsibility for public health. Eventually a system of national regulation was adopted that has dramatically improved water and air quality. It became the basis for pollution regulation worldwide.

It is important to remember how intractable the problem seemed at the time. Industry was predicting a collapse of the economy as a result of increased costs. Fossil fuel industries today make many of the same arguments against EPA rules regulating greenhouse gases, stating that "Investment in American manufacturing and clean energy technologies will come to an immediate halt, putting creation of many new jobs at risk."[25] Certainly opposition to clean energy will continue to be very well funded.

It's a great battle, but one that's been won before. More than a battle, it's an opportunity. We need to rebuild and rewire an entire energy system into one that's clean, renewable, and far less wasteful than the system that we have, to begin the transition from the smokestacks and tailpipes of the 20th century to the whir of turbines and the hum of cars of the 21st. For the sake of this small rock that we all ride around on, it's an opportunity that we can't afford to miss.

APPENDIX: NUTS AND BOLTS

F or those who have interest in going across, or even doing a multiday tour, it's not dangerous, but like most things worth doing, it requires a little planning. There are lots of places to get information, and among the best is the Adventure Cycling Association (adventurecycling.org) based in Missoula, Montana. In this section I'd like to include a few idiosyncratic comments about distance cycling, with an eye toward helping someone else on their way.

Life on the Road

Life on tour is sometimes uncomfortably close to living on the street. I'm continuously wet for long periods of time, either from rain or sweat or some combination. I smell bad. I sleep in sketchy motels or in campgrounds. (There are indeed very few tent campers in campgrounds these days.) Once when we were riding together, my friend Jan and I were doing laundry at the end of the day. He was wringing out his jersey and hanging it in the shower.

"So here we are, two sixty-year-olds washing out clothes in a motel sink."

"Yep," I said, "livin' the dream."

It's a strange thing. Most people would imagine spending time in a cheap motel in the middle of nowhere to be less than inviting. But I find the feeling of lying in bed exhausted, blood pumping through my legs, images of places and people spinning by, to be intensely pleasurable. As for getting out the door in the morning, there was another benefit of my downscale accommodations: in the morning light, another day at the budget motel or campground usually wasn't all that appealing. Turning out of the parking lot, the road brings vividness, freedom, and surprises. A vivid life: not such a bad goal.

That said, there are a few considerations that can ease the way down the road. Pay attention to the bike, to all the little clicks and clatters that sound out of the ordinary. Getting after them early helps. Have your ear attuned to that sound of a dry chain, especially the day after a rain. For me, bike and body melded after a while. I would swear that I could feel a sore spoke, and I considered installing a grease nipple on my knee.

There is a discipline to keeping your dry things dry. After days of sun, a certain laxity sets in. It's like when I was on the ship after a long time in a calm anchorage. People would begin to put things on shelves and tables, unsecured. Then the ship would get under way in big seas and all hell would break loose. I remember falling asleep to cans of food rolling across the galley floor over my head. It's similar to riding the bike after a dry spell: you start to forget to put things in plastic bags. The rain snuck up on me one day, and that night I found the camera strap and parts of the camera body soaking wet. I came close to losing the camera. So don't let the sunshine lull you.

Even in the spring, keep a close watch on water. I heard tales of a gentleman riding across the Plains who needed two days at a motel to rehydrate. Electrolytes are important, too. If you find yourself incorporating leg cramps into your dreams at night, it's time to pack in the bananas and sports drink during the day. It almost goes without saying, but slathering on sunscreen two or three times a day is vital.

Planning

On the coast-to-coast trip, I had seventy-five riding days, with an average of fifty-six miles per day. That's not a bad number for a sixty-something like me. The twenty-somethings typically did more like eighty, but eighty with a big climb tended to fry me even when I was in good shape during the trip.

Figuring out a good route is important. There are lots of roads not suitable for cycling, and getting stuck on a busy four-lane road with no shoulder is one of those times when things really do get dangerous. So how to figure out where to ride? Most state transportation departments have free cycling maps, but they're often not very reliable. The best maps I've seen come from Adventure Cycling. They're drafted by cyclists, updated frequently, and show things like bike shops, accommodations, contours, and road surfaces. In my experience, their information is better for a cyclist than what's on Google Maps. In the case of no information, Google Street View will show most roads, though it's time consuming. Regardless, I like to carry paper maps. Cell coverage is pretty good in populated areas, but some of the most interesting places are the least populated. When the phone comes up with "No Service," pulling a map out of the pack feels pretty good.

Once you've got an idea of where you want to go and how to get there, take time to check it out with a routing app. I use Ride With GPS (ridewithgps.com), which gives a detailed elevation profile and summarizes the total amount of climbing. You don't want to be surprised with a monster climb in midafternoon right after that ice cream stop. That's happened to me. It's not fun.

Just because it's flat doesn't mean that it's easy. It seems odd, but riding on the Plains can be a good deal harder than riding in the mountains. In hill country, eventually there's a downhill to every uphill. But upwind can last for a long, long time. That's one of the reasons I like drop handlebars. When big winds happen, you want to crawl down next to the pavement. A low profile really helps. And the Great Plains are not necessarily flat. As an Easterner, I thought of Kansas as not having much relief. The rollers of eastern Kansas disabused me of that. It's also the middle of a continent, so weather will be some kind of extreme. May can bring sleet in the mountains and blast-furnace winds a week later out on the Plains.

Planning also involves some practical concerns. I've threatened Concetta with riding the Karakorum Highway, one of the world's highest roads, from Islamabad, Pakistan, to Kashgar, China. Along with rockslides and breathtaking climbs, Taliban roadblocks can add to the degree of difficulty. Not only won't Concetta let me ride the Karakorum, she wouldn't let me ride on any "K" road at all, not Kazakhstan, not Kyrgyzstan. I went across Kansas out of spite.

Gear

A few comments about gear, with a preamble. As a certain former Tour winner once said, "It's not about the bike." We Americans can get a bit fixated on gear. I ran into a German rider on the TransAm who noted that he had the experience several times of people coming up and looking over his bike and bags, without asking anything about him. My young friend Maxim, whom I met in Oregon, was riding across with garbage bags bungeed to the back of his rack. I wouldn't recommend it, but then again the last I saw of Maxim, he was riding off up the pass into the distance. Even people with marginal equipment can get an awfully long way.

Anyway, gear is important, but don't let it get in the way of a ride. The people riding the TransAm are largely twenty-somethings and sixty-somethings—both groups with less concerns about kids and jobs—and the sixty-somethings can generally afford better gear. The important thing is to start. There are some truly amazing two-wheel contraptions getting people (and dogs!) across the country. That said, it's more fun not to have things fall apart in the middle of nowhere, and breaking out a sleeping bag that hasn't been soaked in the day's rain is a truly satisfying experience. So I tended to go with solid, reliable gear.

First choice, of course, is a bike. I've had a Trek 520, the horse of the TransAm, since 2000; it's still available. We've gotten used to each other. It has a personal rust spot on the frame under my chin where the sweat drips. It's a touring bike, as opposed to a road, hybrid, or mountain bike, and it's built to carry loads. There are many touring bikes to choose from, and *Adventure Cycling* magazine has an annual review of the models. Like most things, you can spend as much as you like. But there are a few things to consider.

Simple and fixable are the most desirable characteristics for multiday rides. For the bike frame, I like steel. If steel frames break, they can be welded in central Kansas or Nepal or pretty much anywhere else. Not so with carbon fiber or aluminum. Bar-end shifters are simple, with one moving part. Combined shifters (brake and gear) are wonderfully convenient but complex. What if one breaks in Crowheart, Wyoming?

I ran across a westbound cycling group in Montana. I asked their leader about equipment problems. Besides the usual flat tires, their big issues were broken spokes and bent rims. The thin rims of a street bike (say 23mm) are a little risky if you aren't in range of a ride home or have your own support team. The 32mm rims of the Trek 520 could roll over a New York City pothole and not get bent. They are, of course, heavier, and that's a trade-off. Weight on the rim matters far more than static weight. On the other extreme, the knobby tires of a mountain bike dramatically increase rolling resistance. The thinner 32mm tires work well on most dirt bike paths, including the Chesapeake & Ohio Canal in Maryland and the Katy Trail in Missouri. I've had very good luck with Schwalbe Marathon Plus tires. One flat in forty-two hundred miles is a pretty good testimony.

The next question is how to carry your gear, specifically panniers (bags) versus a trailer. I've ridden tours with both, and I tend to go with panniers. Though I love the trailer, on a long tour, one less moving part (the wheel) is a real consideration. You can also carry the world in a trailer, and that temptation can be dangerous. So I ride with a set of Ortlieb panniers, front and back. They're expensive but well-designed and seriously waterproof.

It's a golden rule of cycling: I always, without exception, wear a helmet. In tens of thousands of miles, I've cracked two helmets in falls, losing consciousness both times. The falls happened very fast. In one case I woke up on the road facing the wrong direction. The helmet protected me in each instance from potentially crippling or deadly consequences. Indeed, after one fall, the doctor made the reassuring but mildly offensive statement, "Your brain scan is negative."

Planning for a tour is all about the details. Rich Vertigan is a retired engineer from upstate New York who rode across the United States the year before I did. A most organized man, he generated a packing list that I used as a model for my own. One clever aspect about it is that camping gear is on the right-hand side, so that if you decide to bail out to a motel during a downpour, you need only unpack the left-side bags. So with a bow to Rich, my modified list is below. If you're not camping, gear can fit into the two rear panniers, without need for front panniers.

Front left pannier		Front right pannier	
First aid kit	Spare eyeglasses	On top	Snacks
	Medications	Food bag	Emergency meals (1–2)
	Moleskin		Tea, sugar
	Bandages		Spare sealable bags
	Adhesive tape		Spare grocery bags
	Nail clippers		Paper towels
	Water tablets	Tool bag	Spare brakes
	Wet wipes		Brake cable
	Alcohol swabs		Derailleur cable
	Antiseptic		Spare tubes
	Toothbrush		Electrical tape
	Toothpaste		Kevlar spoke
Electronics bag	Laptop charger		6-inch crescent wrench
	Phone charger		Needle nose pliers
	Earphones		Spoke wrench
	Spare batteries		Presta/Schrader
	USB drive		adapter
	Maps		Frame bolts
Computer bag	Laptop		Shoe bolts
			Shoe cleats
			Zip ties

Handlebar bag
(remove at restaurants)

In Ziploc bag	Camera
	Sunscreen
	Lip balm
	Eye drops
	Electrolyte drops
	Current map
	Smart phone
	Wallet
	Bike touring cards
	Pepper spray

Rear left pannier

Bike clothes bag	Bike shorts
	Tights
	Polypro top
	Bike jerseys
	Bike socks
	Bike gloves
	Glove liners
	Windproof gloves
	Hat
Loose	Fleece pullover
	Rain jacket
	Laundry bag
In rain jacket	Helmet cover
	Reflective leg bands
Off-bike bag	Long-sleeved shirt
	Off-bike shirts
	Underwear
	Zip-off pants
Outside pocket	Rain socks
	Shoe cover
	Cable and lock
On strap	Rear taillight

Right rear pannier

	Fuel bottle
Cookset	Pots
	Cup
	Dish towel
	Pot holder
	Stove
	Eating utensils
Stuff sack	Detergent
	Sponge
	Clothespins
	Needle/thread
Stuff sack	Sleeping bag
	Thermarest pad
	Pad patch kit

Seat bag	Swiss Army knife
	Spare tube
	Patch kit
	Allen wrench tool
	Tire levers

Rear rack	Sandals
Tent bag	Tent
	Tent fly
	Tent poles
	Ground sheet

On bike	Water bottles
	Frame pump
	Front/rear racks

And lastly, every journey needs its talisman. On the ride to Oregon, mine was a small Mary medallion from a nun at the cathedral in Le Puy, France, at the start of my ride on the Way of St. James. The Way is a pilgrimage route that dates from the Middle Ages, and I was just getting started. There was a pilgrims' mass at 7:00 A.M. and a blessing. The nun seemed to pick me out from the crowd and pressed the medallion into my palm. She spoke perfect English. On July 24, the very day I reached the Oregon coast, I noticed that Mary was gone from my neck chain. It seemed that she just needed to see me to the end of the journey.

ENDNOTES

CHAPTER 1: DELAWARE: THE SEA APPROACHES
1. J. A. Church and N. J. White, "Sea-level Rise from the Late 19th to the Early 21st Century," *Surveys in Geophysics* (2011), doi:10.1007/s10712-011-9119-1.
2. S. Harper, "Lawmakers Avoid Buzzwords on Climate Change Bills," *The Virginian-Pilot* (June 10, 2012).
3. A. Harish, "New Law in North Carolina Bans Latest Scientific Predictions of Sea-Level Rise," ABC News (August 2, 2012), http://abcnews.go.com/US/north-carolina-bans-latest-science-rising-sea-level/story?id=16913782.
4. A. Sillers, "Florida Environmental Officials Banned from Using the Term 'Climate Change,'" PBS Newshour (March 9, 2015), http://www.pbs.org/newshour/rundown/.florida-environmental-officials-banned-using-term-climate-change/.
5. J. Walsh, D. Wuebbles, K. Hayhoe, J. Kossin, K. Kunkel, G. Stephens, P. Thorne, R. Vose, M. Wehner, J. Willis, D. Anderson, S. Doney, R. Feely, P. Hennon, V. Kharin, T. Knutson, F. Landerer, T. Lenton, J. Kennedy, and

R. Somerville, "Our Changing Climate," in *Climate Change Impacts in the United States: The Third National Climate Assessment*, eds. J. M. Melillo, Terese (T. C.) Richmond, and G. W. Yohe (U.S. Global Change Research Program, 2014), 19–67.

6. Quoted in J. Gertner, "Should the United States Save Tangier Island from Oblivion?" *New York Times Magazine* (July 6, 2016).

CHAPTER 2: MARYLAND: THE WAY TO GET TO OREGON

1. J. Cook, N. Oreskes, P. Doran, W. Anderegg, B. Verheggen, E. Maibach, J. Carlton, S. Lewandowsky, A. Skuce, S. Green, D. Nuccitelli, P. Jacobs, M. Richardson, B. Winkler, R. Painting, and K. Rice, "Consensus on Consensus: A Synthesis of Consensus Estimates on Human-Caused Global Warming," *Environmental Research Letters* 11, no. 4 (2016), doi:10.1088/1748-9326/11/4/048002.

2. D. Boesch, V. Coles, D. Kimmel, and W. Miller, "Coastal Dead Zones and Global Climate Change: Ramifications for the Chesapeake Bay," in *Regional Impacts of Climate Change; Four Case Studies in the United States* (Pew Center on Global Climate Change, 2007).

3. National Research Council, *Ocean Acidification: A National Strategy to Meet the Challenges of a Changing Ocean* (Washington, D.C.: National Academies Press, 2010).

4. Chesapeake Bay Program, *2014 Bay Barometer* (Annapolis, MD: 2015).

5. Virginia Institute of Marine Science, *Recurrent Flooding Study for Tidewater Virginia*, Report summited to Virginia General Assembly, 2013.

6. L. Montgomery, "In Norfolk, Evidence of Climate Change Is in the Streets at High Tide," *Washington Post* (May 31, 2014).

CHAPTER 3: THE PENNSYLVANIA GOLD RUSH

1. B. Walsh, "Could Shale Gas Power the World?" *Time* (March 31, 2011).

2. Jeff Goodell, "The Big Fracking Bubble: The Scam Behind Aubrey McClendon's Gas Boom," *Rolling Stone* (March 1, 2012).

3. Katie Colaneri, "Transparency About Fracking Chemicals Remains Elusive," NPR StateImpact (August 7, 2014), https://stateimpact.npr.org/pennsylvania/2014/08/07/transparency-about-fracking-chemicals-remains-illusive/.

4. M. Bamberger and R. Oswald, "Long-Term Impacts of Unconventional Drilling Operations on Human and Animal Health," *Journal of Environmental Science and Health, Part A: Toxic/Hazardous Substances and Environmental Engineering* 50, no. 5 (2015): 447–459, doi: 10.1080/10934529.2015.992655.

5. Peter Rabinowitz et al., "Proximity to Natural Gas Wells and Reported Health Status: Results of a Household Survey in Washington County, Pennsylvania," in *Environmental Health Perspectives* (National

Institute of Environmental Health, 2014), http://dx.doi.org/10.1289/ehp.1307732.

6. A. Brandt et al., "Methane Leaks from North American Natural Gas Systems," *Science* 343 (2014): 733–735.

7. A. J. Turner et al., "A Large Increase in U.S. Methane Emissions Over the Past Decade Inferred from Satellite Data and Surface Observations, *Geophysical Research Letters* 43 (2016): 2218–2224, doi:10.1002/2016GL067987.

8. Scott Detrow, "Perilous Pathways: Behind the Staggering Number of Abandoned Wells in Pennsylvania," NPR StateImpact (October 10, 2012), https://stateimpact.npr.org/pennsylvania/2012/10/10/perilous-pathways-behind-the-staggering-number-of-abandoned-wells-in-pennsylvania/.

9. S. G. Rasmussen, E. L. Ogburn, M. McCormack, et al., "Association Between Unconventional Natural Gas Development in the Marcellus Shale and Asthma Exacerbations, *JAMA Intern Med* (published online July 18, 2016), doi:10.1001/jamainternmed.2016.2436.

10.. S. Conley et al., "Methane Emissions from the 2015 Aliso Canyon Blowout in Los Angeles, CA," *Science* 25 (February 2016), doi: 10.1126/science. aaf2348.

11. Robinson Township v Commonwealth of Pennsylvania, Supreme Court of Pennsylvania, J-127A-D-2012, 118, December 19, 2013.

CHAPTER 4: OHIO: TIM HORTONS, ARMADILLOS, AND CLIMATE CHANGE

1. Data from NASA Goddard Institute for Space Studies. GISTEMP Team, 2017: *GISS Surface Temperature Analysis (GISTEMP)*. NASA Goddard Institute for Space Studies. Dataset accessed 2017-02-01 at https://data .giss.nasa.gov/gistemp/.

2. American Association for the Advancement of Science Climate Science Panel, *What We Know: The Reality, Risks and Response to Climate Change* (Washington, D.C.: American Association for Advancement of Science, 2014).

3. UK Royal Society and US National Academy of Sciences, *Climate Change: Evidence and Causes*, 2014.

4. AAAS, *What We Know*, p.14.

5. Intergovernmental Panel on Climate Change, "Summary for Policymakers," in *Climate Change 2013: The Physical Science Basis. Contribution of Working Group I to the Fifth Assessment Report of the Intergovernmental Panel on Climate Change*, eds. T. F. Stocker, D. Qin, G.-K. Plattner, M. Tignor, S. K. Allen, J. Boschung, A. Nauels, Y. Xia, V. Bex, and P. M. Midgley (Cambridge: Cambridge University Press, 2013), Table SPM.2, page 25.

6. IPCC, "Summary for Policymakers," in *Climate Change 2013*.

7.   J. Cook, N. Oreskes, P. Doran, W. Anderegg, B. Verheggen, E. Maibach, J. Carlton, S. Lewandowsky, A. Skuce, S. Green, D. Nuccitelli, P. Jacobs, M. Richardson, B. Winkler, R. Painting and K. Rice, "Consensus on Consensus: A Synthesis of Consensus Estimates on Human-Caused Global Warming," *Environmental Research Letters* 11, no. 4 (2016), doi:10.1088/1748-9326/11/4/048002.

CHAPTER 5: OHIO: AWAKENINGS
1.   Won-Young Kim, "Induced Seismicity Associated with Fluid Injection into a Deep Well in Youngstown, Ohio," *Journal of Geophysical Research* 118, no. 7 (2013): 3506–3518.
2.   A. McGarr et al, "Coping with Earthquakes Induced by Fluid Injection," *Science* 347, no. 6224 (2015): 830–831.
3.   B. Elgin, "Oil CEO Wanted University Quake Scientists Dismissed: Dean's E-Mail," *Bloomberg News* (May 15, 2015). http://www.bloomberg.com/news/articles/2015-05-15/oil-tycoon-harold-hamm-wanted-scientists-dismissed-dean-s-e-mail-says.
4.   J. Fifield, "States' Efforts to Curb Fracking-Related Earthquakes Seem to Be Working," *Washington Post* (August 16, 2016). https://www.washingtonpost.com/national/health-science/states-effort-to-curb-fracking-related-earthquakes-appear-to-be-paying-off/2016/08/15/d0a71108-49ce-11e6-90a8-fb84201e0645_story.html.
5.   Quoted in J. Gillis, "Pope Francis Aligns Himself with Mainstream Science on Climate," *New York Times* (June 18, 2015).

CHAPTER 8: MISSOURI: THE BEST PLACE IN A TORNADO
1.   J. Walsh, D. Wuebbles et al.,"Our Changing Climate," 19–67.

CHAPTER 9: SOUTH DAKOTA: NIGHT ON STRONGHOLD TABLE
1.   Louise Erdrich, "Holy Fury: Lessons from Standing Rock," *The New Yorker* (December 22, 2016).

CHAPTER 11: KANSAS: SMALL HOURS ON THE HIGH PLAINS
1.   T. Egan, *The Worst Hard Time* (New York: First Mariner Books, 2006).
2.   George Marshall, *Don't Even Think About It: Why Our Brains Are Wired to Ignore Climate Change* (New York: Bloomsbury, 2014).
3.   D. Fears, "Prairie, Farmers' Old Enemy, Could Be Their Lifeline," *Washington Post* (August 6, 2016), https://www.washingtonpost.com/national/health-science/iowa-farmers-ripped-out-prairie-now-some-hope-it-can-save-them/2016/08/07/1ff747a2-5274-11e6-88eb-7dda4e2f2aec_story.html.
4.   The Climate Report, "Climate Threatened: Mississippi Kite" (National Audubon Society, 2016). http://climate.audubon.org/birds/miskit/mississippi-kite.

5. J. Mangan, J. Overpeck, R. Webb, C. Wessman, and A. Goetz, "Response of Nebraska Sand Hills Natural Vegetation to Drought, Fire, Grazing, and Plant Functional Type Shifts as Simulated by the CENTURY Model," *Climatic Change* 63, no. 49 (2004): 49–90.
6. T. Egan, *The Worst Hard Time.*
7. Kansas Energy Information Network, Kansas Wind Projects (2015), http://www.kansasenergy.org/wind_projects.htm.
8. U.S. Energy Information Administration, *Electric Power Monthly, with Data for December 2014.* U.S. Department of Energy (2015). 227 pp.

CHAPTER 13: COLORADO: THE FORESTS OF CAMERON PASS
1. John N. Maclean, "The West Is Burning; What Are We Going to Do About It?" *Chicago Tribune* (July 10, 2013), http://articles.chicagotribune.com/2013-07-10/opinion/ct-perspec-0710-fire-20130710_1_suppression-u-s-forest-service-wildland-fire.
2. Jennifer Marlon et al., "Long-Term Perspective on Wildfires in the Western USA," *Proceedings of the National Academy of Sciences* 109, no. 9 (2012): E535–E543.
3. K. E. Pigeon, G. Stenhouse, and S. D. Côté, "Drivers of Hibernation: Linking Food and Weather to Denning Behavior of Grizzly Bears" *Behavioral Ecology and Sociobiology* 70: 1745 (2016). doi:10.1007/s00265-016-2180-5.
4. C. Mooney, "U.S. Forests Are So Full of Dead Trees that Some Scientists Want to Burn Them Instead of Coal," *Washington Post* (September 8, 2016).
5. InciWeb, interagency all-risk incident information management system, "Beaver Creek Fire" (2016), http://inciweb.nwcg.gov/incident/4797/.
6. S. Hart, T. Schoennagel, T. Veblen, and T. Chapman, "Area Burned in the Western United States Is Unaffected by Recent Mountain Pine Beetle Outbreaks," *PNAS* 112, no. 14 (2015): 4375–4380, doi:10.1073/pnas.1424037112.

CHAPTER 14: WYOMING: THE POTTERY STUDIO AT THE END OF THE EARTH
1. C. Davenport, "As Wind Power Lifts Wyoming's Fortunes, Coal Miners Are Left in the Dust," *New York Times* (June 19, 2016).

CHAPTER 16: IDAHO–MONTANA PART I: FIRE
1. P. Mote, A. K. Snover, S. Capalbo, S. D. Eigenbrode, P. Glick, J. Littell, R. Raymondi, and S. Reeder, "Northwest," in *Climate Change Impacts in the United States: The Third National Climate Assessment,* eds. J. M. Melillo, Terese (T. C.) Richmond, and G. W. Yohe (U.S. Global Change Research Program, 2014), 487–513, doi:10.7930/J04Q7RWX.
2. John Miles (Weyawacickan) quoted on White Bird Canyon panel, National Park Service.

ENDNOTES

3. John L. Thomas, *A Country in the Mind: Wallace Stegner, Bernard DeVoto, History and the American Land* (New York: Taylor and Francis, 2002).
4. P. Backus, "Out of the Ashes of 2000, Sula Forest Is Reborn," *Missoulian* (September 18, 2010).
5. A. L. Westerling, "Increasing Western US Forest Wildfire Activity: Sensitivity to Changes in the Timing of Spring," *Philosophical Transactions of the Royal Society B* 371 (May 23, 2016), doi: 10.1098/rstb.2015.0178.
6. National Research Council, *Climate Stabilization Targets: Emissions, Concentrations, and Impacts over Decades to Millennia* (Washington, D.C.: National Academy Press, 2011), 40.
7. US Forest Service, *The Rising Cost of Wildfire Operations* (Washington, D.C.: US Department of Agriculture, 2015).
8. US Environmental Protection Agency, *Climate Change Indicators in the United States* (2015), http://www.epa.gov/climatechange/science/indicators/snow-ice/snowpack.html.
9. L. A. Joyce, S. W. Running, D. D. Breshears, V. H. Dale, R. W. Malmsheimer, R. N. Sampson, B. Sohngen, and C. W. Woodall, "Forests," in *Climate Change Impacts in the United States: The Third National Climate Assessment*, eds. J. M. Melillo, T. C. Richmond, and G. W. Yohe (U.S. Global Change Research Program, 2014), 175–194, doi:10.7930/J0Z60KZC.
10. National Research Council, *Climate Stabilization Targets*.
11. US Forest Service, *The Rising Cost of Wildfire Operations*.

CHAPTER 17: IDAHO–MONTANA PART II: ICE
1. E. Holmes, *Trail of the Coeur d'Alenes Unofficial Guidebook* (Spokane, WA: Gray Dog Press, 2016).
2. Sena Christian, "Bunker Hill Superfund Site Is Still a Toxic Mess, with a Legacy of Suffering," *Newsweek* (June 24, 2016).
3. Julie Weston, *The Good Times Are All Gone Now: Life, Death, and Rebirth in an Idaho Mining Town* (Norman: University of Oklahoma Press, 2009).
4. C. White, *The Melting World: A Journey Across America's Vanishing Glaciers* (New York: St. Martin's Press, 2013), 12.
5. M. Zemp, I. Gärtner-Roer, S. U. Nussbaumer, F. Hüsler, H. Machguth, N. Mölg, F. Paul, and M. Hoelzle eds., *Global Glacier Change Bulletin No. 1 (2012–2013)* (Zurich, Switzerland: World Glacier Monitoring Service, 2015).
6. N. M. Kehrwald, L. G. Thompson, Y. Tandong, E. Mosley-Thompson, U. Schotterer, V. Alfimov, J. Beer, J. Eikenberg, and M. E. Davis, "Mass Loss on Himalayan Glacier Endangers Water Resources," *Geophysical Research Letters* 35 (2008), L22503, doi:10.1029/2008GL035556.
7. D. Benson and M. Cummins, "Move, Adapt, or Die: *Lagopus leucura* Changes in Distribution, Habitat, and Number at Glacier National

Park, Montana," in *Gyrfalcons and Ptarmigan in a Changing World*, vol. 1, eds. R. T. Watson, T. J. Cade, M. Fuller, G. Hunt, and E. Potapov (Boise: The Peregrine Fund, 2011), http://dx.doi.org/10.4080/gpcw.2011.0121.

8. M. Zimova, L. S. Mills, and J. J. Nowak, "High Fitness Costs of Climate Change–Induced Camouflage Mismatch," *Ecology Letters* 19 (2016): 299–307, doi:10.1111/ele.12568.

CHAPTER 18: TO OREGON AND THE SEA

1. M. M. Dalton, P. W. Mote, and A. K. Snover, eds., *Climate Change in the Northwest: Implications for Our Landscapes, Waters, and Communities* (Washington, D.C.: Island Press, 2013).

2. Jerry M. Melillo, Terese (T. C.) Richmond, and Gary W. Yohe, eds., *Climate Change Impacts in the United States: The Third National Climate Assessment* (U.S. Global Change Research Program, 2014), 563, doi:10.7930/ J0Z31WJ2.

CHAPTER 19: CLIMATE AND THE FUTURE

1. World Meteorological Organization, *Assessment for Decision-Makers: Scientific Assessment of Ozone Depletion: 2014*, Report No. 56 (Geneva: World Meteorological Organization, Global Ozone Research and Monitoring Project, 2014).

2. M. A. Cane, S. C. Dolan, and S. E. Zebiak, "Experimental Forecasts of the 1982/83 El Niño," *Nature* 321 (1986): 827–832.

3. National Research Council, *Climate Change Science: An Analysis of Some Key Questions* (Washington, D.C.: National Academy Press, 2001).

4. Intergovernmental Panel on Climate Change, "Summary for Policymakers," in *Climate Change 2013: The Physical Science Basis. Contribution of Working Group I to the Fifth Assessment Report of the Intergovernmental Panel on Climate Change*, eds. T. F. Stocker, D. Qin, G.-K. Plattner, M. Tignor, S. K. Allen, J. Boschung, A. Nauels, Y. Xia, V. Bex, and P. M. Midgley (Cambridge: Cambridge University Press, 2013).

5. Carling C. Hay, Eric Morrow, Robert E. Kopp, and Jerry X. Mitrovica, "Probabilistic Reanalysis of Twentieth-Century Sea-Level Rise," *Nature* 517 (January 22, 2015): 481–484.

6. B. H. Strauss, S. Kulp, and A. Levermann, *Mapping Choices: Carbon, Climate, and Rising Seas, Our Global Legacy* (Climate Central Research Report, 2015), 1–38.

7. O. Wiggins, M. Hui, and J. Cox, "Two Dead After Severe Flash Flood in Maryland," *Washington Post* (July 31, 2016).

8. C. Mooney, "What We Can Say About the Louisiana Floods and Climate Change," *Washington Post* (August 15, 2016).

9. L. A. Joyce, S. W. Running, D. D. Breshears, V. H. Dale, R. W. Malmsheimer, R. N. Sampson, B. Sohngen, and C. W. Woodall, "Forests,"

in *Climate Change Impacts in the United States: The Third National Climate Assessment*, eds. J. M. Melillo, Terese (T. C.) Richmond, and G. W. Yohe, (U.S. Global Change Research Program, 2014), 178 doi:10.7930/J0Z60KZC.

10. A. L. Westerling, M. G. Turner, E. A. H. Smithwick, W. H. Romme, and M. G. Ryan, "Continued Warming Could Transform Greater Yellowstone Fire Regimes by Mid-21st Century," *Proceedings of the National Academy of Sciences* 108 (2011): 13165–13170.

11. National Academy of Sciences, Royal Society, *Climate Change: Evidence and Causes* (Washington, D.C.: National Academy Press, 2014).

12. W. McKibben, "Global Warming's Terrifying New Math," *Rolling Stone* (July 19, 2012).

13. J. Moyer, "The Legacy of Oil Executive Christophe de Margerie, Dead in Freak Moscow Plane Crash," *Washington Post* (October 21, 2014).

14. Christopher Hayes, "The New Abolitionism: Averting Planetary Disaster Will Mean Forcing Fossil Fuel Companies to Give Up at Least $10 Trillion in Wealth," *The Nation* (May 12, 2014).

15. C. Le Quéré et al., "Global Carbon Budget 2014," *Earth System Science Data* 6 (2014): 1–90, www.earth-syst-sci-data-discuss.net/6/1/2014/, doi:10.5194/essdd-6-1-2014.

16. Reuters, "China Plans a Market for Carbon Permits," *New York Times* (August 31, 2014).

17. T. Bruckner, I. A. Bashmakov, Y. Mulugetta, H. Chum, A. de la Vega Navarro, J. Edmonds, A. Faaij, B. Fungtammasan, A. Garg, E. Hertwich, D. Honnery, D. In eld, M. Kainuma, S. Khennas, S. Kim, H. B. Nimir, K. Riahi, N. Strachan, R. Wiser, and X. Zhang, "Energy Systems," in *Climate Change 2014: Mitigation of Climate Change. Contribution of Working Group III to the Fifth Assessment Report of the Intergovernmental Panel on Climate Change*, eds. O. Edenhofer, R. Pichs-Madruga, Y. Sokona, E. Farahani, S. Kadner, K. Seyboth, A. Adler, I. Baum, S. Brunner, P. Eickemeier, B. Kriemann, J. Savolainen, S. Schlömer, C. von Stechow, T. Zwickel and J. C. Minx (Cambridge: Cambridge University Press, 2014).

18. Chris Mooney, "Why Storing Solar Energy and Using It at Night Is Closer Than You Think," *Washington Post* (September 16, 2015).

19. K. Bleich and R. Guimaraes, *Renewable Infrastructure Investment Handbook: A Guide for Institutional Investors* (Geneva: World Economic Forum, 2016).

20. W. McKibben, "A World at War," *New Republic* (August 15, 2016).

21. M. Jacobson, M. Delucchi, G. Bazouin, Z. Bauer, C. Heavey, E. Fisher, S. Morris, D. Piekutowski, T. Vencill, and T. Yeskoo, "100% Clean and Renewable Wind, Water, and Sunlight (WWS) All-Sector Energy Roadmaps for the 50 United States," *Energy and Environmental Science* 8 (2015): 2093–2117.

22. H. Paulson Jr., "How to Raise Trillions for Green Investments," *New York Times* (September 20, 2016).

23. J. Maxwell and F. Briscoe, "There's Money in the Air: The CFC Ban and DuPont's Regulatory Strategy," *Business Strategy and the Environment* 6 (1997): 276–286.

24. E. Brown, "A Conversation on Conservation," *Washington Post* (September 8, 2016), B1.

25. Coalition for American Jobs, a group sponsored by the American Petroleum Institute, http://www.sourcewatch.org/index.php/ Coalition_for_American_Jobs.

ACKNOWLEDGMENTS

J an Kublick, my classmate and best man, joined me on many of these rides, often against his better judgment. We've ridden through eleven states, France, Spain, and Switzerland by bike. This book has been hashed out on long walks by his upstate New York home. It's rare when I don't see a 6:00 A.M. email from him.

Rick Sullivan and I have been riding partners and climate activists for some years now. Rick joined me on the Underground Railroad route in Mississippi. Along with his folding guitar, we explored the Delta Blues Trail. A house concert in a motel room is a rare luxury.

Our kids each brought their own gifts. Tom flew into Portland to meet me at the end of the cross-country ride. Laura calmed me down on the way into the Bitterroot fires and later rode with me on El Camino de Santiago. Andrew came out to Yellowstone for the first familiar voice in a thousand miles.

I encountered instances of thoughtfulness along the road almost too numerous to mention. Twice during the ride, I opened my bag to discover that my hosts of the night before had stashed brownies. Several times I discovered on approaching the cashier that strangers had picked up my lunch. I know from my time in Europe that, for all our flaws, Americans are known there as a kind and open people. I can vouch for that.

The Writers Center of Bethesda, Maryland, has been an incubator for this book and for me. Over the years, I've taken workshops there with Ellen Herbert, Sara Taber, John Morris, David Taylor, and Lynn Stearns. Lynn has been instrumental in reviewing and editing early chapters of this book, and in encouraging the first submission of a chapter for publication. That first publication happened courtesy of Julie Wakeman-Linn, editor of the *Potomac Review* and a friend ever since. A version of "Kansas: Small Hours on the High Plains" first appeared in the winter 2013 issue of the journal.

My writing group, born at the Writers Center, consists of Sarah Birnbach, Andrea Hansell, Darci Glass-Royal, Sherlyn Goldstein-Askwith, Jane Oakley, Bonnie Rich, Janna Bialek, Arch Campbell, and Paul Carlson. They have worked over the entire manuscript at one time or another, providing that perfect mix of hard criticism and encouragement.

A version of "Delaware: The Sea Approaches" was published in *The Humanist*, November–December 2014, with the kind assistance of Jennifer Bardi and Fred Edwords.

Rick Piltz was my former colleague at the U.S. Global Change Research Program. He revealed how a George W. Bush White House staffer and former American Petroleum Institute lobbyist dramatically watered down government science assessments of climate change before their public release, and how the assessment process was undermined. As a whistleblower, Rick left the government to found the blog *Climate Science Watch* (later *Climate Science and Policy Watch*). He passed on too early in 2014. With the help of Michael Termini, an early version of chapter 16, "Montana: In the Time of Fire," was published in September 2015 on *Climate Science and Policy Watch* as a tribute. An owl-eyed photo of Rick has looked over me as I wrote this book. I hope that I can live up to his courage.

ACKNOWLEDGMENTS

John Silbersack of Trident Media has been both quiet and relentless in representing me. It's an honor to be on his illustrious client list. One has the sense of a steady hand on the tiller.

Jessica Case of Pegasus Books took a chance on a new writer and opened doors that I never could. I've been blessed with a thoughtful and energetic editor. She assembled a thoroughly professional team to produce the book. Lara Andrea Taber's maps grace the pages, while Judy Gelman Myers provided a meticulous copy edit. Maria Fernandez designed the book, while Derek Thornton from Faceout Studio did the jacket.